D0874164

Mr Secretary Thurloe

John Thurloe, *Secretary to Oliver Cromwell*

MR SECRETARY THURLOE

Cromwell's Secretary of State
1652–1660

Philip Aubrey

The Athlone Press
London
•
Fairleigh Dickinson University Press
Rutherford • Madison • Teaneck

First published 1990 by The Athlone Press Ltd
1 Park Drive, London NW11 7SG
© R. Aubrey 1990

British Library Cataloguing in Publication Data

Aubrey, Philip, *d. 1984*
    Mr Secretary Thurloe 1616–1668.
    1. England.   Politics.   Thurloe, John, 1616–1668
    I. Title
    942.06′092′4

    ISBN 0-485-11347-3

Library of Congress Cataloging-in-Publication Data

Aubrey, Philip.
    Mr Secretary Thurloe : Cromwell's Secretary of State, 1652–1660 /
Philip Aubrey.
        p.   cm.
    Bibliography: p.
    Includes index.
    ISBN 0-8386-3388-9
    1. Thurloe, John, 1616–1668.   2. Cabinet officers—Great Britain—
Biography.   3. Great Britain—History—Commonwealth and
protectorate, 1649–1660.   4. Cromwell, Oliver, 1599–1658.
I. Title.   II. Title: Mister Secretary Thurloe.
DA407.T5A92   1990
941.06′4′092—dc20
[B]   89-45379
                                                                      CIP

Associated University Presses
440 Forsgate Drive
Cranbury, NJ 08512

The paper used in this publication meets the requirements of the American
National Standard for Permanence of Paper for Printed Library Materials
Z39.48—1984.

Typeset and printed in the United States of America

CONTENTS

PREFACE

A substantial documented biography of John Thurloe is long overdue. Somewhat of a factotum, he was a very acceptable Secretary of State to the successive regimes of the 1650s – to the Rump of the Long Parliament from 1652, to the Nominated Assembly (or Barebone's Parliament) during 1653, and to the Protectorate of Oliver, then of Richard, Cromwell from 1653 to the spring of 1659. Thrown out by the restored Rump on the resignation of Richard, he was brought briefly back by George Monck, who admired his work, in the hectic weeks that culminated in the unexpected Restoration of Charles II. Thurloe may have lacked charisma and intellectual fire, but he was loyal, indefatigable (though often ill) and well-organised. Almost imperceptibly he became an indispensable element in the formulation and conduct of policy, domestic and external. By the time the turn of events thrust him back into the comparative obscurity from which other events had pushed him, he was the unique repository, in his head and in his vast accumulation of papers, of much of the history of the British Isles of his times. As Secretary and Postmaster General, he controlled a network of agents at home and abroad dedicated – some more, some less – to serving the interests and preserving the security of very nervous governments. He has been called 'Cromwell's master-spy', but Thurloe was no James Bond nor, indeed, an M. Even so, from intercepted mail and a plethora of reports, all needing his sort of intelligent interpretation, he came to know more than anyone else what was going on and who was doing it. A serious investigation of his career can provide the historian with sharp insights into the inwardness of the developments of the 1650s in politics, administration, finance, economics and foreign relations. Such was the objective of the late Philip Aubrey whose posthumous publication this is.

Thomas Philip Aubrey was born in Kent in 1912. Entering Dartmouth at 13, he went on to a diverse and distinguished naval career, until invalided out in 1949. He had already shown a strong historical bent with a survey of the part played by the Royal Navy in the suppression of the slave trade between 1811 and 1870, *Prevention Squadron* (1948). Government work, insecurity at home and abroad in the 1950s and 1960s brought him into close contact with the intelligence services, awakening an interest in their history. His book on *The Defeat of James Stuart's Armada of 1692* (1979) owed much to his naval and governmental skills and experience, and testified, too, to the fascination the seventeenth century had for him. Given this background it is not surprising that Philip Aubrey should be drawn to the career of John Thurloe.

When, about a decade ago, he told me at a meeting of the Cromwell Association, of which he was an enthusiastic life-member, that he felt an urge to write a full-length biography of the Secretary of State, I offered him every encouragement. A good one would meet a long-felt want among students of the Interregnum who, in no doubt that Thurloe was important, have often found his character and personality and the details of his activities outside of the council chamber, the House of Commons and his private office hard to come by. Philip Aubrey and I were in contact on the project over the next few years during which it became clear to me that he was pursuing his research with a skill and assiduity worthy of his subject.

I was saddened to learn of his death in 1984 but delighted to know that he had been able to complete what he had set out to do. His family, quite rightly, has been determined that his book should be published. It was pleasing that, when The Athlone Press took it on, I was asked to help to prepare it for publication by making, as far as I could, the sort of minor factual and stylish revisions that Philip Aubrey would have made himself had he lived to see it through. In this task I have been much assisted by my former research students, Drs Peter Gaunt and Sarah E Jones, both specialists in the Interregnum, who have read and commented constructively upon the typescript. The latter has also compiled the Index. Mrs Hilary Tolley expertly typed the final recension of the text. Throughout Mr Brian Southam of The Athlone Press has been helpful and encouraging.

At last the book is in print, embellished with a reproduction of an engraved portrait of 'the little Secretary' which suggests a more sensitive human being than is commonly accepted among those who would dismiss this dedicated public servant as 'dry as dust'. Philip Aubrey's biography aims to bring out the man struggling to emerge from the bureaucrat. The book is essentially Mr Aubrey's own, reflecting his scholarly zeal, his enterprise in research and reconstruction, his absorption in the men and movements of the age, his experience in intelligence diplomacy, naval and military security, policy and administration. It has been for me a privilege to have been associated with him and to have had a small share in the making of *Mr Secretary Thurloe* and now in bringing it to the attention of (I hope) the many who can find, as the author himself did, excitement and satisfaction in contemplating not only 'our chief of men' like Oliver Cromwell but the secondary, still valuable, figures like John Thurloe.

Exeter   Ivan Roots
July 1989

ACKNOWLEDGEMENTS

The material for this book has been collected with the help of a number of libraries and record offices and I wish to express my thanks to their staffs for their courtesy and assistance. In no particular order they are: the National Register of Archives, the Public Record Office, the British Library Departments of Printed Books and of Manuscripts, the British Museum Department of Coins and Medals, the Cambridgeshire County Record Offices at Cambridge and Huntingdon, the Buckinghamshire, Essex and Hertfordshire County Record Offices, the Greater London Record Office, the Guildhall Library, the Wisbech Museum and Library, the Bodleian Library, the House of Lords Record Office, the India Office Library and Records, Lambeth Palace Library, the Library of the University of Reading, Kensington Public Library, and the Camberley branch of the Surrey County Library, which obtained several works for me through the interlibrary loan service, including six of the seven volumes of the Thurloe State Papers from the London Library and an unpublished MA thesis from the University of Wales. As a member, I have also made use of the Library of the Society of Genealogists.

Perhaps my most unusual acknowledgement for help in the preparation of a book about seventeenth-century Britain is to the librarian and staff of Auckland Public Library, New Zealand, which opened its doors in the 1880s. The library holds four holograph letters of Thurloe and several others addressed to him. Although they were all printed in the *English Historical Review* in 1892, it was interesting to see the originals and to find in this unlikely spot the Latin text of an agreement of July 1659 made between the English Commonwealth and the United Provinces, complete with the signatures and seals of the negotiators. It appears that the manuscripts formed part of the library of Sir George Grey, twice Governor of New Zealand and later its Premier, who gave his entire collection to Auckland Public Library.

Private individuals to whom I am grateful for assistance include: the Marquess of Bath for permission to use the Whitelock papers at Longleat and his archivist there, the Marquess of Bute for permission to quote from Whitelock's diary and Ruth Spalding for identifying references to Thurloe therein, the Master and Registrar of the Charterhouse, the Librarian of Lincoln's Inn Library, the Archivist of the University of

Glasgow, the Secretary of the Chequers Estate, the Keeper of the University Archives at the University Library, Cambridge, Rouge Dragon Poursuivant at the College of Arms, the incumbents of the parishes of Fen Ditton and Hatfield Broad Oak, the Archivist of Corpus Christi College, Cambridge, and Mr. J. R. Ravendale of Landbeach, Cambridgeshire.

Any modern historian or biographer owes a huge debt to earlier writers in the same field. Without their work it would have been much harder to locate many of the available sources, both primary and secondary. I have been particularly fortunate in receiving advice and encouragement at an early stage from Professor Ivan Roots of the University of Exeter, to whom I am extremely grateful. I have also enjoyed useful discussions with Mr Howard McKenzie, a member of the Cromwell Assocation. At a later stage, Dr Anne Pallister of the University of Reading read and commented upon two drafts and has earned my deep gratitude for her most helpful advice.

PREFATORY NOTE

All dates are rendered in Old Style according to the calendar in use in seventeenth-century England, which was ten days behind the Continental calendar, but the years have been taken to begin on 1 January, not 25 March. Spelling and punctuation have been modernized in quotations from contemporary sources, and surnames are reproduced in a consistent and recognizable form, regardless of the (often variable) spelling which their owners and contemporaries adopted; for example, it is Montagu, not Mountagu, Montague or Mountague. However, seventeenth-century place names have been retained, even where the vagaries of history and language have produced changes since. The towns of Constantinople, Danzig, Elsinore, Leghorn, Memel, Smyrna and Stettin would now be rendered as Istanbul, Gdansk, Helsingör, Livorno, Klaypeda, Izmir, and Szczecin respectively.

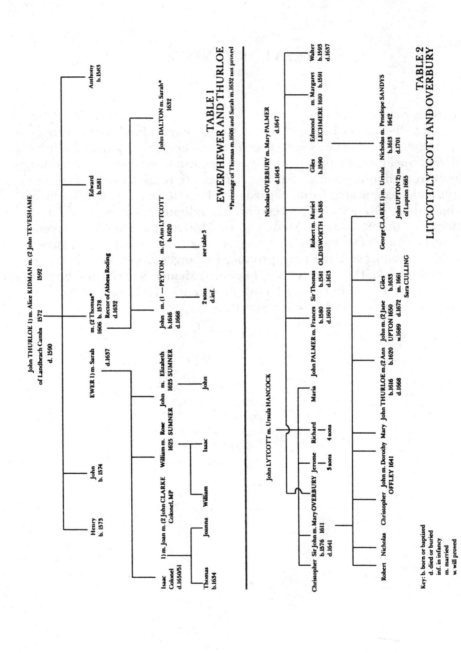

TABLE 1

EWER/HEWER AND THURLOE

*Parentage of Thomas m.1606 and Sarah m.1632 not proved

John THURLOE 1) m. Alice KIDMAN m. (2 John TEVESHAME
of Landbeach Cambs   1572   1592
d. 1590

Henry b.1573 — John b.1574 — EWER 1) m. Sarah d.1637 — Edward b.1581 — Anthony b.1583

m. (2 Thomas* 1606 b. 1578 Rector of Abbess Roding d.1652

Isaac 1) m. Joan m. (2 John CLARKE Colonel, MP — William m. Rose 1625 SUMNER — John m. Elizabeth 1625 SUMNER — John

Isaac Colonel d.165051 — Thomas b.1654 — Joanna — William — Isaac

John m. (1 —PEYTON   m. (2 Ann LYTCOTT b.1616 d.1668   b.1620

John DALTON m. Sarah* 1632

2 sons d.inf.   see table 3

TABLE 2

LITCOTT/LYTCOTT AND OVERBURY

Nicholas OVERBURY m. Mary PALMER d.1643

John LYTCOTT m. Ursula HANCOCK

Robert m. Muriel b.1585 — Sir Thomas b.1581 d.1613 — Giles b.1590 — Edmond m. Margaret LECHMERE 1610 b.1591 — Walter b.1593 d.1637

John PALMER m. Frances b.1560 d.1601

Christopher — Sir John m. Mary OVERBURY b.1576 d.1641 1611 — Jerome 3 sons — Richard 4 sons — Maria

Robert — Nicholas — Christopher — John m. Dorothy OFFLEY 1641 — Mary — John THURLOE m.(2 Ann b.1616 b.1620 d.1668 — Jane UPTON 1650 w.1689 d.1672 — Giles b.1635 m. 1661 Sara CULLING

George CLARKE 1) m. Ursula
John UPTON 2) m. of Lupton 1665

Nicholas m. Penelope SANDYS b.1615 1642 d.1701

Key: b. born or baptized
d. died or buried
inf. in infancy
m. married
w. will proved

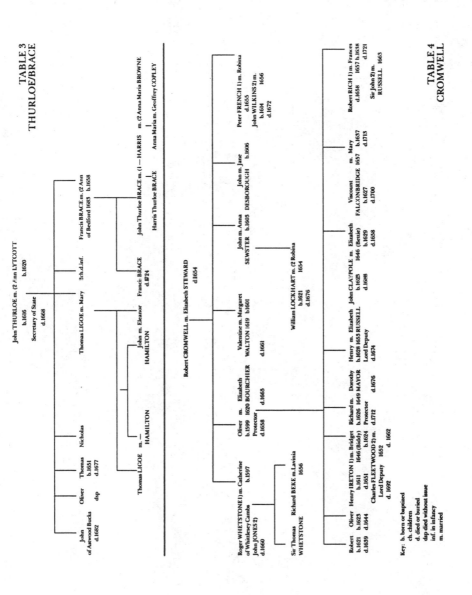

TABLE 3
THURLOE/BRACE

John THURLOE m. (2 Ann LYTCOTT
b.1616   b.1620
Secretary of State
d.1668

John   Oliver   Thomas   Nicholas   Thomas LIGOE m. Mary   Francis BRACE m. (2 Ann
of Astwood Bucks   dsp   b.1651   of Bedford 1683   b.1658
d.1682   d.1677

Thomas LIGOE   m. —   John m. Eleanor   John Thurloe BRACE m. (1 — HARRIS   m. (2 Anna Maria BROWNE
               HAMILTON   HAMILTON   Francis BRACE
HAMILTON   d.1724   Harris Thurloe BRACE   Anna Maria m. Geoffrey COPLEY

Robert CROMWELL m. Elizabeth STEWARD
                                    d.1654

Roger WHETSTONE 1) m. Catherine   Oliver   m.   Elizabeth   Valentine m. Margaret   John m. Anna   John m. Jane   Peter FRENCH 1) m. Robina
of Whitdesey Cambs   b.1597   b.1599 1620 BOURCHIER   WALTON 1619 b.1601   SEWSTER b.1605 DESBOROUGH b.1606   d.1655
John JONES 2)   Protector   d.1665   d.1661   John WILKINS 2) m.
d.1660   d.1658   b.1614   1656
                                                                                                                               d.1672

Sir Thomas   Richard BEKE m. Lavinia
WHETSTONE   1656

Robert   Oliver   Henry IRETON 1) m. Bridget   Richard m.   Dorothy   Henry m. Elizabeth   John CLAYPOLE m. Elizabeth   Viscount   m. Mary   Robert RICH 1) m. Frances
b.1621   b.1623   b.1611   1646 (Biddy)   b.1626 1649 MAYOR   b.1628 1653 RUSSELL   b.1625   1646 (Bettie)   FALCONBRIDGE 1657   b.1657 b.1638
d.1639   d.1644   d.1651   b.1624   Protector d.1676   Lord Deputy   b.1629   d.1658   b.1627   d.1713   d.1658 d.1721
         Charles FLEETWOOD 2) m.   d.1712   d.1674   d.1688   d.1700   Sir John 2) m.
         Lord Deputy   1652   RUSSELL 1663
         d. 1692   d. 1662

William LOCKHART m. (2 Robina
                    b.1621   1654
                    d.1676

Key: b. born or baptized
      ch. children
      dsp died without issue
      inf. in infancy
      m. married

TABLE 4
CROMWELL

Mr Secretary Thurloe

INTRODUCTION

John Thurloe, son of an obscure country rector, was thirty-five years old when in March 1652 he was appointed by the Council of State of the Commonwealth as its secretary. Less than two years later he became Secretary of State to the Protector, Oliver Cromwell, and soon afterwards one of the most powerful men in the country, at once feared and respected. At the Restoration in 1660, shortly before his forty-fourth birthday, he managed to avoid retribution and disappeared into a retirement as obscure as his beginnings, to die at the age of fifty-one.

Thurloe had taken the precaution of hiding a great deal of the official correspondence of his eight active years. It is largely through those papers, discovered after Thurloe's death, that his name and activities are known to later generations. His principal object in concealing them was no doubt to safeguard his own life and those of friends, agents and informants. Though thoughts of posterity may not have been uppermost in his mind, it is interesting that he chose to conceal rather than simply to destroy the papers and he must surely have desired that some authentic record should survive the reaction of the Restoration. Had he not done so, it is certain that our knowledge of the Protectorate period would have been much the poorer. It was fortunate that when the hoard of papers was discovered and reached Lord Somers, Lord Chancellor to William and Mary, he recognized the importance of the collection and had it carefully preserved and bound in sixty-seven folio volumes. Nearly half a century later most of the important and interesting items, together with a few contemporary papers from other collections, were transcribed and published by Thomas Birch in his seven-volume series. *A Collection of the State Papers of John Thurloe, Esquire.*

Birch, born of Quaker parents in 1705, had no university education but became an Anglican priest and eventually a doctor of divinity. He devoted much of his time to the study of English history and published many biographies. Dismissed by Horace Walpole as a 'worthy good-natured soul, full of industry and activity . . . with no parts, taste or judgement', he was dull in his prose style but minute in detail, a quality which made him such an excellent editor of the Thurloe material. His seven folio volumes, published in 1742, are still a fruitful source for all aspects of government during the 1650s.

3

Even so, Thurloe himself has never before been the subject of a detailed biography in English. Birch provided a short biographical note as a preface to his first volume of papers, and two monographs have appeared since. The first, by Sigismund von Bischoffshausen, was published in German in 1899, though an appendix reproduced a score or more of Thurloe's letters in their original English. Its cumbersome title translates as *The Statecraft of the Protector Oliver Cromwell, as shown by the ideas and actions of his minister, Secretary of State John Thurloe.* In seven chapters, it covers all aspects of Thurloe's work from the period preceding the Protectorate until his death. The second 'life', written by D.L. Hobman and published in 1961, is based almost exclusively upon the state papers. Entitled misleadingly *Cromwell's Master Spy,* it deals mainly with Thurloe's intelligence activities, which have also inspired a number of articles, scholarly and otherwise. A first-class account of Thurloe's role in Cromwell's government was published anonymously in *Macmillan's Magazine* in 1894.

Although so much of Thurloe's official correspondence has survived in the state papers and other collections, it is remarkably uninformative about his private life. The main facts of his parentage, marriages and offspring were fortunately recorded by Birch within eighty years of his death. From these foundations modern genealogical research has uncovered a little more information, but Thurloe's own reticence remains a formidable obstacle.

Besides Birch, one other scholar must be mentioned: Richard Rawlinson, who collected manuscript documents in huge quantities. Though Jacobite in his sympathies, he acquired the Thurloe papers when they came up for sale in 1751. In a letter of 14 May announcing his bid, he remarked that although seven large volumes had been printed, he would be glad to see the original documents if he could procure them at a moderate price.[1] At his death in 1755 they were left, with the rest of his collection, to the Bodleian Library at Oxford. There, in the Rawlinson MSS and in smaller quantities in a handful of other collections, Thurloe can still communicate his thoughts, tell us of his work and relate the minutiae of government during the 1650s, all in his rather thin and slanting hand.

An English Secretary of State in the seventeenth century was responsible for carrying forward government policy in almost every sphere, at home and abroad. A strictly chronological approach to Thurloe's life and work would entail a constant and complex interchange between foreign policy, domestic affairs, internal security and intelligence work, with many other distractions on the way. For this reason, the first and second chapters of this study are devoted to his early life and first official employment. For the active years as Secretary of State, each main aspect of his work is dealt with in turn, going over the same period perhaps several times but avoiding repetition as far as possible. First, the political and parliamentary background to Thurloe's work is examined to gauge his influence on events. Secondly, an account of foreign affairs seeks to estimate Thurloe's contribution to the formulation of policy and to assess his successes and failures. Next, his control of intelligence is explored, with some account of the advances in technique under his direction, justifying, it is hoped, his great reputation in this field. Finally, though the almost complete lack of private letters and papers inhibits a full assessment, some account is attempted of his family and personal affairs.

The occupant of a high position of state at a time of revolutionary change is bound to attract obloquy from political opponents as well as praise from supporters of the regime. Perhaps after more than three centuries, it is now possible to make a dispassionate and reasonably fair assessment of Thurloe's qualities and failings. Thurloe was entrusted with extensive, ill-defined and potentially corrupting powers and knew few restraints beyond his own conscience and his respect for the law. It has been pointed out that 'unlike other officers of State whose authority is prescribed by patent, by custom or by oath, the Secretary can never have a warrant long and universal enough to cover him.'[2]

In a study of the office of Principal Secretary between the reigns of Elizabeth I and Charles II, Florence Evans remarks that 'secretarial history is sadly lacking in heroes'. 'The two most heroic figures', she goes on, 'are Walsingham and Thurloe, zealous spirits inspired by high ideals. Yet in the minds of both was that curious twist which enabled them to sink to very unheroic methods.'[3] The words 'very unheroic' could be misinterpreted, for Thurloe certainly did not employ the most unattractive powers at his disposal. There is no evidence, for example, that he used the rack or any other form of torture to extract confessions or information from captives and his methods of acquiring intelligence have, in fact, been followed by every reputable security organization to this day.

We need look no further than this, however, to determine why Thurloe has been neglected by biographers. He appears in most histories as no more than a name; few historians have even summed up his qualities and failings. Among those who have attempted some assessment of the man and his career, François Guizot writes of Thurloe as

> more than any other in the confidence of Oliver Cromwell, charged with all his police and with his personal correspondence both official and private, a keen, active and discreet servant, with no pretension to independence or glory, which made him as convenient as he was useful to his master.

Dr G. E. Aylmer sees Thurloe as the archetypal pliant bureaucrat, portraying him as prudent and useful, by no means a complete mediocrity or a mere hack, but essentially a man of limited abilities and power. Out of his depth as a political and parliamentary leader, concludes Aylmer, he remained the perfect secretary and an exemplary gatherer and processor of news and intelligence. Lord Dacre concurs, admitting Thurloe's skill in counterespionage but stressing his pathetic lack of originality in echoing his master's sentiments and errors. An industrious secretary does not necessarily make a good Secretary of State, he concludes. Godfrey Davies, while accepting that Thurloe was Richard Cromwell's ablest adviser, condemns him for being cautious to the point of timidity and for lacking in initiative.[4]

All these historians agree that Thurloe was not an originator of policy, that he did not directly influence decisions or initiate ideas leading to changes in home or foreign statecraft. In contrast, Professor Woolrych writes that Thurloe, above all his contemporaries on the Council, did make a contribution to the collective character of the Cromwellian regime, even in its early stages.[5] There is no record of the detailed discussions which went on in Council or in its committees, but there is plenty of evidence, as this account may demonstrate, of Thurloe's many-sided involvement in governance, of his gradual domination of the conduct of foreign policy and of his undisputed mastery of intelligence operations. His touch was scarcely less sure in domestic affairs, including those of Scotland and Ireland. Even in parliament, he was not so ineffective as has been made out. He was, in fact, an interesting personality and an intimate partaker in – and to some extent moulder of – great events at home and abroad during a particularly eventful decade of British history.

1
A LONG APPRENTICESHIP, 1616–1652

Thurloe was then my private servant . . . Having bred him
from a youth in my service *(Oliver St John)*

The Church of St Edmunds at Abbess Roding in Essex, where John
Thurloe was baptized in 1616, was an early English foundation. The
village, like others in its vicinity, takes the second half of its name from
the valley of the Roding, which rises near Thaxted and drains both the
edge of Epping Forest and a wide expanse of flat agricultural land less
than three hundred feet above sea level as it flows south-westwards
towards Woodford, to enter the Thames at Barking creek. The first half
of the name derives from the abbey of Barking, founded in 675 by
Earconwald, Bishop of London, who appointed his sister Ethelburga as
its first abbess, though he had to bring over an experienced abbess from
Gaul to train her. The abbey became Benedictine under the Normans.
At the time of the Dissolution it held several manors in Essex, including
that of Abbess Roding.

The manor passed through several hands in the decades after 1540
and was for a time held jointly by Robert Thornton and Oliver St John, a
member of the extensive St John clan and thus both namesake and
distant forebear of the Oliver who was to play a significant part in John
Thurloe's life. The advowson, originally from Barking Abbey, settled
from about 1590 with the Capel family, who lived at Rockwood Hall,
three-quarters of a mile south-west of the village. It was Sir Gamaliel
Capel, a former deputy-lieutenant, sheriff and MP for the county, who
presented Thomas Thurloe as rector of Abbess Roding in 1612.[1] As the
Capels later proved themselves to be staunch royalists – Arthur, Baron
Capel, followed Charles I to the block in 1649 – their choice of a Puritan
in 1612 seems somewhat surprising.

Thomas Thurloe, who came from Cambridgeshire, had been admitted in 1593 to Corpus Christi College as a sizar (a student charged
reduced fees in return for performing certain menial duties). Though
neither identification can be proved, it is probable that he was the
Thomas baptized on 11 February 1578 at Landbeach, a village a few
miles north of Cambridge on the Ely road, the third of five sons of John

and Alice Thurloe, and that he had first been admitted to the university at Queens' College in 1591 at the age of thirteen. There was a strong connection between Corpus Christi and Landbeach, one of the college's principal properties. College masters were also rectors of the parish. The university had long been a centre of radical religious thinking, and Corpus Christi was a college with a strong Puritan element, so Thomas no doubt imbibed Puritan doctrines there. He graduated as a Bachelor of Arts in 1598 and became Master of Arts in 1610. No record of his ordination as deacon and priest in the Church of England seems to have survived.

On 10 July 1606 at Margaret Roding Thomas Thurloe married Sarah Ewer, a widow with three young sons, Isaac, William and John. Six years later Thomas took up his duties as rector of Abbess Roding, an event recorded in Latin in the parish register on 11 October 1612, roughly a month after his presentation. He would have found a medieval church with flint rubble walls and a sloping slate roof. It is still standing, but with a western bell tower and other minor nineteenth-century additions. On the south side of the sanctuary are two fifteenth-century windows, one depicting a bishop and the other St Margaret. A rood screen of intricate tracery is believed to have been brought from Barking Abbey and cut down to fit its new position. An elaborate monument, erected during Thomas's incumbency within the chancel but now on the north wall of the nave, commemorates Sir Gamaliel Capel, who died in November 1613, and his wife Jane, who died on 22 August 1618 and was buried at St Edmund's two days later; the couple, to whom Thomas Thurloe owed his position, are shown kneeling at prayer with their nine children. In Thomas's day, one wall of the church was decorated with repetitions of the letters 'IHS' separated by orbs, though these later disappeared beneath layers of whitewash. It was at the ornate square font, dating from the time of the Crusades and richly decorated with carving of the sun, moon, stars, foliage and flowers, that Thomas baptized his only son on 12 June 1616.

Little is known of John Thurloe's boyhood and schooling. He was probably taught by his father at home in the old rectory house – of which no trace remains – that stood immediately south of the churchyard. In view of his later connections, it is likely that John visited Cambridgeshire from time to time. Assuming the identification of Thomas Thurloe with Landbeach is correct, John would have had little difficulty visiting his father's old haunts and relations – the forty-five miles from Abbess Roding could have been covered in a day's riding. Although John's paternal grandparents had died or left the village long before, two uncles remained and raised families there and John would have had several cousins of about his own age at Landbeach.

In 1625 Thomas Thurloe married two of his Ewer stepsons to Rose and Elizabeth Sumner, probably sisters; the remaining stepson, Isaac, married somewhat later. Their half-brother John also made an early marriage, though it was short-lived and poorly documented. No official record of the marriage has been found and although the bride was apparently of a family called Peyton, she cannot be identified. Sir Robert Peyton, knight of the shire and high sheriff of Cambridgeshire, owned property around Wisbech and had three daughters, all of whom would have been of an age to marry Thurloe. If one of these was Thurloe's bride it may explain his later connection with the town, perhaps because he had retained an interest in property there which had come to him through his long-deceased first wife. Certainly, at least one historian of Wisbech has asserted that his bride came from there.[2] However, the name was fairly common in East Anglia and there were many other Peytons in Cambridgeshire and Essex; Thurloe's first wife may easily have been a local girl from the Rodings. Whoever she was, her married life was brief – no more than three or four years – and the two sons she bore soon followed her to the grave.

Thurloe's father died in November 1633. It appears that John, who was still in his teens, continued to live at Abbess Roding with his widowed mother. Thomas Thurloe had left no will, but in January 1634 his son secured administration of his estate on behalf of the widow Sarah,[3] who survived until 1637. The parish register of St Mary, Chelmsford, records her burial on 29 June of that year. By then John must have been spending the times of legal terms in London working as a sort of personal assistant to Oliver St John, boarding at Furnival's Inn on the north side of Holborn, one of the recognized training establishments for Chancery clerks.

St John, fourteen years older than his assistant, had been at Queens' College, Cambridge, in 1615, was admitted to Lincoln's Inn four years later and was called to the bar in 1626. A thoughtful, taciturn and moody young man, he visited the Netherlands during a vacation and imbibed some republican views. His first connection with the Essex countryside came in 1629, when Lady Masham of Otes, High Laver, wrote to her mother Lady Barrington, a Cromwell by birth, about a possible match for Joanna, her daughter by her first marriage. The couple were soon married and their first child was baptized at High Laver in January 1631.[4]

It is not clear how Thurloe came to St John's attention, but presumably St John heard in some way of a bright lad in a parish neighbouring those of the Mashams and Barringtons. Thurloe was evidently working for St John by 1637, the year in which he attained his majority, for in May he was a vouchee on a legal deed concerning lands belonging to Sir Thomas

Barrington and his son John in Essex, Yorkshire, Hampshire and London.[5] Less than two years later Sir Thomas made a settlement of manors and farms in Yorkshire, Hampshire and Essex on four gentlemen, one of whom was Oliver St John, and these four in turn released their shares to four others, St John's nominee being 'John Thurloe, servant to Oliver St John, in trust for his sons'.[6] Thurloe thus early became possessed of an independent income from land, though these two children of his first marriage did not long survive.

Only canon and civil law were taught at the universities of Oxford and Cambridge and education in the common law was begun in London. By the end of the fourteenth century a distinction was well established between the law of equity administered by the Court of Chancery and the common law dispensed in its own courts. Teachers and students resided at the Inns of Court, so called because of the connection between the teachers, who were practising lawyers, and the royal courts of justice at Westminster. The inns had a collegiate character. To gain admission a young man must first become proficient in the administration of the law; it was to fill this role that Inns of Chancery such as Furnival's arose. Furnival's had initially been occupied by the exchequer clerks when Sir William de Furnival, Baron of the Exchequer, acquired the place in 1376. By 1408 it was an Inn of Chancery, later leased by Lincoln's Inn and bought in 1547 for £120. Thurloe served his apprenticeship there until he was admitted to Lincoln's Inn in 1646, shortly after his thirtieth birthday.

His second marriage, to Ann Lytcott, must have taken place at about this time. He was still dependent on Oliver St John, who was playing a prominent part in these turbulent years for church and state. St John's first wife had died in childbed in 1637, and on 21 January 1638 he was remarried at High Laver to Elizabeth Cromwell, a first cousin of Oliver Cromwell, thus enlarging his links with the family which was to share in the triumph of parliament over the crown. St John had already made a name as an advocate by his defence of John Hampden in the Ship Money case of 1637–8 before he was elected (rather oddly) for Totnes in Devon in the Short Parliament of 1640. In what became the Long Parliament (from November 1640) St John again sat for Totnes.

During the opening months of 1641 Charles, in an attempt to balance his administration by admitting 'opposition' members to the Privy Council, appointed the Earl of Bedford, a leading Presbyterian, as Treasurer, John Pym to the Exchequer and St John as Solicitor-General. In 1642 parliament refused permission for St John to join the king at York and passed an ordinance enabling him to carry on with the duties of Solicitor-General in spite of the king's exasperated appointment of Sir

Thomas Gardiner in his stead. Parliamentary and official business can have left St John little time for his private legal practice, and he must have come to rely more and more on Thurloe to safeguard his interests.

St John, who had no military ability or inclination, did not consider fighting when the civil war broke out in August 1642. Years later he wrote to Cromwell congratulating him on the victory of Dunbar and excusing himself that 'indisposition of body and other employments will not suffer me to do more than tarry by the stuff'. The biblical allusion, which would have been immediately apparent to the general, was to David's ordinance that those that tarried by the baggage were to have an equal share of the spoils with those who went down to battle.[7] Nor did Thurloe himself seek to emulate several of his contemporaries at the Inns of Court by going off to join one or other of the opposing armies. The Earl of Essex, who initially commanded the parliamentary army, for example, formed his lifeguard from volunteers from the Inns. 'I was never a soldier', Thurloe was to confess to the House of Commons in later years.[8]

The fortunes of war favoured first one side, then the other, with two rival governments and for a time two parliaments at Oxford and Westminster. The executive arm of the latter became the Committee of Both Kingdoms (England and Scotland) in February 1644 with St John a member. A year later Thurloe made his entrance on the political stage by accompanying St John to treat on behalf of parliament with the king's representatives at Uxbridge. On the list of the parliamentary retinue he is named first of three servants to Mr Oliver St John, but it soon became apparent that he was filling a more important role as one of two secretaries of the English commissioners, another being designated secretary to those representing Scotland in the negotiations.

Uxbridge at that time consisted of a single street of houses on a road leading to a pair of wooden bridges over two arms of the Colne river, which divided about a mile above the town and formed the boundary between Middlesex and Buckinghamshire. Just short of the bridges stood a large mansion, formerly the seat of Sir John Bennet, now to be the centre for the negotiations. Part of the house still stands and bears an inn sign with the words 'Built 1576 Ye Old Crowne Inn formerly ye celebrated Treaty House AD 1645'. It is a two-storeyed brick building; its bay windows have moulded brick mullions and transoms and its three chimney stacks have clustered shafts. As it stood in 1645 it was well adapted for its temporary purpose. A large room at the centre of the house was furnished with an almost square table giving room for the opposing commissioners on two sides each. The divines and secretaries sat behind the commissioners. Retiring rooms were available for private discussion and secretarial work. Since the king's party used the front door and the parliamentary representatives the back, there was no necessity for either side to meet the other except across the table.

Uxbridge was very crowded on the evening of 29 January 1645. Even some of the commissioners lay uncomfortably two to a room on field beds with quilts. The secretaries must have had even more cramped quarters. But everyone seems to have been well fed at the two inns allocated to the opposing sides. At the parliamentary inn, The George, one of the ministers prayed before each meal. The commissioners did at least exchange calls on arrival in the town.

The first day, a Thursday, was market day. Many on both sides joined the townspeople and market visitors at the church of St Margaret, the royalists seemingly overcoming their distaste for the banning of the Book of Common Prayer and vestments by parliamentary ordinance. A young man from London (inappropriately called Love) preached violently against the king and his commissioners, and finally upset both sides by condemning the proposed treaty itself. He was afterwards admonished by the local justices and sent out of town, but he had soured the opening of the negotiations. The gulf between the opposing viewpoints was in any event so wide and the rival commissioners' positions so firmly entrenched that hopes of compromise on any of the main subjects of debate were almost negligible. The king's initial declaration lamenting the continuation of the war and its mischiefs and urging that 'some reasonable conditions of peace might be thought upon', and parliament's declaration to have agreed to the conference 'out of their passionate desire for peace'[9] seemed equally unrealistic.

Twenty days had been allocated for the treaty negotiations. After some preliminary sparring about precedence, and queries by both sides about various clauses in their opponents' instructions, the Earl of Northumberland proposed that three days should be devoted to religion, three to the militia and three to Ireland. After any other business had been settled the conference would return in rotation to the three main topics. This agenda was agreed and on 2 February the negotiations began. The same evening Thurloe wrote and signed his first official paper.

Parliament had effectively poisoned the atmosphere for any discussion of religion by hurrying through the trial and execution of Archbishop Laud during the preliminary talks about the Uxbridge treaty. The archbishop, who had been four years in the Tower, was brought to the bars of both Houses of Parliament and accused of high treason. In spite of a reasoned defence he was condemned to death, a pardon from the king under the Great Seal of England being ruled of no effect.

To understand the negotiations on religion at Uxbridge it is necessary to look back over the preceding years and appreciate the changes which had already taken place. The Scots had rejected the use of a new prayer book in July 1637 and had introduced the National Covenant in February of the following year. The so-called Bishops' Wars of 1638 and 1639 had done nothing to defuse or resolve the situation. In February 1641 the English parliament began to debate the removal of bishops from the House of Lords and the Star Chamber. The main argument advanced by St John was that bishops ought not to sit in any assembly capable of passing a death sentence. However, the so-called Root and Branch bill abolishing episcopacy, drafted by St John as Solicitor-General, was not passed until January 1643. The king at Oxford declined to give his assent to this and all other legislation passed since the previous summer. Other ordinances (that is, Acts of Parliament without the king's consent) forbidding pictures and crucifixes, the use of vestments, and singing and organ music in cathedrals were passed at intervals in 1642, 1643 and 1644, whilst on 22 September 1643 the Scots succeeded in persuading the English parliament to swear to a Solemn League and Covenant in St Margaret's church at Westminster, thus making more or less inevitable the adoption of a Presbyterian form of church government in England and Wales.

Towards the end of 1644 the Westminster Assembly of Divines, which included Scottish representatives, prepared for the Uxbridge treaty a series of measures to introduce a directory for public worship in England, Scotland and Ireland, suppress the Book of Common Prayer, confirm its own powers and impel the king to take the Covenant of Both Kingdoms. Accordingly, when the discussion opened the parliamentary representatives proposed that bishops, deans and chapters be abolished and replaced by government 'more agreeable to God's word and the practice of the best churches', that the prayer book should be 'taken away and totally suppressed' and replaced by the directory, and that the king should take the Covenant and consent to an Act of Parliament obliging everybody to take it too.

The royalist response was that the Church of England had enjoyed a settled and continuous government since Christianity was first established here. If the aim was to be like a foreign Protestant church, who could tell which was the chosen model since the directory proposed a liturgy unlike any other known? Without bishops there could be no ordinations and hence eventually no administration of the sacraments or performance of priestly functions. Finally, it would be contrary to the king's coronation oath in England to order such changes.

The debate on religion continued until late on its third day. The Scots commissioner, after inveighing against episcopacy, argued that since the king's commissioners had been quite unmoved by parliament's view that abolition was 'absolutely necessary for the preservation of the kingdom', clearly they were not committed to peace. His speech, ending with studied insolence, drew the mild rejoinder from Edward Hyde, the King's Chancellor, that his side could hardly be expected to give up after a mere three days' debate everything they had learnt from the cradle. It was nearly midnight when the commissioners adjourned, chatting together for a little time longer before the fire. No doubt Thurloe and the other weary secretaries had to work on through the night, writing and copying reports on the day's proceedings and covering letters for Westminster and Oxford.

Discussion of the militia, the next topic, centred on control, an issue that had led to the final break between king and parliament and the outbreak of the first civil war in 1642. That March parliament, after failing to obtain royal assent to their militia bill, had passed a militia ordinance appointing its own lords lieutenant to lead, conduct and employ the county militia as directed by parliament. This the king could not concede, and in May at York he forbade the militia to obey parliamentary orders and appointees, and instead issued his own commissions of array. At Uxbridge nearly three years later Hyde declared that by the law of England control of the militia rested solely with the king, a contention disputed by Bulstrode Whitelock, MP and lawyer, who would later represent the Commonwealth abroad and, as a holder of high offices in the state, become one of Thurloe's firm friends.

After a solemn fast on 5 February, the king's commissioners proposed next day that control of the militia should be in the hands of a committee of twenty, ten chosen by the king and ten by parliament, each to serve for three years. Scotland was not mentioned. Whitelock and others attempted to obtain some modifications, but the royal commissioners were bound by their instructions. Parliament, fearing vengeance if control were lost, remained determined to keep the command of the militia and of all forts and ships. This second part of the negotiations was remarkable for short conferences and lengthy papers. It ended, like the first, with no sign of agreement. On the third day Thurloe drafted a note to the royal commissioners expressing the disappointment of the parliamentary side, which had received no response to its own proposals.[10]

On Sunday there were what Whitelock described as 'very seasonable' sermons both morning and afternoon. A certain amount of fraternization between the two sides had no lasting effect. The discussion of Ireland again brought no meeting of minds. Parliament accused the king of supporting the Irish rebels; the royal commissioners, charging parliament with having diverted troops and supplies to fight the king, refused parliament's demand to prosecute the war against the Irish rebels. Thus deadlock was reached for the third time.

When the conference returned to the subject of religion, the king's commissioners would not sanction the removal of bishops, though they offered some limitations of their powers. They would not agree to the directory of worship, and expressly repudiated the Covenant. Progress on the other two subjects was equally disappointing. The notes from the king's commissioners and Thurloe's draft replies, preserved in the Whitelock papers, show that each side expected its own proposals to form the basis of agreement and tended to ignore those of its opponents.[11] Two parliamentary commissioners returned from Oxford and asked officially for more time, to be told that nothing had yet been agreed and no more could be expected. Moreover, the parliamentary commissioners presented a document insisting that the Princes Rupert and Maurice, the king's nephews, and many other peers and gentry who had taken arms for him, should be excepted from any act of indemnity. In no circumstances could Charles agree to sacrifice his followers in this fashion.

The third Sunday was spent in rest, sermons being heard at the commissioners' lodgings. Both sides had worked hard for three weeks, often until two or three in the morning, but they had achieved nothing. Hyde recorded that the commissioners 'parted with such coolness towards each other, as if they scarce hoped to meet again'. He had earlier remarked on the lack of trust among the opposing commissioners, who had no authority to give way on the smallest point. St John and Sir Henry Vane junior appeared to be acting as watchdogs to prevent their more moderate colleagues from becoming friendly with the royalists.[12]

Early the next morning the king's party took coach for Oxford, reaching the royal headquarters on the same day. The parliamentary commissioners reported next day to the Commons, where their conduct was approved. They had discharged their duties with singular judgment and fidelity, and had earned the thanks of parliament.[13] Thurloe's official work was over and he returned to St John's private law practice, but he had received a valuable introduction to the difficulties of conducting government business in an age of revolutionary change. No doubt he had also made an impression upon several influential people.

The war had continued throughout the negotiations, and the New Model Army did not have long to wait to prove its superiority. Charles was routed at Naseby in June 1645, and by May of the following year, after a bitterly cold winter with seven weeks of frost in London, the king had fled north to surrender to a Scottish army near Newark. The first civil war was all but over.

That summer, with the worst plague in London for ten years and the prospects of a poor peacetime harvest, Thurloe was admitted to Lincoln's Inn for a fee of £3 10s., of which the bulk went to the Society, with standard deductions for the chapel, the keeper of the black book of records, the head butler and the second.[14] Thurloe was of a temperament to enjoy the disciplined collegiate life of Lincoln's Inn, even though at thirty he must have been much older than the sons of gentlemen admitted in his year. Cap and gown were the proper wear in hall, but in these troubled times many appeared booted and spurred, wearing hats, cloaks and swords.

Throughout the rest of 1646 and the whole of 1647, while parliament pressed ahead with measures to impose Presbyterian church government and the army continued to increase its power, it must be presumed that Thurloe was fully engaged in furthering his legal knowledge and experience while still assisting St John privately. Not until March 1648 did he receive an official appointment. It was as receiver of cursitors' fines under the Commissioners of the Great Seal, an office reportedly worth at least £350 a year. His job was to endorse 'the fines paid upon all fineable writs made out by the cursitors of the High Court of Chancery'.

There were twenty-four cursitors, chosen by the Lord Chancellor and the Lord Keeper from among the clerks. They had to show familiarity with the Latin form of writs and an ability to write in a conventional Chancery hand. They kept commons together in their own hall on the corner of Chancery Lane and Cursitor Alley (now Cursitor Street), almost opposite the gatehouse of Lincoln's Inn. It appears that while the fines for writs in real actions went to the crown, those for writs in personal actions were divided in two, with one half retained by the cursitors (no doubt the source of the receiver's income) and the other itself equally divided between the Lord Chancellor and the Master of the Rolls. Since actions in the Chancery court were normally brought by members of wealthy and notable families, Thurloe's appointment served to bring him into contact with men of influence, while widening his reputation as an able administrator. The diary of Bulstrode Whitelock, one of the Commissioners of the Great Seal, shows that he received from Thurloe in June and July 1648 some dividends presumably representing a share of the crown's receipts.[15]

A glimpse of Thurloe's work for St John around this time can be found in papers that have survived concerning the estate of the third Earl of Essex, who had died in September 1646 after resigning his command of the parliamentary army a day before the self-denying ordinance was passed. His will, dated 4 July 1642, named as executors the earls of Northumberland and Warwick, John Hampden (who had since died) and Oliver St John, each of whom was to receive £100. Thurloe was a witness to an agreement dated 3 February 1648 about a sum of over £4,000 due to Essex for money he had lent to parliament. It seems that, as usual, parliament was slow to repay the loan, and beneficiaries under the will became impatient. In August Thurloe wrote to

William Jessop, who six years later was to become his own assistant secretary for foreign affairs, telling him that £147 remained to be paid to Essex's servants and £200 to the poor of Clement's. (As a good Puritan Thurloe struck out the 'St' from the name of the church and parish.) Northumberland and St John had agreed to pay these legacies out of their own purses rather than expect any further sum out of the estate. Jessop, who had been with Warwick since his days as parliamentary Lord Admiral, was asked to entreat his employer to order his share to be paid. Thurloe added that the servants were importunate and that the church-wardens of Clement's had been to see him about it a dozen times.[16]

In the same month that Thurloe dealt with this minor administrative matter, the second civil war was being brought to an end by Cromwell's defeat of the invading Scottish-Royalist army at Preston. Thereafter the English army became supreme, presenting its 'remonstrance' to parliament in November and then reducing the Commons to a rump of some seventy active members who remained after Pride's Purge had not only barred from the House those inimical to army policy but also caused many others to withdraw.

St John meanwhile had accepted the post of Chief Justice of the Common Pleas, an appointment which debarred him from parliament under the self-denying ordinance and put him at a distance from any hand in the trial and execution of the king. Moreover, he kept himself remote from the newly established Commonwealth, designed to be a free state governed by the representatives of the people in parliament without any king or House of Lords. He remained in London for the legal terms and spent his vacations at Longthorpe, his country house near Peterborough. Yet his hand is again discernible in the next appointment to come Thurloe's way, when in February 1650 he was made one of the treasury officials for the drainage of the Isle of Ely.

The project was not new, but had been held in abeyance during the civil wars. Parliamentary interest had, however, been maintained; a committee appointed in August 1645 reported two years later that it would be possible and profitable to drain a large part of what was then known as the Great Level, but was soon spoken of as Bedford Level after the two earls who successively led the adventurers of capital in the project. The additional 95,000 acres to come under cultivation would repay the charge of drainage and maintenance. By the terms of an Act for draining the Great Level of the Fens, passed in May 1649, Bedford and the adventurers were to undertake to drain the level on or before 10 October 1656 without prejudice to navigation of adjacent rivers and ports, making the level 'winter ground' instead of an area constantly subject to flooding. The economic objectives of this ambitious plan were the cultivation of rapeseed for soap and oils to be used in the clothing and spinning industries, of corn and grain, of hemp and flax for linen cloth and cordage, and of grass for pasture. Equally important, perhaps, significant employment would be provided.[17]

On 10 February 1650 Bedford and two other members of the company met to lay down rules for its treasury. Thurloe was one of four 'officers of the treasury' who were to employ Jessop as receiver at a salary of £100 a year. The receiver was responsible for taking in and paying out all moneys on behalf of the company, sending a weekly abstract of transactions to the company secretary. Rather optimistically, he was directed to inform one of the treasury officers if the balance reached £1,000. The rules were formally approved without delay and the officers were told to agree on a fit place for the receiver to work, and to provide him with a chest and ledgers.[18]

Local opposition to the drainage scheme was considerable. Oliver Cromwell had spoken passionately on behalf of the commoners in a Commons committee in June 1641, reproaching Hyde, the chairman, for partiality.[19] Petitions came in from the ports, Cambridge University and nearby towns. But the Act of 1649 gave new impetus, and a month before Thurloe's appointment the Dutch-born engineer Sir Cornelius Vermuyden was reappointed as director of works. Vermuyden had been employed on a number of drainage projects before the civil wars and had been rewarded with a large gift of land in the fens after reclaiming 360,000 acres there. Wages for labourers on the works were constantly in arrears, but after Cromwell's victory at Dunbar in September 1650 a number of Scottish prisoners were added to the labour force, which at later dates was augmented by Dutch prisoners and by a few Huguenot refugees.

By the time Thurloe took an official interest the drainage of the north and middle levels of Bedford Level were almost completed. The first of these comprised land north-east of Peterborough and north of the river Nene, flowing north-eastwards from Peterborough to Wisbech and thence to the sea; the middle level stretched between the villages of Whittlesey and March. Vermuyden's new task was to complete the drainage of the south level, fenland lying north of Ely itself. This was to be achieved by cutting a forty-foot channel known as Vermuyden's drain running roughly east and west between Ramsey and the old Bedford river, and a smaller sixteen-foot trench known as Thurloe's drain running at right-angles northwards for about nine miles to join the main drain of the middle level south of Upwell. It was customary to name artificial rivers in this way after influential members of the company, and it was proposed to give St John's name to a stretch between Denver sluice and Stowbridge. However, for some reason the Lord Chief Justice declined this aquatic honour. The order book of the company records on 25 April 1651 a memorandum 'that a letter be written to Sir Cornelius Vermuyden upon the motion of Mr Thurloe on behalf of Lord Chief Justice St John that the name "St John Eau" may be spared and some other name given.' Since the water flowed past the village of Downham Market it was called Downham Eau instead.[20]

The commissioners from London, meeting on 25 March 1651 at Peterborough, first at the minster church and then at the Angel, adjudged 30,000 acres north-west of the Bedford river as effectively drained, and handed over their proportion of land to Bedford and the other adventurers. The necessary deeds were signed the next day.[21]

Meanwhile the Commonwealth government, like all revolutionary regimes, was anxious about its reception and recognition by other states. It had got off to a bad start when two of its envoys were murdered. Anthony Ascham, its first ambassador to Madrid, was set upon at an inn as soon as he reached the city in May 1650. The five men arrested for this crime were all British soldiers in Spanish service. A year earlier Isaac Dorislaus, a doctor of laws from Leyden who had spent many years in England and had become thoroughly anglicized, was sent to The Hague to confer with Walter Strickland, the resident there since 1642, about preparations for an alliance between the two Protestant republics. He, too, was assassinated. There were no arrests and Strickland was recalled in June 1650, the Dutch ambassador in London being sent home three months later.

The Council of State was not content to leave the matter there. Early in 1651 they selected Oliver St John and Walter Strickland as ambassadors to the Assembly of the United Provinces to negotiate an alliance and possibly a political union. Reluctant to accept the appointment, St John pleaded indisposition, though he later admitted that the murder of Dorislaus and his own potential loss of earnings as a judge were the main influences. Nevertheless parliament resolved by 42 votes to 29 that he should go. It was, he declared later, a command from the *de facto* government and no appeal was permitted. Though he had earlier visited the Low Countries, he had no previous experience of foreign affairs. Dorislaus's son, another Isaac, was to accompany the embassy to demand justice upon his father's murderers. Thurloe went too, in attendance on St John, his first and only visit to a foreign country. The number of embassy papers in Thurloe's hand show him acting as secretary to both ambassadors. (Throughout his life he signed himself as 'Jo: Thurloe', a practice that has caused him occasionally to be indexed as 'Thurloe, Joseph'.)

The embassy was to be no hole-and-corner affair. One thousand pounds was advanced for the ambassadors' preparations and transport, they were to have £3,000 in cash and a further £3,000 in bills of exchange, and they were provided with plate worth £2,000 engraved with the arms of the Commonwealth. Whitelock prepared their commissions and letters of credence for approval by parliament. On 14 February 1650 the House agreed to heads of instructions for the ambassadors and to a draft letter to 'the high and mighty lords of the States General of the United Provinces', signed by the Speaker and sealed with the seal of parliament. The ambassadors were given permission to use the public barges to embark on 8 March. The frigates *Advice* and *Providence* carried them over, with three other vessels for the baggage. They were becalmed for a time off Margate but were off the Dutch coast by 12 March, completing their journey in local schuyts – flat-bottomed river-boats.[22]

The embassy reached Rotterdam a hundred and fifty strong early on Friday 14 March, and were entertained over the weekend by the English merchant adventurers, exchanging calls with a representative of the States General and with the burgomaster of Rotterdam. On Monday the Dutch master of ceremonies conducted them to The Hague, where they were met by an escort of thirty coaches.

The first official audience, at which St John spoke, was on the following Thursday. Pleased with their initial reception, the ambassadors gave credit for it to the Lord, who had smoothed their way, though they were surprised at the hostility shown to them in the streets of the capital. The Queen of Bohemia, sister of the late King Charles and herself a refugee from the Palatinate, was resident at The Hague, as were numerous English royalists in enforced exile. The Commonwealth representatives faced frequent public abuse and an insult by Edward, one of the younger Palatinate princes, caused the ambassadors to complain officially to their hosts, a stand later fully supported by the English parliament.

Serious negotiations were delayed by complaints and accusations from both sides. The English focused on the murder of Dorislaus and the presence of Tromp's fleet around the Scillies, the Dutch on the seizure of one of their ships at Limerick in 1646 and the repayment of loans advanced during the 1640s.[23] But more fundamental difficulties soon surfaced, for the Dutch showed themselves profoundly unsympathetic to the English proposals for a closer alliance and union between the two states, preferring a simple treaty of common interest. At Westminster, the Council urgently considered fresh instructions and despatched them by express messenger on 12 April. However, they failed to break the deadlock, for they did little more than approve the ambassadors' insistence on reparation for affronts suffered, while urging speedier progress.

Perplexed at the negative attitude of the Dutch, the ambassadors had already decided to send Thurloe back to obtain a prolongation of their powers to treat. The small craft in which he made the crossing had reached the mouth of the Orwell making for Harwich on the afternoon of Thursday 24 April. For some reason, possibly the foreign appearance of the vessel, the guns of Languard fort on the Orwell opened fire, forcing the ship seaward. Eventually, Thurloe was put ashore at 'Bodsey cliff' (modern Bawdsey) at about nine o'clock that evening. By riding post he reached London in just over twenty-four hours.

Thurloe reported to the Council on 29 April and was directed to submit a narrative to the committee which had prepared the ambassadors' instructions. This met early the next morning and by 3 May Thurloe had received new orders extending the period of negotiation by up to forty days. Contrary winds delayed his sailing, but on the 6th he set off from Gravesend on the eighteen-gun *Love*. She reached the Dutch coast on the following day and Thurloe was landed by pilot boat. After a further delay caused by storms, on 8 May he reached Rotterdam, from where he wrote a hurried account of his journey before proceeding to The Hague.[24] He had been away for a little over a fortnight.

Thurloe was immediately reimmersed in the work of the embassy, writing within hours of his arrival to inform the States General that the English parliament expected justice and reparation for the affronts and indignities offered to its ambassadors since their arrival. None the less, to manifest their own sincerity the ambassadors would stay a short time longer. Detailed proposals were presented the next day. Under the first article the two commonwealths were to become 'confederated friends', allied to defend the liberties of their two peoples; under the second, neither country was to attack the other. There followed five more articles, all designed to guard against aid or even residence being granted to 'rebels'.[25]

The Dutch would not listen to requests to expel the royalist refugees, though they eventually undertook to give no assistance to 'rebels'. At a conference on 12 May the Dutch submitted a paper resolving to renew all ancient treaties. They said that eight days previously they had proposed seven articles, most of them merely bringing up to date the treaty of 1495 between Henry VII and Philip, Archduke of Austria, but they had received no response from the English commissioners. No progress seems to have been made and on 19 May the Queen of Bohemia intervened, asking the States General to include a special article in the treaty about the payment of arrears of the allowance from England settled on her by King James, her father, and continued by her brother Charles I. This was referred to the English ambassadors, who sat on it until the eve of their departure. They then replied that they were incensed by the queen's use of the style Charles I, they disputed the liability of parliament to pay any allowance and, observing that the queen had expressed the greatest enmity to parliament, they would not even forward her request.[26]

This letter reflects the exasperation reached by the latter stages of the negotiations. On 6 June the ambassadors wrote home for ships to be sent, since they were instructed to leave in fourteen days' time. By the same despatch Thurloe wrote to Gualter Frost remarking that the Dutch seemed to have learnt from the Scots and French to profess much and perform nothing unless to their own advantage. This was a perceptive observation from someone making his first incursion into foreign negotiations. It suggests that Thurloe was already keen to come to grips with the problems of international intercourse. He went on to say that he saw no hope of agreement and hoped God would give wisdom to the commissioners to manage their farewell without loss of honour or interest.[27]

Meanwhile the negotiations dragged on. On the 19th the Dutch proposed a whole series of new articles of advantage to the States General and waved aside earlier English drafts. In desperation the ambassadors suggested that rather than go home empty-handed they should at least renew the treaty of 1495 with provision for its revision and enlargement, but the Dutch, who had already agreed to renew articles 1 to 5 of that treaty with one amendment to article 2, rejected the proposal. The ambassadors concluded that they could do no more and on the following day took leave of their hosts with mingled thanks and regrets. On the same day the Dutch negotiators made a lengthy recapitulation of their stand. A time limit for negotiations was unheard of, they said. Good progress had been made. Why could not the ambassadors stay and conclude an agreement? This long statement, written in Dutch, reached the ambassadors at midnight on 20 June. A copy in French did not arrive until Sunday the 22nd, when they were already under sail. They had the last word with a long and rambling statement of dissent.[28]

St John declared at a later date that he had obtained no advantage from the embassy. All the plate and furniture had been returned and a gratuity of £1,000 in gold had been refused. His only reward had been his successful plea for the preservation of the minster at Peterborough, threatened with sale and demolition.[29]

Ten years later Thurloe wrote a summary of the negotiations that shows, far more clearly than the contemporary records, the fundamental difference of approach between the two sides. The English, anxious for the future of the Protestant cause, sought nothing less than union with the Dutch in a perpetual league for mutual preservation. On the other hand the Dutch, resentful of competition, were looking for advantages in commerce, navigation and fishery; they wanted stiffening of the laws on freedom of the seas, on the privileges of merchants resident in a foreign country, on definition of war contraband and lawful prize, and on reprisals for wrongs. Hyde, viewing the negotiations from a distance and from a royalist standpoint, observed that St John had 'pressed such a kind of union as must disunite the Dutch from all their other allies'.[30]

This excursion into diplomacy completed Thurloe's long preparation for his life's work, and gave him very valuable experience. He had seen at first hand the difficulties of international negotiations. An entirely novel concept of relations between states, such as was put forward by St John and Strickland on behalf of the English parliament, requires very careful practical preparation and an appreciation, made on the basis of accurate intelligence reports, of the likely reaction of the other party. In fact, the English had laid no diplomatic foundation and had been deprived of intelligence by the withdrawal of their resident. Moreover, treaty-making had been hampered by the presence at The Hague of members and supporters of the House of Stuart, to which all those of the parliamentary party were sworn enemies. Thurloe must also have observed the petty jealousies and bickering between the Dutch provinces, and may thus have been influenced to keep in close touch in later years with central government representatives in Scotland and Ireland. Four crossings of the narrow seas, one of them in a craft that can hardly have been larger than a ketch or lugger, had brought home to him the realities of life afloat, the effects on movement of winds, tides and visibility, the dangers of shoals and lee shores, all of which might prove useful in his future career. Above all, it had brought him to the attention of the Council of State, some of whose members may also have remembered him from Uxbridge.

Thurloe remained in St John's service for a further year or so. One piece of work completed at this time made him a trustee of the income of the manor of Biddlesden in Buckinghamshire on behalf of the widow and children of Henry Ireton, Lord Deputy of Ireland and Cromwell's son-in-law, who had died of plague in Ireland a month after the surrender of Limerick. His widow, Cromwell's daughter Bridget, was shortly to find a second husband among the parliamentary military leaders in Charles Fleetwood, who was to be sent to Ireland in July 1652. Any contact with the Cromwell family was likely to prove valuable to Thurloe and, as it happened, this was not his first. As long ago as the summer of 1647, Thurloe, no doubt at St John's instigation, had acted as sponsor for Richard Cromwell, 'son and heir apparent of Oliver Cromwell of Ely', on his admission to Lincoln's Inn. In October 1650 Thurloe had been ordered to appear in the Admiralty court on behalf of the Lord General's interest in a vessel from Waterford, which had been driven into Swansea by stress of weather and there condemned as prize. In January 1651 he had presented to the Committee for Compounding a petition to recover rents on property in Monmouthshire that had been settled on Cromwell. Six months later he represented the Lord General again in securing another estate settled on him by parliament.[31]

Cromwell's defeat of Charles Stuart at Worcester on 3 September 1651, the anniversary of his victory over the Scots at Dunbar, caused parliament to despatch another strong team of commissioners to Edinburgh to make proposals for giving legislative effect to a union of the two countries. St John was again selected as one of them; they left London for the north in January 1652 and submitted proposals from Dalkeith on 3 March.[32] As it happened, St John did not take Thurloe with him to Scotland – a fortunate decision, for before the end of the month Thurloe's big chance came.

2
THE COUNCIL OF STATE, 1652–1654

There is a tide in the affairs of men,
Which, taken at the flood, leads on to fortune *(William Shakespeare)*

Thurloe's life and prospects were changed by the death of Gualter Frost, the Secretary to the Council of State. On 29 March 1652 the Council decided that Thurloe should be presented to the Commons in his place and that young Gualter, Frost's eldest son, should remain as assistant clerk at a salary of £365 a year. Members had evidently been impressed by Thurloe's reports on the Dutch negotiations, while entertaining some misgivings about the younger Frost's suitability for promotion. On 1 April Thurloe's salary was fixed at £600 a year for the lifetime of the existing Council. It was understandably somewhat less than his experienced predecessor had been receiving, but must have represented a big increase in Thurloe's income. The Councillors reminded him that he had no right to demand fees on their behalf, no doubt a necessary caution for one who had hitherto depended on fees from the cursitor's office. It was this government's policy to move towards a salaried civil service.[1]

Thurloe wrote to St John on 3 and 6 April to tell him about his good fortune. He must also have let him know that he was about to go to Cambridgeshire, for St John directed his reply of the 13th to be left with the postmaster at Stilton in Northamptonshire, so that Thurloe might receive it on his way. St John had already heard the news before he received Thurloe's letters and reacted generously: 'God forbid that I should repine at any of his works of providence'. Rejoicing at the news, he encouraged Thurloe with an enthusiasm that was typical: 'go on and prosper; let not your hands faint, wait upon him in his ways, and he that hath called you will cause his presence and blessing to go along with you.' Knowing that he had lost Thurloe's services did not prevent St John from continuing to discuss his private business and to issue instructions. He told him of the state of his negotiations for the purchase of Osterley Park, a property in Middlesex at 'a good distance from London'. Thurloe was to inspect the north of the Bedford river, where work had

25

not yet started, and to let St John know whether the bottoming of Bedford river itself had been completed.[2]

It seems likely that it was, in fact, business connected with fen drainage that had brought Thurloe away from Westminster so soon after assuming his new duties. On 9 April the Council had approved his request for ten days' leave in the country 'on private business of concern', subsequently extending it by another week. He was back at work on 27 April.[3] As well as inspecting general operations, Thurloe may also have cast an eye over progress on St John's estate. The adventurers had complained in October 1651 about the difficulties and expense of looking after the Scottish prisoners sent as labourers, twenty of whom had been sent as additional servants on the estate of Oliver St John, who was responsible for providing them with clothing.[4]

Ten months after this visit, Thurloe was present when members of the company met and resolved to demand adjudication of the south level. A committee was appointed to attend the commissioners in Middle Temple Hall. There it was decided that the commissioners should leave London on 21 March and reassemble at Ely on the 24th. The company was to be responsible for 'horse meat and man's meat' and Jessop was to take charge of a sumpter horse to carry the deeds and other legal documents. Later Thurloe was asked to procure a letter from the Lord General requiring his troops quartered at Ely to meet the commissioners.[5]

On 21 March 1653 the commissioners for the fen drainage set out by road from London to make their official inspection and adjudication of the south level work. Thurloe, who a few days previously had been directed by the Council to speak to the adventurers about the employment of Dutch prisoners, did not accompany them as they made their way to Earith, where they embarked to complete the journey by water to Ely. They were escorted into the level by a troop of horse. At Ely after their survey they listened to Vermuyden's account of what had been done and gave their approval, glad to note that 40,000 acres of the north and middle levels had now been in cultivation or carrying stock for two years without flooding. A service of thanksgiving, at which the notorious Independent divine Hugh Peter was the preacher, was held in the cathedral.[6]

All was not well, however, Vermuyden's work had been much criticized and had aroused considerable opposition. The Earl of Bedford and five other adventurers reported to Thurloe in detail during July. Glad though they had been to get the Dutch prisoners of war, they had found them in practice to be more trouble than they were worth. The country people opposed to the scheme encouraged them to run away. Troops rode after them and brought them back, but had no power to punish them. The major in charge had instructions not to quarter his men beyond the Isle of Ely, but the opponents and disturbances emanated from villages just outside the Isle. At the end of the year Thurloe received a letter from Ely complaining that the local people were contributing nothing towards the maintenance of the south level works, insisting that their own conditions had not been improved, a plea which had never been raised in the other two levels. The latter blamed young lawyers in Cambridgeshire and Norfolk for encouraging the locals. The writer ended with a tribute to Thurloe's wisdom 'that hath been a principal guide to us hitherto', and expressed the hope that it would 'at last bring us to a safe harbour where we may (without any more chargeable contention) enjoy the benefit of our long labour and expense.'[7] It is apparent that it was not only in government circles that Thurloe was establishing a reputation for getting things done.

If Thurloe had led a busy life when he was employed by St John, as Secretary to the Council of State he now had to work very hard indeed. Though the frequency of meetings varied slightly according to the activity of each succeeding Council, the Councillors often met five days a week, sometimes twice a day, and occasionally even on Sunday. Few meetings went by without Thurloe being directed to look up precedents or draft instructions. In addition he had to supervise all the work of the office, for the Council had laid down that all bills were to be certified by him or his assistant before being submitted for signature and that all letters, warrants or papers to be signed by the Lord President or other members of the Council were first to be examined and countersigned by the Secretary or his assistant.[8]

In September 1652 Thurloe was directed to inform Lord Chief Justice St John that he was to be President of the Council for a month. St John evidently turned down the honour, for someone else was appointed the next day.[9] The record of St John's attendances at Council meetings at this time bears out the suggestion that he was out of sympathy with the regime and confining himself to his legal duties.

In addition to his role in central government, Thurloe was also being called upon to oversee or participate in local administration, particularly in Cambridgeshire. Thus when the Rump Parliament issued an ordinance in December 1652, assessing contributions to raise £120,000 per month for six months for the maintenance of the army and navy, Thurloe's name appeared with that of Cromwell and twenty-five others as commissioners for the Isle of Ely.[10]

Like all revolutionary governments, the Commonwealth had from its beginning been seriously concerned about counter-revolution, whether from those who thought things had gone too far or those who would have liked to see them go a good deal further. In this continuing struggle to keep themselves informed of any subversive plot or movement the council were much alive to the value of intercepting correspondence.

As early as 1642 Parliament had intercepted letters from the royalist Digby in the Netherlands and had later derived useful information from a letter to the king's secretary from one of the queen's court giving details of expected foreign aid to the royalist cause. But it was the capture of all Charles I's correspondence at Naseby that opened the eyes of members of the executive – at that time, the Committee of Both Kingdoms – to the immense value of this source of intelligence. Its value was redoubled when it was found that the learned Dr John Wallis, later Savilian Professor of Geometry at Oxford University, was able to break the substitution codes that were widely used by both sides to conceal the more sensitive portions of letters. This service of cryptography was later described by Thomas Scot, the Commonwealth's first intelligence chief, as 'a jewel for a prince's use'. Wallis recorded that he had never seen a cypher before 1642, when he managed to break a letter using a single alphabet letter substitution. This he accomplished 'after supper', though figure substitution caused more difficulty and took longer to crack. But he persevered, both to satisfy his own curiosity and to gratify his friends.[11]

The Commonwealth's first attempts to exploit the value of interception were ordered without any tact or finesse. On 14 May 1649, for example, the Council of State issued a warrant to Captain Edward Sexby 'to go to the foreign post, seize the letters of persons holding correspondence with the enemy, and bring them' to the Council.[12] (It is noteworthy that even when the country was later at war, first with the Dutch and then with Spain, the term 'the enemy' in Commonwealth papers almost always refers to the royalists.)

In March 1650 the Council confirmed that the office of Postmaster should be in the sole power and disposal of parliament and appointed Edward Prideaux, the Attorney-General, to manage the business of the inland post, accounting quarterly to the Commonwealth for the profits. On 29 June the Council ordered their sergeant-at-arms to go to a post stage twenty miles from London on the road to York, seize the outward mail, then ride to the next stage and take possession of the inward mail for presentation to the Council. Similar orders were issued for the Chester and western roads. It seems that the biter could be bit at this game, for in 1651 there was an enquiry into the opening of packets between England and Scotland sent on the business of Captain George Bishop, Scot's assistant.[13]

By October 1651 a committee under the Lord General Cromwell was on parliament's order reconsidering the whole business of foreign and inland post. Thurloe's first contact with the intelligence aspect of postal interception seems to have been made in June 1652, after he had been three months in office, when Bishop was directed to make an extract of intelligence from intercepted letters and deliver it to the Secretary. At that time all suspect letters were brought to Whitehall to be opened, but procedures improved when Isaac Dorislaus joined the staff in January 1653. Given the cover appointment of Solicitor to the Admiralty Court at £250 a year, Dorislaus was allocated a room next to the sorting office and soon became expert at recognizing the hands and seals of persons of potential interest to the authorities. His knowledge of languages was invaluable and his flair for intelligence work an asset. At this period he made no attempt to conceal from recipients that their mail had been opened, read and possibly copied.[14]

The Commonwealth shared with most governments, particularly perhaps those of revolutionary origins, a profound distaste for criticism. Part of its interest in the post sprang from its concern to prevent the dissemination of propaganda material directed against itself. For self-promotion the government relied largely on the skills of the poet John Milton. It was in March 1651, while Thurloe was labouring at The Hague, that Milton was (to quote his earliest biographer) 'without any seeking of him, by means of a private acquaintance, who was a member of the new Council of State, chosen Latin secretary'.[15] His appointment was initially as secretary for foreign tongues, but the Commonwealth decided to drop the use of French and to concentrate on Latin for its international correspondence.

The activities of royalists at home and abroad – partly countered by interception, counterintelligence and propaganda – constituted just one of many threats to the Commonwealth regime. Religion was still a divisive rather than a unifying strand within English society. After the failure of the Uxbridge negotiations early in 1645, the Long Parliament went ahead with imposing a Presbyterian system, first on the City of London and the Inns of Court and later on the counties, which were divided into classical presbyteries with approved elders. At Thurloe's native Abbess Roding, for instance, the incumbent who had succeeded his father in January 1634 was turned out and replaced as minister in January 1648. The village classis, the building block of the Presbyterian system, was too small to have any elders.[16]

Presbyterian influence waned after Pride's Purge, replaced by the growing ascendancy of the Independent members of Parliament, who had the backing of Cromwell and the army. Early in 1650 the Rump passed a series of religious Acts and in September, with the repeal of the Recusancy Act, it was no longer an offence not to attend church, provided that one was present at some other place of prayer or preaching.

But toleration did not extend to supporters of Roman Catholicism or episcopacy. Since 1646 no episcopal functions had been exercised; in April 1651 the offices of deans and chapters were abolished and their estates seized. By the time Thurloe took up his appointment, religion in England and Wales was in a thoroughly confused state. Laud's policies had long been in ruins and the prayer book officially out of use. Tithes, it had been conceded, must continue until some more fitting means of financing the church could be devised and introduced. But Presbyterianism had not taken root; there were many Independent and Baptist ministers in livings, whilst in some country districts the same minister remained throughout all the turmoil and change. At Wisbech, for example, where Thurloe was later to reside, William Coldwell was vicar for fifty-one years – from 1651 to 1702 – and at Whittlesey, where Thurloe held the manor during the Interregnum, Richard Mason succeeded his father William as incumbent until his own death in 1683.

One piece of religious business which Thurloe handled in January 1653 was the preparation of a paper to be sent to all foreign ambassadors and ministers instructing them not to permit 'any people of this commonwealth to hear mass in their houses, it being contrary to the laws of the nation'.[17]

There were at this time no organized political parties as such, and all members of parliament valued their freedom to vote as their consciences dictated. Those who tended to support the executive power were labelled the 'Court party', and those who questioned or criticized its policies the 'Country party', but there were no rigid division into moderates and radicals. The dyed-in-the-wool republicans, such as Vane and Sir Arthur Heselrige, were chiefly concerned to maintain the supremacy of the House of Commons as the voice of the elected representatives of the people. One extreme of political thought outside parliament, and for a while strongly represented in the army, was to be found amongst the Levellers, who sought a much wider franchise. However, Leveller influence in the army greatly declined after Cromwell's suppression of the mutinies of 1647–9.

There remained the Fifth Monarchy men. Basing themselves on their particular interpretation of Daniel's vision of the four beasts representing kings, they held that there had been four empires or monarchies in the history of the world – the Assyrian, Persian, Greek and Roman. The Roman empire had been perpetuated in the papacy, the destruction of which they believed to be imminent. They therefore looked for a fifth universal monarchy of God's servants, when 'the saints of the most High shall take the Kingdom, and possess the Kingdom for ever', as a preliminary to the Second Coming.[18] They may be portrayed as true revolutionaries intent on the overthrow of established society, who would not recognize power derived from the people instead of from Christ. Subversive to the Rump government, they were added to Thurloe's burden in watching the royalists, his principal enemies.

Before Thurloe came on the scene Scot had been successful in smothering two royalist conspiracies. In the first he made use of an *agent provocateur* to persuade one Eusebius Andrews, who planned the seizure of the Isle of Ely, to commit his project to paper. Andrews was executed in August 1650 and in the following year the capture and interrogation of nine more conspirators, two of whom were subsequently executed, greatly hindered the plans of Charles Stuart in England. After his defeat at Worcester in September 1651 there was a lull in royalist plotting for almost two years and in February 1652, just before Thurloe's appointment, parliament was prepared to pass an Act of Oblivion pardoning almost all treasons and felonies committed before the battle. But the use of horse races at Salisbury as cover for a meeting of royalist sympathizers from the south-west alerted the authorities to the danger of allowing these apparently harmless sports to continue in time of tension.[19] Bull- and bear-baiting were suppressed by the Nominated Assembly in May 1653 in part on grounds of needless cruelty, in part because they, too, provided opportunities for plotters to gather and foment disorder.

The pressure of the Secretary's work in disposing of business arising from Council meetings and in preparing for almost daily meetings at eight o'clock in the morning made it essential that he should be provided with lodgings in Whitehall. This was done in June 1653. His salary had been increased in the previous December to £800 a year, when the post of clerk to the Committee for Foreign Affairs was added to his duties. His talents were now becoming fully recognized, and on 8 July 1653 the new Council gave him the sole management of foreign intelligence, with power to use such instruments as he should think fit. Bishop was discharged from 'intermeddling' in that field.[20]

It seems that Bishop had been indiscreet. A fortnight earlier, after a full night's work on the post, Dorislaus went to Whitehall and informed Bishop that he was to have no more to do with the post letters. Dorislaus himself would manage the business in future with secrecy and dexterity, resolving not to impart a syllable of what he knew to any living soul but the Secretary. Bishop was transferred to an allied field as secretary to the Committee of Examinations, responsible for interrogating suspects. He complained bitterly to the Council in September that the appointment had brought him

little advantage except the loss of my calling, the prejudice of my estate, the wearying out of body, breaking of my health, neglect of my family, and encountering temptations of all sorts, prejudices, censures, jealousies, envies, emulations, hatreds, malice, and abuses, which the faithful discharge of my duties has exposed me to, in no small measure, besides the mischiefs designed on me by the enemy, and the keeping of £600 and sometimes £1,000 always ready by me of my own money, to carry on my correspondence when Council had no money in their treasury.[21]

The Councillors were unmoved by this comprehensive appeal and Bishop did not get his job back.

Thurlow had other problems in the office. In March 1653 Frost and his two younger brothers (who were also in government employment) had some possessions, probably money, stolen from their chamber at Whitehall. Thurloe was ordered to investigate the theft and at the same time reminded to take care of money in his own charge, possibly by recruiting a watchman to lodge where the iron chest was kept and by ensuring that one of the palace guards was always within call. The Frost family were not yet out of trouble; they were being pestered and sued for debts incurred by their father on behalf of parliament in Ireland. The elder Frost had died intestate, leaving, besides his debts, a widow, four sons, two daughters and seven grandchildren to be maintained. The younger Gualter, who had achieved a reputation as a mathematician at Emmanuel College, Cambridge, seems to have served under Thurloe without resentment and later to have found his niche as treasurer of the Council's contingencies. The Frost petition about the debts was just one of a constant stream of petitions and applications for licences, passes and warrants that passed through Thurloe's hands.[22]

But it was the foreign work that had proved the heaviest burden. In October Thurloe recruited Philip Meadow, ten years his junior, as assistant to Milton at £100 a year. When the Council told Thurloe to name two or three persons to assist in the business of foreign affairs, he chose to bring in his friend William Jessop as an additional assistant secretary and to upgrade Meadow's post to take in foreign affairs as well as Latin translation, increasing his salary by £100 a year. Milton was to remain. All these appointments were confirmed by the Council.[23]

The executive had not yet achieved the control of the post that it wanted, and the interim Council of May–June 1653 – which held power in the interval between the ejection of the Rump and the inauguration of the Nominated Assembly – tackled the problem anew. It was decided in May 1653 that the carriage of inland letters, both private and public, should be at the sole disposal of the state, public letters being carried free; existing claims were dismissed and in June the Council entered into a contract with John Manley, Dorislaus's brother-in-law, that he farm the post by paying a fixed sum and making what profit he could. The Council's committee had recommended an annual rent of not less than

£6,300 a year, payable in half-yearly instalments, but Manley seems to have been forced to pay considerably more – £10,000 quarterly. In November Thurloe was directed to report the state of the contract but no alteration was made at that time, for the Commonwealth was on the eve of great constitutional change.[24]

On 20 April Cromwell had dismissed the Rump Parliament and its fifth Council of State, but he retained the secretarial staff to service the new, smaller, interim Council. Two intercepted letters seen by Thurloe in May showed an underlying distrust of Cromwell's intentions in some quarters. His declaration that he would govern by the Council of State only until a new form of government could take over showed, in the view of one correspondent, 'what henceforth he aims at'. Another was more forthright: 'he intends to be king in effect, though loath to take upon the title'. The new assembly which he and the Council of Officers summoned consisted of one hundred and twenty-nine English, six Irish and five Scots members nominally chosen by local congregations. In practice, however, few were proposed in this way, and most were selected by Cromwell and the Council of the Army. The majority had served as justices of the peace and although only about twenty had previous parliamentary experience, they were by no means the mindless and destructive fanatics of tradition. They met for the first time on 4 July and most were given lodgings in Whitehall, at Somerset House, formerly the queen's palace, and in the Mews, where the National Gallery now stands. Just before the Nominated Assembly met there were reports that Cromwell would lay down his commission as General and receive some other title. But his authority appeared secure. 'It is impossible now', one commentator wrote a week later, 'that any change, risings or alteration can be imagined.' All these reports were being intercepted and translated for Thurloe, who decided on the appropriate response.[25]

Soon after they had assembled, the members declared themselves to be the Parliament of the Commonwealth of England, and elected a Speaker to ensure that things be done in a parliamentary way. They were divided over proposals to dispense with church patronage and tithes. They made tentative moves to codify the Chancery law and the rates of excise. They set up a High Court of Justice to deal with royalist plotters. Their achievement included a Marriage Act, which required lawful ceremonies to be conducted by justices of the peace and an able and honest person in each parish to register marriages, births (not baptisms) and burials. Altogether they enacted over thirty statutes, a far better record than that of the elected parliament which followed them in 1654. But after five months of often bitter internal divisions, and following some judicious nudging from John Lambert, they surrendered their powers to the Lord General in early December. Cromwell meanwhile had been given Hampton Court Palace. Accordingly, the sale of its land, which Thurloe had earlier been instructed to arrange through trustees, was stayed.[26]

At this critical time St John was seriously ill at his home in Northamptonshire. He had been there since October, at times apparently near death, and did not return to full duty until the following May. If one is to believe St John's later defence of his activities during the Commonwealth and Protectorate, he was always opposed to arbitrary power and as a judge refused to act on ordinances passed by the Nominated Assembly of 1653 or later by the Protector and Council. It is doubtful, however, whether he could have restrained Cromwell at this time even had he been well and disposed to make the attempt. Thurloe, too, complained of sickness in a letter to Richard Bradshaw, the resident at Hamburg, on 9 September. It was the first recorded sign of the ill-health which dogged him for the rest of his active career and would bring his life to its premature close at the age of just fifty-one. This particular attack appears to have lasted almost two months and to have been severe. When it was over General George Monck, at anchor off St Helen's after failing to intercept a Dutch convoy, wrote that he was

> glad to hear that the Lord hath delivered you from the pit's brink, to which you were brought by the hand of sickness, whereby you may be yet further instrumental for his glory.[27]

There was a general air of discontent abroad in the autumn of 1653. Among the intercepted letters that Thurloe saw at this time was one describing a riotous incident in St Paul's churchyard when boys had stoned an Anabaptist soldier who was preaching one Sunday morning and who had threatened a sheriff when asked for his authority. An intercept on the following day contained the words: 'some rail, some groan, all complain; the poor saints begin to droop, and hang up their harps upon the willows', though the writer did go on to say that he himself had never seen so great a spirit of faith and prayer.[28]

The seamen in the fleet were mutinous; two were hanged and another whipped. On 27 October Thurloe signed an order by the Council prohibiting upon pain of death seditious assemblies of the sort which the seamen had recently held on Tower Hill and at Charing Cross. It promised speedy adjustment of moneys due for shares of prizes and encouraged voluntary engagement to continue in service. In November General John Desborough, Cromwell's brother-in-law, was sent to Portsmouth with back pay to quieten grievances there.[29]

In November, too, there was an important meeting of dissidents at Blackfriars. Cromwell received a report on it and had it copied for Thurloe. There had been aspersions from the pulpit on parliament, the army, the Council and all now in power. This, said the author of the report, might render their affairs contemptible 'when ambassadors and residents, who lie here as honourable spies, shall transmit these things oversea to their superiors'. He went on to note the distinguishing mark of all political factions: that each strives solely for the establishment of its own members, principles and opinions. He advised Cromwell to oblige all to 'fasten those fundamentals' – the rest would hum and buzz, he foretold, but soon die. Cromwell did in fact see the principal preacher at the Blackfriars meeting and warned him that the Anabaptist opposition was serving to encourage enemies at home and abroad. ('Anabaptist' was a term of opprobrium used, as a modern writer has suggested, much in the way that the word 'red' is employed in the second half of the twentieth century.) This preacher earned but a temporary respite: by late January 1654 he and another had been committed to prison 'for so insolently proclaiming' against the new Protectoral government, as Thurloe reported in a letter to Whitelock.[30]

In retrospect the idea of a parliament of saints seems a fanciful notion with little or no chance of success. The hope that holy desires would lead naturally to good counsels and that good counsels would as assuredly give rise to just works was one that appealed to idealists and it was, of course, a step towards that ideal form of government for which the Puritan element under Cromwell was striving. They did not all expect instant success. Some, indeed, comparing the king's execution to the Israelite crossing of the Red Sea, contemplated a period of forty years 'in the wilderness' before reaching the promised land. The saints fell short of expectations that an assembly of God-fearing men of proven integrity would encourage all God's people, reform the law and impartially administer justice. Thus it was hoped that the people would forget the monarchy and come to appreciate that their true interest lay in the election of successive parliaments. At a conference on the eve of dissolution St John condemned the Commonwealth's attempts to govern, but Thurloe, immersed in the detail of daily administration as a servant of one of the most active of successive Councils, can have had little time for political theory and probably maintained few contacts with the Nominated Assembly.[31]

The Assembly's demise provided an opportunity for the introduction of a written constitution covering the three countries of England, Scotland and Ireland. Drafted by John Lambert, a successful and popular military leader, assisted by a group of mainly military advisers, it was a distillation of several earlier proposals, particularly the Heads of the Proposals of 1647, which had been drafted and discussed since the end of the first civil war. Secretly in preparation for a couple of months, the constitution was put to Cromwell in 13 December, the day after the dissolution. Entitled the Instrument of Government, it vested the supreme legislative authority of the Commonwealth of England, Scotland and Ireland, and of the dominions and territories thereunto belonging, in one person, the Lord Protector, and the people assembled in parliament. Not surprisingly, Cromwell was to be the first to hold the Protector's office, which was to be elective, not hereditary.

Parliament was to have four hundred English members, most of them representing counties and elected by holders of £200 real or personal property. (Roman Catholics and any who had fought against parliament were excluded.) The Protector and Council were to decide on a method of selecting up to sixty members representing Scotland and Ireland. The House was to assemble for the first time on 3 September 1654, the date of Dunbar and Worcester and an anniversary that was to assume a sort of religious significance in the Cromwellian age. it was to sit for a minimum of five months in the first instance and be subject to triennial elections.

Under the new constitution, executive authority, together with all governmental functions during the intervals between parliaments, were entrusted to the Protector and a new Council of State. A permanent body of between thirteen and twenty-one members – the founder members were named in the Instrument itself – the Council possessed extensive powers to oversee the actions of the Protector, to execute the will of parliament, and to make and implement policies of its own, if necessary issuing conciliar legislation.[32]

Though smaller than its predecessors, the Protectoral Council was thus far more influential than the succession of Councils of State of the period 1649 to 1653, a series of short-lived bodies possessed of strictly limited powers and heavily reliant upon the ever-present parliament or assembly. And if the new Protectoral Council held far more power than its predecessors, so its Secretary naturally acquired a much enlarged status and authority of his own. But with the advent of the Protectorate, Thurloe gained a role in government far beyond that of mere chief clerk to a newly powerful Council. Although there is no formal record of his appointment, from the outset he combined the office of head of the conciliar secretariat with that of chief minister to the Protector, his right-hand man in almost every aspect of government. Thurloe can, indeed, be described as Cromwell's principal – and probably only – Secretary of State.

On 16 December 1653, after further discussion of the Instrument, Oliver Cromwell was installed as Lord Protector in a short ceremony in Westminster Hall. When the Instrument of Government was subsequently read out to the assembled Commissioners of the Great Seal, judges and barons of the Exchequer, the new Council of State, army leaders and the Lord Mayor and aldermen of London, it was Jessop who spoke, while Thurloe took his place among the Councillors in anticipation of his enhanced position in the new government. After John Lisle had administered the Protectoral oath, the whole assembly moved to the Banqueting Hall for a sermon.

The Protector's new Council, in which the real power resided, contained a mixture of military and civilian members including several friends and relatives of Cromwell. Henry Lawrence became its permanent President, but Lambert was probably its dominant personality. They appeared in attendance on the heralds when the Protectorate was proclaimed in London on 19 December, while the printed proclamation was despatched to the sheriffs with a covering letter from Thurloe.

Cromwell had been given authority, with the consent of the majority, to fill his Council to the permitted twenty-one members by adding to the fifteen names in the Instrument. Although three new members were, indeed, added in 1653–4, it seems that Thurloe did not formally become a Councillor at this time. He was, however, accorded wide powers and was far more than a mere Council servant. As Secretary of State he was on the staff of the Protector and one of the most powerful men in the country. The Councillors quickly acknowledged the elevated status of their Chief Clerk or Secretary, and on 22 December 1653 Thurloe 'took his place at the board, being thereunto called by the Council'. He was, in fact, a full Councillor in all but name. His first important task was to perfect the Instrument of Government, at first called 'the Government of the Commonwealth' and finally 'the Government of England, Scotland and Ireland', and to incorporate amendments for its engrossment and enrolment.[33]

To the disgust of the diarist John Evelyn – and, no doubt, of many other devout Anglicans – Cromwell was feasted by the Lord Mayor in the City of London on Ash Wednesday 1654 'in contradiction to all custom and decency'. Thurloe himself revelled in the reception of his master, attended by thirty other coaches, half of which had six horses, and two hundred horsemen, including the life guard. The shops were shut, Thurloe reported, and everybody seemed to be in the streets, but there was no disorder. In reporting 'no disorder' Thurloe was putting the best complexion on the day's events. In fact the cavalcade was received in silence by the populace. To Thurloe it appeared that the new government had been accepted 'beyond what was expected'. The people, he boasted, would be 'governed by the good old laws and all arbitrariness in government laid aside'. As always, English tongues were wagging and giving credence to all sort of constitutional developments. 'Some say', read a letter intercepted in April, 'that our Protector intends to be Emperor within this three weeks.'[34]

Thurloe's forecast that the introduction of the Protectorate would cause the laying aside of all arbitrariness in government reads strangely to a modern mind accustomed to think of single rulers, even when advised by an elected assembly, as despots or dictators, and therefore the embodiment of arbitrary decisions. But Thurloe was writing against a background of five years of government shared between a Council of State and parliament. No new laws had been passed in a strictly constitutional fashion, because the old pre-war constitution had been dismembered. Government had been carried on by enactments resting on a majority vote in a single chamber and by ordinances prepared by successive parliaments and Councils of State. Small wonder that other lawyers besides St John looked askance at their validity as representing the law of the land. To Thurloe the introduction of a written constitution meant that new legislation would in future require the approval of Commons and Protector, and should therefore command the consent of the governed.

In February 1654 the Council called on Thurloe to submit his office establishment for scrutiny and approval. It is remarkable for the disappearance of Jessop at a time when the foreign work showed no sign of diminution. However, Jessop still continued in employment as one of two assistant secretaries, the other being Henry Scobell, until then Clerk to the Commons. Both appear in an authority to pay a quarter's wages on 31 December 1654, when they were each to receive £125 compared with Thurloe's £200. Frost, who as treasurer of the Council's contingencies was to make the payments, was to have £100, Milton £72 4s. 7d., Meadow £50, James Nutley £30 6s. 8d. as clerk of the patents, eight other clerks the same and eleven messengers £22 15s. each. The payments were not made until 13 February, six weeks late, a delay that must have meant real hardship to the families of many of these men in supposedly good employment. They often had to wait even longer.

It will be observed that sergeant-at-arms Colonel Dendy is absent from this list, as unaccountably as Jessop from the earlier one. The full list of February contained Philip Meadow, Latin secretary; Dendy, sergeant-at-arms; Frost, treasurer; Milton, the amount of his salary left blank (though it is evident from the later payment that his duties continued so far as his blindness permitted); seven under-clerks at 6s. 8d. a day; eleven messengers at 5s. a day and 6d. a mile riding; nine sergeant's deputies at 3s. 4d. a day and 8d. a mile riding; a man to make the fires in the clerks' rooms at 2s. a day; four attendants in the Council chamber, one at 7s., one at 3s., and two at 2s. a day; and two women cleaners at 2s. a day. The establishment was approved as it stood by the Council, but the Protector personally added one more messenger and one more sergeant's deputy, and increased one of the Council chamber attendants' daily pay from 3s. to 4s.[35]

Although Thurloe, as Clerk of the Council, had occasionally been sent to Cromwell as Lord General and must have been periodically in personal touch with him about his land and other legal matters, he now began an almost daily contact with the Protector, presenting papers for signature, reports and petitions of all kinds, and letters from ambassadors and foreign governments. Besides the Great Seal, now in commission, and the Privy Seal, in royal days there had also been a signet for the personal correspondence of the monarch, with the Principal Secretary as its keeper. Cromwell continued his practice and the clerks of the signet were added to Thurloe's staff. The number of letters written by Thurloe to recipients of Cromwell's correspondence makes it evident that he was privy to the majority of the Protector's most confidential and personal writings. Cromwell employed William Malyn as his private secretary from 1650, but he appears to have been no more than a personal assistant and to have exerted little, if any, influence on policy or events.

The Protector aroused some anxietyy at the beginning of April by requiring the commissioners to return the Great Seal. One of them, Bulstrode Whitelock, was in Sweden. George Cokayne, his chaplain, agitated that his master might be affronted in his absence, called on Thurloe between nine and ten o'clock at night, and was reassured. 'Indeed Mr Thurloe hath played his part gallantly and like a true friend, for which I shall love him as long as I live', Cokayne told Whitelock. Cromwell kept the Seal himself for a couple of days to seal the Dutch treaty, before placing it again in commission with Whitelock, Sir Thomas Widdrington and John Lisle.[36]

The management of the post was still causing problems. The previous Council had supported Manley and had given him authority to seize all mail carried by others, including carts, wagons and pack horses. Now the Protector's Council issued an ordinance on 20 January confirming Manley's contract and forbidding any other carriers. After two members had considered the matter, Manley's rent was continued at £2,500 for the quarter begun in January. At the end of the month the Council had to deal with plaintive petitions from former farmers of foreign mail and others whom Manley had turned out for attempting to provide a cheaper service.[37]

Now that Thurloe had become a man of power in the land as Secretary of State to His Highness the Lord Protector, Lincoln's Inn made haste to honour him by making him a bencher on 10 February 1654. His name had come forward for call to the bar in the previous June, though he had been a member for only six years instead of the customary eight, but the council of Lincoln's Inn had omitted him because he was not in commons and they concluded that he did not wish to be called. It was, in fact, in the same month that he was given lodgings at Whitehall. He must have made his excuses to the Society, for they called him to the bar on 9 November.[38]

St John, though still not fully recovered from his illness, was back in London at the end of February 1654. Thurloe sent a messnger to his chamber with £300 for some undisclosed purpose and a note to say that he would wait on him in the afternoon to receive his quittance. St John scribbled on the note an invitation to dinner, naming the place. He must speak with Thurloe, he added, so the Secretary should come to his chamber if unable to dine. When they met, St John had with him a printed copy of the Instrument of Government, which he said he had just read. 'Is this all the fruit the nation shall have of their war?' he demanded rhetorically, throwing the document aside in disgust. He then developed the argument and left Thurloe in no doubt of his thorough disapproval of the form of government set up under the Instrument.[39]

If Thurloe had by then modified his earlier views on constitutional arrangements, he left no record of it. Up to March 1652 he had owed everything to Oliver St John's patronage and protection and this meeting demonstrates that their friendship continued, even though Thurloe was serving a regime of which St John disapproved. As for Thurloe, he had unreservedly transferred his loyalty to the Protector. In a society dominated by patronage he now had the favour of the most powerful patron of all. While St John, harking back to the ideas of Pym and Hampden, could be critical of recent political developments, Thurloe would have been foolish as well as churlish to have spurned the confidence extended to him by the head of state. His importance in the government was steadily growing now that he had a voice in Council and was its chief executive. Nowhere was this more apparent than in the conduct of foreign policy.

3
FOREIGN AFFAIRS, 1652–1657

The same arts that did gain
A power, must it maintain *(Andrew Marvell)*

When Britain, looking with a just disdain
Upon this gilded majesty of Spain . . .
Our nation's solid virtue did oppose
To the rich troublers of the world's repose *(Edmund Waller)*

The English response to the breakdown of negotiations with the Dutch early in 1651 was to pass the Navigation Act. St John, still smarting from his refuff, was determined to break the Dutch monopoly of the carrying trade. The Act, largely the work of convinced republicans in parliament, admirers of Venice such as Heselrige and Scot, became law on 9 October 1651 and made it obligatory to carry English exports in English bottoms and imports either in English ships or in those of the country of origin. Its effects, in reducing Dutch and increasing English commerce, were felt almost immediately. In response the States General sent three ambassadors to London to reopen negotiations. They reached Gravesend on 15 December bearing complaints of interference with their shipping, even when French rather than English or Dutch goods were being carried. Discussions covering the same ground as those of 1651 dragged on through the early days of Thurloe's tenure of the Secretary's office. There was little talk of union, and though the English made some concessions – for instance, that Dutch subjects of reformed religion might settle in England and enjoy the same privileges as natives – tension continued to mount.

The two countries drifted into war through a four-hour naval action between Tromp and Blake in the Downs on 20 May 1652. Four days later Thurloe was directed to extract the salient points from detailed reports of the action and to submit them next day to the foreign affairs committee. The Dutch ambassadors, still in London, were bombarding parliament with papers. Thurloe and Sir Oliver Fleming, the Master of Ceremonies, had to deliver replies on 5 June.[1]

A naval war with the United Provinces brought difficulties with other maritime powers. Thurloe became embroiled in disputes with Denmark, the Senate of Hamburg, the Hanseatic agent, with Spain and with Sweden under her young queen, Christina. The Peace of Westphalia, which brought to an end the Thirty Years War in 1648, had left much of eastern Europe devastated and exhausted. Philip Sydney, Viscount Lisle, a former Lord Lieutenant of Ireland and a Councillor of State, was selected as ambassador to the Swedish court in January 1653. Thurloe prepared his instructions from parliament, which in essence were to explain the quarrel with the Dutch and to protest if Queen Christina received any representative of Charles Stuart. To these the Council added another important point of English policy: that there should be free trade through the Sound, unhindered by the Danes or the Dutch. The Danish closure of the Baltic to English shipping was causing great anxiety about the supply of masts, yards and other naval stores. Their provision from Scotland was a subject constantly before the Council at this time. In August 1653 Richard Bradshaw at Hamburg managed to buy and ship some masts, powder and shot.[2]

The political upheavals of 1653 hampered progress, Lisle proved far from enthusiastic and his departure was repeatedly postponed. Towards the end of the year the Nominated Assembly decided to send Bulstrode Whitelock in his place to negotiate a treaty with the Swedish queen. He left for Gothenburg in November on board the forty-four-gun *Phoenix,* with four other ships and a ketch. Into a very full account of his embassy, written later, he made a point of inserting a letter written by Thurloe in the following March

> to show by it the constant way and course of intelligence, and the generality and clearness of it, between Thurloe and Whitelock, whereby his business and reputation in this court was very much admired; and Whitelock made great use and advantage of it.

Normally they conversed in French. He was forced by circumstances to remain a long time at Christina's court at Uppsala, where he had arrived and been made welcome just before Christmas.[3] His embassy therefore extended over the closing weeks of the Nominated Assembly and the opening month of the Protectorate, reflecting a consistency of policy which survived the shifting regimes.

Thurloe had inherited from Scot a number of correspondents overseas, most of whom were not trained or full-time intelligence agents but merely reporters of the local political scene and sometimes the military situation as an army advanced here or a fortress fell there, a fleet was prepared, sailed or returned to harbour. Some correspondents were merchants and some were consular agents. In this he was following in the footsteps of Mr Secretary Walsingham, for whom the office of

Principal Secretary had been created in the reign of Elizabeth I, and of Mr Secretary Cecil, who took the tradition into the Stuart age.

Besides maintaining several correspondents at various times and places in Flanders and the Netherlands, Thurloe received reports from such centres as Danzig, Hamburg, Zürich, Paris, Marseilles, Madrid, Genoa, Leghorn and Rome. From these and from intercepted diplomatic and private correspondence he was able to build a fairly balanced picture of the European scene and to report on events to the Protector and Council, and later to parliament, as well as keeping the Protectorate's diplomatic representatives overseas up to date.

To this extensive correspondence he added regular letters to and from the military commanders to Scotland and Ireland (and later in Flanders) and the generals at sea. He also supplied Marchamont Nedham, a journalist and writer ready to sell his talents to the highest bidder, with material for the only two news sheets officially permitted for much of the Protectorate period: *Mercurius Politicus,* published on Thursdays, and *The Public Intelligencer,* on Mondays. The former had previously been supervised by Milton and Frost, but it now made better sense for Thurloe to do it himself.

The naval war went well for England. There were actions between the opposing fleets off Portland in February 1653, near the Gabbard shoal and off Scheveningen in June, and off the Texel at the end of July; in most the Dutch fleet suffered heavier losses than the English. In the final action off the Texel, part of the Dutch fleet was accused at home of cowardice. One of the intercepted letters seen by Thurloe listed the sentences on the culprit officers, ranging from three years in the workhouse; through fines of between thirty and a thousand guilders, keel-hauling three times and standing with a halter round the neck, to a kick in the breech.[4]

The English lost a number of merchant vessels to Dutch warships in the Mediterranean. Longland, Thurloe's correspondent at Leghorn, more than once urged him to send 'a nimble squadron' to protect trade. There were also losses of ships from the Newfoundland fisheries. In home waters the Dutch managed safely to escort their convoys to and from the Indies as far as Shetland, and to give safe passage to their trade from Bergen and the Sound, but elsewhere they lost an enormous number of merchant vessels. Thurloe reckoned their losses above 1,400 prizes by February 1654, of which 120 were warships. Modern historians have put the total at 1,500.

By that time the Dutch had twice sent commissioners to treat for peace, but England was continuing to equip a fleet for the following summer. With a certain disregard for the singular and plural – typical of his style – Thurloe boasted that 'this State intends their preparations at sea as if the war were to continue', that seventy warships were already at sea and there would be a hundred and twenty by the beginning of March. The Dutch had none, he crowed, and their merchants dare not enter the Channel 'so perfectly is this State masters and lords of the narrow seas'. Nevertheless his anxiety showed in a severely worded letter of 3 March 1654 to an intelligence agent in the United Provinces calling for exact weekly reports of Dutch warship readiness and movements.[5]

When the four Dutch commissioners first arrived in June 1653 they were introduced to Thurloe by Hugh Peter, who had been busy striving for peace between the two Protestant nations. They found the Council still insistent on some form of merger. This the Dutch totally rejected. Though lodged in a handsome house in the newly fashionable area of Covent Garden, they complained that all their actions were spied upon and reported that friends in England had told them that all the secret transactions of the States General at The Hague were presented weekly in writing to the Council of State, an allegation that quickly reached Thurloe.[6]

Two of the ambassadors returned to The Hague at the beginning of August, just as reports were being received of the final action off the Texel and of the death of Tromp. They arrived back in London towards the end of October with proposals for a defensive league, but were met by a draft treaty drawn up in imperious terms. Again it was unacceptable to the Dutch. One of their commissioners died on 4 December and the three survivors left on 3 January 1654. At Gravesend the next day they heard from Thurloe that Cromwell had at last given way. They returned in February and finally got down to serious negotiation for a peace treaty, though even then there was coolness when Cromwell refused to receive their leader, who had to send to The Hague by express for amended credentials.

The Protector received the ambassadors at the Banqueting House, the only building of a projected new Whitehall palace that had been completed. The procedure was for Cromwell, attended by the Lord President and five members of the Council, the Secretary of State and Master of Horse, to enter the hall by the privy door from the older part of the palace and to take his place in a raised and carpeted area, the Councillors and Secretary standing on either side of his chair of state. The ambassadors, conducted by the Master of Ceremonies, made three bows on entering, advanced halfway to the dais and again bowed three times, then bowed a further three times at the foot of the steps. 'Good God! What damn'd lick-arses are here!' was a forthright comment in an intercepted letter seen by Thurloe at this time, reporting that the French ambassador was also pressing to be heard by the Protector.[7] It was the open recognition of the usurper that so outraged this correspondent, rather than simply the number of 'legs' made by the ambassadors. Such matters were governed by strict rules of protocol, as were occasions for standing or remaining seated and for covering or uncovering the head. The Protector and his entourage, insistent that the English head of state was equal to any other, attached importance to these things. Their quarrel with the Dutch over salutes in the narrow seas stemmed from the same cause.

The Dutch negotiations took another month. On one occasion the ambassadors asked Thurloe to meet them in St. James's Park on a Saturday, as if to outwit eavesdroppers. Thurloe could afford to adopt a firm attitude. Reports from Holland, while showing preparation for a fleet in case of a renewal of hostilities, revealed public opposition to any continuance of the war. When he went to see the ambassadors after dark on 30 March he was able to force them to accept the English reply to their latest memorandum. On 5 April they signed the treaty and sent it to the States General for ratification.[8]

Thurloe later summarized the terms of the Treaty of Westminster. The first English draft consisted of twenty-seven articles; after debate and amendment the final treaty contained thirty-three. The first four, dealing with peace, did indeed refer to a confederacy under which each country would assist the other with men and ships and would conclude no treaty alone – an agreement quickly ignored as England made bilateral treaties with Sweden, Portugal and Denmark, causing complaints from the Dutch ambassador in December. There was to be oblivion of all injury suffered since war broke out in May 1652, but in a later article the Dutch were held responsible for reparation of damages they had inflicted, notably in the East Indies, between 1611 and 1652. Prisoners of war were to be released. The Dutch had complained several times about their treatment and had pointed out that they included subjects of a number of other states. The vexed question of salutes in the narrow seas was settled by article 13, which laid down that ships and vessels of the United Provinces, military as well as civilian, should, on meeting any Commonwealth man-of-war 'in the British seas', strike their flag and lower the topsail, as had always been the practice under any other form of government. Eight articles referred to trade in Europe, trade with each other's plantations being forbidden, and a further three provided for warships protecting each other's trade.

Cromwell – who had, according to Thurloe, agonized over the lamentable state of the Protestant cause while the war continued – made provision for the Anglo–Dutch alliance established by this treaty to be joined by the Swiss Protestant cantons, the Duchies of Holstein and Courland, the Count of Oldenburg and the Hanseatic towns. A secret clause was added between England and the United Provinces in furtherance of the Protectorate's implacable harrying of the House of Stuart. It was agreed that neither the United Provinces nor any one of them at any time to come would appoint the Prince of Orange, grandchild of 'the last King of England', or any of his descendants to be captain general, stadtholder, commander of their armies or governor of any of their towns, castles, forts or fleets. That individual provinces raised serious objections to the terms of this clause soon became common knowledge. Man may propose, but God disposes. The young prince, not yet four years old, was destined to become not only Stadtholder of the United Provinces but, as William III, King of England, Scotland and Ireland.

Thurloe's summary ends with some reflections on the difficulties of negotiations with the Dutch, who tried persistently over many years to alter the English stance on the right of visit and search, and to persuade England to repeal the Navigation Act. Moreover, they quibbled over the designation of seas as 'British' or 'English'. (What is now called the English Channel was shown on the 1651 Great Seal of the Commonwealth as the British Sea.) The Dutch also argued that salutes accorded British ships were given in respect for the dignity of the kingdom and not in recognition of British dominion over the sea.[9]

On the evening the treaty was signed, members of the Council, with the Secretary of State and Scobell, their clerk, drove in the Lord Protector's coaches, carrying the documents from Whitehall to the Dutch ambassadors' lodging. The leading coach had six horses, and running alongside were footmen in the Protector's grey livery, their coats velvet-collared and welted with velvet, silver and black silk lace. Cromwell and his ministers, Thurloe among them, were certainly aware of the value of ceremony and dignity. The treaty was ratified without delay by both sides.

On 25 April Thurloe was ordered to arrange heralds to proclaim peace on the following day at Whitehall, Temple Bar, St Paul's and the Old Exchange. There were celebratory bonfires at night, and cannon boomed from the Tower and on board ships in the river. The Dutch ambassadors had nearly eighty barrels of pitch burnt in the riverside garden of their house. Two days later they were invited to dinner at Whitehall, travelling there in two coaches, and were received with a fanfare of trumpeters. The Protector sat with the three ambassadors and three of his Council at one table, the rest of the Council at another, while Cromwell's wife, with one of her daughters and Mrs Lambert, entertained two Dutch ladies at a third. Music was played during dinner and afterwards the company heard a rendering of a psalm.[10]

Hostilities were to cease on 4 May. Earlier instructions had been sent to

New England for an attack on Manhattan island, whose Dutch inhabitants were to be encouraged to stay under the English flag or return to Europe, but Thurloe wrote immediately cancelling the project in light of the peace treaty. News of the peace reached Boston on 20 June, a week before a force of nine hundred foot and a troop of horse was to advance towards the Hudson.[11] Not until the reign of Charles II did this valuable Dutch enclave fall to the English.

The slow negotiations with the Dutch had held up Whitelock's treaty in Sweden, for the Swedes, understandably, would not sign until they knew the outcome in London. Thurloe had been writing weekly to his friend to keep him up to date. 'I perceive you have to do with a wise woman', he observed at an early stage. Towards the end of February 1654 he assured the ambassador that the Council was very satisfied with what he had so far achieved and

> commit the issue thereof unto the Lord, who will either bless the endeavours by bringing things to a desired issue or otherwise dispose of this affair to the glory of God, the good of the Commonwealth and the comfort of yourself who are employed in it.

The tedious talks with the Dutch were trying Thurloe hard. 'It is now midnight and I am extreme weary', he ended his letter of 15 March. In his next he said that Whitelock's wife had been with him to urge the ambassador's speedy return, 'wherein I should be glad to be instrumental', a note that caused Whitelock to offer apologies. 'I presume Mrs Thurloe will join me', he wrote, 'in asking your pardon for the importunity of a loving wife who troubles you daily soliciting for an order for her husband's return.' This importunate wife was Mary, Whitelock's third. She had borne him her third child just as he was sailing from the Thames, and in addition was responsible for the care of several stepchildren. Whitelock left a record in his diary that Thurloe had been one of those who had encouraged Mary to accept him.[12]

An additional anxiety for both Whitelock and Thurloe at this stage was Queen Christina's decision to abdicate in favour of her cousin Carl Gustav. Thurloe had heard of her intention three months earlier, but could not at first believe it and still wondered at it. When at last the Dutch treaty was signed, new instructions were sent off to Sweden and Whitelock was told that he was at liberty to return home. He had evidently expressed in writing his appreciation of Thurloe's care in keeping him informed, for Thurloe ended his letter of 13 April by returning humble thanks for the ambassador's acceptance of his endeavours to serve him. Among the recurring Swedish complaints about England's detention of their ships and cargoes there was apparently one concerning goods belonging to the queen. Whitelock wrote about it to Cokayne, who went immediately to Whitehall on 26 May and discussed the matter over a private dinner with Thurloe.

Whitelock signed the Swedish treaty at the end of April, sailed from Stockholm on 31 May and, after travelling overland from Lübeck to Hamburg, reached England on 1 July at the end of a perilous voyage during which the frigate sent for him by Thurloe was grounded in fog off the English coast.[13] He arrived in London on a Saturday. Cromwell, who had become Protector since Whitelock's departure the previous year, was at Hampton Court and agreed to receive him on the following Monday. Early that day Whitelock presented himself at Thurloe's Whitehall lodging, accompanied by most of his retinue in their official attire and liveries. Together they went for the audience and were none too pleased to be kept waiting for an hour and a half.

When the first Protectorate parliament met in September Whitelock, who sat for Buckinghamshire, was voted £2,000, a sum which he calculated gave him only £500 profit for nearly a year's demanding work. Soon after his return home the movements of ex-Queen Christina began to excite and puzzle the chancelleries of Europe. She was reported to have arrived at Antwerp at the end of July disguised as a page in an all-male party.[14] Thurloe, who would in time have trouble enough with her successor on the throne of Sweden, could now afford to ignore her, since she retained no power and little practical influence, though she continued to be treated with deference, particularly in Italy after she had professed conversion to the Roman persuasion.

Thurloe was exultant at the way things seemed to be developing. There was peace with Denmark, the Swiss, the Hanseatic towns, Oldenburg and Holstein besides the United Provinces, and the new alliance with Sweden meant that there was now good understanding between most of the Protestant states. France and Spain, still at war with each other, were vying for friendship and a military alliance with the Protectorate. Portugal, fighting for independence from Spain, was pressing for a treaty. But negotiations with Portugal soured when her ambassador and his brother, believing themselves cheated at the New Exchange (built on the site of the stables of Durham House, where the Adelphi stands today), went there in arms. Two men were killed in the resulting affray. The brother was accused and tried for murder. The ambassador had to leave the country on the very day the treaty with England was signed, while his brother, found guilty by a jury composed half of English and half of Frenchmen, was promptly executed on Tower Hill. By the terms of the treaty English trade gained access to Portuguese territories in the Americas, Africa and the Far East.[15]

The Count of Oldenburg, a small Protestant state in the plain of lower

Saxony, had in January 1654 asked the States General to be included in the peace settlement between the Dutch and the English. On 9 March he presented his compliments in Latin to the Protector and three months later he and his son made a short visit to England, where they were given passes to travel freely around the country and to facilitate their return to Flanders.[16]

The count brought a gift to the Protector: a team of six grey Friesland horses. On a fine afternoon in late September 1654 Cromwell invited Thurloe to accompany him when he tried them out on his coach in Hyde Park. According to one account Cromwell was troubled with a stone in his kidney and deliberately rode hard or jolted his body in a coach, 'that by such agitation he might disburden his bladder'. Whatever the reason, Cromwell dismissed the coachman and took his place on the box. A private newsletter of the previous May had remarked on the way in which members of the Protectoral court used to gallop round and round the park. On this occasion Cromwell apparently used the whip unwisely and the horses bolted, the leading horse unseating its postilion. Cromwell was tossed from his seat on to the pole and then on to the ground, though one of his feet became entangled in the harness so that he was dragged for some distance before his shoe came off and freed him. To add to the confusion, his pocket pistol was discharged. Fortunately the horse guard at the park gate had seen what was happening and came to his assistance. Thurloe was lucky to escape with an injured ankle when he jumped from the runaway vehicle, but he and the Protector were severely bruised.[17]

A contemporary piece of satirical verse, headed *Elegy on the unhappy accident,* has survived and is worth quoting:

Foreign ill-tutored jades! Had you but known
Whom you rebelled against, whom you have thrown,
You would have pined to nothing, loathed the day
And left the crows a memorable prey.

It refers later to one

Whose army braves the land, whose fleets the main;
And only beasts did think unfit to reign,

and it goes on to suggest that members of parliament would gladly have prevented the accident:

They would themselves have drawn the coach and borne
The awful lash, which those proud beasts did scorn.

It would have been

> A most magnificent and moving sight
> To see the brother both of Spain and France
> Sit in the coach box, and the Members prance.[18]

The Protector's popularity was far from universal. A year earlier leaflets with what were termed 'barbarous libels' and pictures of 'our noble general' hanging on a gallows had been thrown about the streets of London. Now a lampoon appeared repainting this image in new tones:

> Every day and hour
> Hath shown us his power
> But now he hath shown us his art;
> His first reproach
> Is his fall from a coach
> His next will be from a cart.

When the Anabaptists issued a broadsheet addressed to Cromwell, rhetorically putting to him a number of questions to be answered 'to his own conscience', the twenty-fifth (and last) query was 'whether the six coach horses did not give you a fair warning of some worse things to follow, if you repent not, seeing God often forewarns before he strikes home?'[19]

The Count of Oldenburg sent a further present of horses in January 1655. The Protector was embarrassed and incensed when the vessel bringing them over was intercepted by an English privateer, two of the horses were injured and a trunk of clothes was plundered. The master of the privateer pleaded that the theft had been committed without his knowledge, but the trunk was found at his house and restored to the count, the owners of the privateer being ordered to pay compensation.[20]

Horses, both for riding and for drawing coaches, were at that date part of the trappings of greatness. The French ambassador brought thirteen into England and the Portuguese ambassador took with him twelve, together with a mare and foal, when he left. Thurloe was later in correspondence with Longland at Leghorn about the Protector's purchase of two horses and four mares from Naples. The total bill, including shipping costs and expenses for two Neapolitan grooms to look after them on passage, was over £700. Cromwell later sought to improve English bloodstock by bringing in four Arab stallions from Turkey and another from Rotterdam.[21]

The coaching accident had been an unfortunate end to a rare afternoon's recreation, but it serves to demonstrate how close Thurloe had come to the Protector. He was, in fact, a member of the small circle of intimate friends with whom Cromwell was prepared to discuss events and policy. There is a much-quoted description by Whitelock, relating to a slightly later period, of the way in which Cromwell would sometimes pass an evening with his friends.

The circle included Roger Boyle, Lord Broghill, who in 1649 had returned to London from active service in Ireland resolved to join Charles Stuart and work for his restoration. But a meeting with Cromwell had completely changed his view, turning him into a devoted admirer of the General and, incidentally, a close friend of Thurloe. Another of Cromwell's intimates was the young baronet Sir Charles Wolseley, who had served on two Councils of State and had in December 1653 presented the motion that led to the resignation of the Nominated Assembly. A third was Philip, Lord Wharton, three years Thurloe's senior and a cultured Puritan. Whitelock and Thurloe reportedly completed this small circle. Whitelock describes how Cromwell would decide to break off discussions, 'lay aside his greatness', have pipes and tobacco brought, and play a game of making verses before resuming consideration of great affairs.[22]

At the end of 1655 Sir Edward Nicholas, secretary to Charles Stuart, was told that Oliver St John was a member of the inner cabinet (though this seems unlikely) together with Thurloe, 'who had been St John's clerk', Henry Lawrence, President of the Protector's Council, Nathaniel Fiennes, a son of Viscount Saye and Sele, and from time to time William Pierrepont, a leading Independent member of the Long Parliament, who had consistently deplored the division of the country into warring factions.[23]

Cromwell's son-in-law Fleetwood, commander-in-chief in Ireland, paid tribute to Thurloe's position when he wrote in July 1654 that he felt free to express opinions to the Secretary, assured that he would not divulge them to others, 'knowing the confidence and trust which deservedly is put upon you, as one my lord hath a more particular affection unto, and opinion of'. This is a striking recognition both of Thurloe's qualities and of the relationship built up only months after Cromwell had become Protector. Fleetwood certainly expressed himself very freely on the subject of the Irish, begging Thurloe to deny any of them access to the Protector's person. 'These people are an abominable, false, cunning and perfidious people', he had written in the previous month. Even the best of them were merely to be pitied, certainly not trusted. At the same time he claimed to be doing his best to rehabilitate a fine country; its greatest want, he declared, was a better people. Fleetwood and two other commissioners reported that at a time when scarcely a house was left undemolished outside the walled towns and hardly any timber was left standing, the Dutch were prevented by the Navigation Act from bringing over timber from Norway and the few English who did import wood had fixed their prices beyond the reach of ordinary folk.[24]

One of the first audiences Cromwell gave as Protector in December 1653 was to Alonso de Cardeñas, the Spanish envoy. Cardeñas proposed a closer understanding between England and Spain in the expectation that it would induce France to make peace, restoring stability and peace to all Christendom, which had been disturbed by the ambition of the French. Spain would undertake to secure the Protector in power to the exclusion of Charles and all his line, in return for military and naval help against France. The English contribution was initially set at four thousand troops and twelve warships, but Spain later raised the demand for a whole army on horse and foot, the Spanish themselves paying two-thirds of the costs of this army and of the fleet. In return the English wanted a port in Flanders for safe landing and as a base for operations. By the end of February 1654 Cardeñas felt he had made much progress, though Cromwell's personal preference, supported by some of his Council, was to steer clear of any entanglement with Spain, the power traditionally seen as the main obstacle to advancement of the Protestant cause in Europe.

France was concerned about the outcome of the English peace negotiations with the Dutch, and in January 1654 Cardinal Mazarin despatched to London Paul, Baron de Baas, reputedly brother of the man who served as model for d'Artagnan in Dumas's novel *The Three Musketeers*. Mazarin had by that time been chief minister of France for almost twelve years. Succeeding Richelieu towards the end of the reign of Louis XIII, he had ruled the country during the minority of his son, overseeing the latter stages of the Thirty Years War, and had recently emerged victorious from the protracted civil wars of the Fronde. The French king, not yet sixteen years of age, was already represented at Westminster by Baron Bordeaux, raised to ambassadorial rank in March, but he was now to be assisted by de Baas, whom Thurloe described as 'a great confidant of the cardinal's and a very crafty man'.

The French were quite willing to comply with England's first demand: that Charles Stuart should be turned out, in spite of the close family ties between the houses of Stuart and Bourbon. Thurloe received numerous reports that he was about to leave, and he eventually did so in July 1654. The exclusion of Charles from France would necessarily cast him on Spain, but Cromwell's government reckoned that this would make restoration with the support of foreign troops more unlikely, for the Spaniards were hated by English and Scots alike, and acceptable only to the papist Irish. De Baas offered Cromwell the backing of four thousand horse if he would besiege Dunkirk. It was ironic that Cromwell had intervened in 1652 by sending Blake to frustrate the French relief of Dunkirk, which had been surrendered to Spanish forces on 5 September of that year. Now he saw the prospect of securing 'a sure and good footing on the continent' by the capture, with French help, of Dunkirk or some other port in Flanders.[25] Nearly a century after the loss of Calais, England stood to regain a gateway to Europe.

There followed a period of active horse-trading between the French and Spanish representatives, with large sums of money promised by both sides for England's favour. But when Cromwell set out the English demands for de Baas on 1 May 1654 he received an outspoken rebuff. Disregarding Thurloe's advice, Cromwell immediately turned to Cardeñas, told him that he was resolved on war with France and asked what financial contribution Spain would make. The promised aid now reached £300,000 and on 19 May Cardeñas was told that the Spanish offer was accepted. England would supply thirty ships for the sea war, but her troops were currently heavily engaged in Scotland and could not intervene in Flanders during the present campaigning season.

At this critical period for France de Baas was suspected of intrigue with 'persons tending to public disturbance'. Summoned before a board of enquiry comprising Cromwell, Thurloe and five Councillors, he refused to answer any questions and was summarily expelled early in June. Diplomatic civilities were nevertheless observed. A warship was provided to ferry him and his six servants across the Channel, and the commanding officer was directed by Thurloe to allot them the best accommodation available.[26] It was an opportune moment for Bordeaux to reopen talks, and he did so on the 18th. Cardeñas had by then found the demands of the English too much to swallow. Besides some concessions on trade and currency, they wanted satisfaction for attacks on their ships going to and from their plantations in America. Moreover, they condemned the Inquisition as a danger to English merchants in Spain, who should be allowed their own religious books. Cardeñas replied colourfully that this was to ask for his master's two eyes.

One of Thurloe's admirable summaries of foreign affairs, invaluable to later students and historians of the period, sets out the seven considerations which eventually swayed the government in favour of a treaty with France. First, and always the most important in the eyes of Protector and Council, it would frustrate the French royal interest in restoring the House of Stuart. Then there were the facts that France had a Protestant minority and ancient ties with Scotland. A French alliance looked the better means of keeping the Dutch in check and might also prevent Spain from retaking Portugal. It would halt the losses of English merchant vessels to French privateers in the Mediterranean. Finally, it would advance Cromwell's dreams of leading a united Protestant world against papist Spain and the House of Austria. Against these favourable arguments was the certainty that very valuable trade with Spain would be interrupted. Thurloe had appreciated this point at the beginning of the rivalry for alliance, declaring from the outset that Spain would be 'the steadier friend' with 'the better and more considerable trade'.[27]

The decision was taken by 18 August 1654, when Cromwell authorized the despatch of an expedition to the Caribbean. At that time the fleet was administered by commissioners of the Admiralty and navy, but its operational employment was under the control of the Council. Thus it was Thurloe who signed the instructions for Penn. Venables was appointed to command the troops but received his commission much later. Fourteen warships with transports carrying three thousand foot and a hundred horse were to attack Spanish possessions. Two people were to be sent ahead to Barbados to make preparations and to consider what follow-up forces should be sent, and when.[28]

The expeditionary force did not sail until almost the end of the year. It reached Barbados late in January 1655 and took its first offensive action by landing near San Domingo in April. Achieving nothing there, it went on to capture Jamaica in May. Cardeñas, who had remained in London unaware of the expedition's objective, took leave of the Protector on 30 April and went to the Spanish Netherlands. In Jamaica the commanders fell out and returned separately to England, where they both lost their commissions.

In October Cromwell issued a manifesto justifying what he termed the 'defensive' action in the West Indies. In this century we are quite accustomed to political statements using words in a sense directly opposite to their commonly accepted meaning, but in the seventeenth century this practice must have raised a few eyebrows. The excuse for sending the expedition had been well summarized in the preamble to the commission issued to Venables: to counter a threat to the English plantations. But to do so by attacking Spanish settlements and shipping was very far from a defensive measure.

While Bordeaux grew increasingly restive at the repeated delay, the Spaniards made one more attempt to reach a treaty and avoid open war by sending over the Marquis of Leda as soon as Cardeñas had left. Thurloe told Henry Cromwell that an alliance had been offered 'on extraordinary terms' but made clear his personal distrust by crediting the Spanish with an intention to murder His Highness. It would be necessary to deal with them, he said, 'as the Irish are dealt with in Ireland'. Leda left empty-handed a month later, but he did so in style in the Protector's own coach with six white horses escorted by ten more coaches-and-six.[29]

Amidst much rumour and speculation, an English fleet had been sent under Blake to the Mediterranean in October 1654. Rumour quickly redoubled, perhaps because of the coaching accident, and stories spread on the Continent that Cromwell was to be assassinated as he left the parliament House, that he had indeed been killed, and that his sons had also perished. In Paris the accident was reported in an exaggerated form: the postilion was dead and neither the Protector nor the Secretary was expected to live. Cromwell had certainly been severely shaken by his fall and ran a slight temperature for a little while, but he was out in St James's Park in a sedan chair taking the air on 19 October. A few days later Thurloe wrote that His Highness was perfectly recovered and himself nearly, though still very lame.

Other rumours had the royalist Middleton alternately reported victorious or defeated in Scotland. In these circumstances, the employment of Blake's fleet added a further subject for intense speculation. The French had a fleet under the Duc de Guise at sea with troops to attack the Kingdom of Naples. Many in France and the Netherlands thought this fleet was Blake's objective, especially when he called at Gibraltar to receive orders transmitted via Madrid. At Basel hopes were expressed that Blake would attack the territory of the Duke of Savoy. The English were also widely thought to have captured Canada from the French. All this was reflected in the stream of intelligence from informants and intercepted correspondence passing over Thurloe's desk. He was laid up for over a month until his restored ankle permitted him to resume a more active life, but the volume of paperwork never slackened.[30]

In April 1655 Blake did considerable damage to Tunisian ships and batteries without securing the release of the captives held by the Dey, but he was better received at Algiers, where he redeemed all the English prisoners, while several Dutchmen managed to escape by swimming to the English ships. He took the opportunity to retrieve the guns of Prince Rupert's ships wrecked over Cartagena in 1650, accepting the help of Spain in this and much else in her Mediterranean dominions at the very time when her colonies were being attacked by the English on the other side of the Atlantic. The Spanish government was remarkably slow to react to these transatlantic hostilities. It was not until March of the following year that English merchants in Spain were ordered to leave within a month. In June 1655 Blake received secret, if not unexpected, orders to intercept the Spanish American treasure fleet, always a magnetic target for English naval forces, but he missed the main convoy and returned to England in early October after an exhausting year's voyage. As usual the Commissioners of the Admiralty and navy had insufficient money to pay off the crews. Blake's was not the first penetration of the Mediterranean by an English fleet; Penn had cruised in the western basin in summer 1651 in pursuit of Rupert.[31]

Venice still possessed the most potent Christian navy in those waters and was interested in securing English help against the Turks, but relations with the infant English Commonwealth had got off to a bad

start in 1650 when Venice gave great offence to the English parliament
by receiving a representative of Charles Stuart. Later, the Venetian
ambassador in Paris was instructed to send Lorenzo Pauluzzi to London,
but he arrived without credentials, a fatal error which caused him to be
dismissed unheard by Fleming, the Master of Ceremonies. Not until
June 1652 were his credentials passed by the Venetian senate and
Charles's repesentative there dismissed on the pretext of smuggling. On
18 March 1653 Thurloe was directed in Council to look up the 'for-
malities of a consulship' so that one could be appointed to Venice. An
exchange of ambassadors was agreed just before Cromwell became Protector, but further progress was hindered when in February 1654
Charles appointed an English consul at Venice on the recommendation
of the late resident.[32]

Pauluzzi remained in London as resident and was received by Cromwell in January 1654, Fleming acting as interpreter, and again at the end
of July, when a guard of one hundred halberdiers of household troops
lined the entrance. Some forty gentlemen were in attendance, but only
the Secretary of State stood close to the Protector. Pauluzzi quickly
accepted and repeated Fleming's description of Thurloe as 'the soul of
the government and of the Protector'. The Secretary of State, he complained in a letter of 9 October, was the only minister acquainted with
everything and there was great difficulty in conferring even with him
because he was seldom apart from Cromwell. In July of the following
year he echoed Fleming's words in one of his own letters when he
referred to Thurloe, 'who may be called the soul of the Protector's body'.

By that time Sagredo, formerly the Venetian ambassador in Paris, had
been ordered to transfer to London. An English warship carried him
from Dieppe, sixteen barges brought him from Greenwich to the Tower,
and six coaches with an escort of fifty horse took him to his lodgings. But
when he saw Cromwell a few days later he found no support for his
requests that English troops be sent to Crete to help defend the island
against the Turks, whom many saw as rivals to the Pope as antichrist on
earth. It was probably unnecessary for Thurloe to point out that an
earlier scheme to despatch three thousand royalist prisoners for Venetian service had foundered on the opposition of the Levant Company,
nor could government or City afford to forgo the rich pickings of the
Smyrna trade. Sagredo eventually saw that there was no point in pressing his case. He asked to be recalled and departed by Dutch warship
from Dover in March 1656, leaving his secretary Guavarina as resident.
Pauluzzi had left in the previous November after taking the unusual step
of asking Thurloe to provide him with a testimonial of good service from
the Protector.[33]

By then the long-awaited treaty with France had at last been signed. By

October 1654 Bordeaux was exasperated by the continual delays, which he attributed to the domestic problems of establishing the new English regime and its constitution. In practice, the treaty had been held back by French treatment of the Protestant minority known as the Vaudois or Waldensians residing in the territory of the Duke of Savoy. In January 1655 the duke ordered all those living outside the Vaudois mountain valleys, where their religion was tolerated by an edict of 1651, to return to their enclave, giving them only three days to move on pain of death. In April they were attacked and a large number massacred, causing an outcry in England, where 30 May was observed as a day of humiliation to mark the 'late sufferings, present condition and future relief' of these Protestants.[34] Milton not only composed a sonnet beginning 'Avenge, O Lord! thy slaughter'd Saints', but in his official capacity drafted a stiffly worded protest to Louis XIV. Thurloe informed Bordeaux that Cromwell would sign nothing until the king's reply was received.

The envoy chosen to carry this missive and to distribute the substantial aid subscribed for the Vaudois came to play an important part in Thurloe's career. His name was Samuel Morland. Some nine years younger than Thurloe, and like him the son of a country parson, he had been called from Cambridge University to serve on Whitelock's mission to Sweden. Whitelock found him modest and respectful, very civil and an excellent scholar, and on his return recommended him to Thurloe as suitable for employment.

Morland received barely three days' notice of his mission. He left on 26 May and arrived at the French king's court at La Fère on 1 June. He had to wait no more than three days for a satisfactory reply before travelling on to Turin with a similar letter for the Duke of Savoy. After reporting to the ducal master of ceremonies he rode in his coach to the court about ten miles outside the city. There he was received by the young duke in the presence of his mother and spoke at length, not sparing his words in describing the massacres and atrocities and resultant misery, 'which', he was careful to add, 'no man can say was done by the will of your Highness'. Then he presented the Protector's letter. Ironically, it was the duke's mother, a sister of Henrietta Maria and aunt of Louis XIV, who replied as Regent, applauding Cromwell's concern but denouncing the malice with which the just chastisement of rebellious and insolent subjects had been misrepresented. Nevertheless she promised to prove Savoy's respect for England and the Protector by pardoning the Vaudois and according them the privileges sought on their behalf. After an exchange of letters with the duke's secretary of state, Morland left for Geneva on 19 July, carrying a reply to Cromwell confirming a pardon without precedent and according the Vaudois the free exercise of their religion.[35]

Cromwell had already despatched an ambassador to the Swiss Protestant cantons, a forty-three-year-old doctor of divinity called John Pell, a skilled linguist and mathematician who, after leaving Cambridge, had spent six years at the University of Breda. Pell took up his post at Zürich in May 1654 and exchanged regular correspondence with Thurloe, whom he addressed as Mr Adrian Peters, a merchant at London. Letters sometimes got through in a fortnight but could take as long as seven weeks in transit. Thurloe kept Pell well informed about domestic affairs in England, Scotland and Ireland, permitting him to make translations into German (or High Dutch, as it was then known in England) for publication in an effort to counter the mass of rumours in circulation, many of them started deliberately by royalist sympathizers on the Continent.

Pell had little success in his negotiations with the Swiss cantons and earned a reproof from Thurloe for omitting to send copies of letters exchanged with their deputies, but the Secretary was pleased with the addition to his network of this strategically placed intelligence centre. 'I desire to have from you all the news you hear', he wrote on 4 August when Pell indicated that he was forbearing to report some matters which he imagined Thurloe had already heard from other sources. Even in these circumstances, Thurloe wanted confirmation and corroboration, and so demanded all the news. After a while Pell made a practice of forwarding snippets of news from European capitals, ports and centres of commerce. In April he obtained prior warning of the Duke of Savoy's intention to massacre the Vaudois, but it had taken place even before he sealed his despatch, so he had to report it in a postscript. Cromwell, self-appointed leader of Protestant Europe, immediately despatched letters of outrage to the kings of Sweden and Denmark, to the States General and through Pell to the six Protestant cantons of Switzerland.[36]

Pell had been warned by Thurloe in early July of Morland's impending arrival at Geneva and told to prepare to meet him there. Morland reported his coming to Pell on 4 August, reminding him that they had once met in Edward Montagu's chamber at Whitehall.[37] The Protector now sought to reinforce his representation at Geneva still further by sending over George Downing. Downing, whose uncle John Winthrop was Governor of Massachusetts, had graduated at the new University of Harvard in 1642. Returning to England, he had served first as a chaplain and then as a soldier in Cromwell's army in Scotland. In November 1649 at the age of twenty-six he was appointed Scoutmaster-General, or chief of military intelligence.[38] The expedition to Geneva was his first diplomatic mission; he was subsequently elected to parliament. As a property developer after the Restoration he was to give his name to perhaps the best-known street in the metropolis.

Downing left London on 1 August and was at Boulogne five days later. He found the French court at La Fère and was received by the cardinal, conversing with him in Latin for over two hours. A letter from Thurloe dated 23 August 1655 acknowledged Downing's decision not to wait on the French king but to travel direct to Geneva; however, with Pell and Morland already in residence there was no role for Downing to play at Geneva, especially once news reached London that a settlement had been concluded. The Treaty of Pignerol imposed disadvantageous conditions on the Vaudois, but brought the crisis to an end. The news reached London in late August and Thurloe recalled Downing in September. In fact, he had already left for Lyons and London well before this letter could have been received. He was back in England on 24 October, and reporting to the Council the next day.[39]

There was £16,500 in hand to be distributed to the poor Vaudois. Morland would later write a 'clear and exact account' of its receipt and disbursement. In November he and Pell received instructions from Thurloe. Two thousand pounds had already been sent and distributed, £5,000 remained in the hands of Mr Ludwig Calandine, and a further £2,500 would be sent by bill of exchange. At first they thought it more sensible to make use of Calandine's correspondents rather than take the money from him and arrange transfer through their own agents. But finding that the first £2,000 had been sent to Grenoble a little at a time in packs and panniers, they thought this too dangerous a method and engaged one James Tronchin to take the whole sum at his own risk at two-thirds of one per cent.

Thurloe wrote on both 20 and 27 December approving the method of distribution proposed by Pell and Morland, who replied that the £5,000 paid to a commissioner at Grenoble would soon be spent on corn, cloth, shoes, linen and other things of which 'these poor wretches' had need. But Thurloe's letter of 3 January 1656 contained a sharp rebuke to Morland, who had presumed to criticize Pell's diplomatic indolence and to interfere by negotiating behind his back with the Swiss deputies. This reprimand caused him to acknowledge his fault, to apologize in the most abject fashion and promise to do better in future. In the following month Pell and Morland took over the entire business upon the death of Calandine, whose burial they reported on 13 February.[40]

Morland's detailed accounts showed that a total of £446 out of £9,500 distributed by then had been lost in fees and expenses. Tronchin offered to advance future sums at Geneva, Lyons or Grenoble at two per cent on an assurance of repayment in London with fourteen days at the current rate of exchange. There was, in total, a further £7,000 for disposal. In February Thurloe sent new instructions concerning payments, and he queried the rate of exchange. Morland's methods were later criticized in

London, causing him to defend them vigorously and to plead for
Thurloe's support since he was unknown to His Highness and most of
the Council. He claimed to have made a fair profit for the state by
lending the money at interest until orders for its allotment were received, but 'we here are much afraid that you have endangered the
money by letting it out to a private hand', Thurloe told him. As so often,
those at headquarters were more inclined to caution than the man on the
spot. In March Morland was advised that he was to assign only £2,000
out of £5,000 sent to support the Protestant cantons in the inter-cantonal
war, now apparently at an end. In August, however, Thurloe told him to
allocate the full £5,000.[41]

Morland was repeatedly pressed by Thurloe to write a history of
events in the Vaudois valleys and he did eventually publish a book in
1658, dedicating it to Cromwell in adulatory terms. 'If ever man de-
served a crown,' he had written in April 1657, 'I think he does.' The
book describes the suffering of the 'slaughter'd Saints', reproduces the
official correspondence from authentic copies supplied by Thurloe and
prints the constitution of the committee appointed to administer the
relief fund. The latter was composed of thirteen Councillors plus
Thurloe, seventeen peers and prominent civilians including Richard
Cromwell, St John and Whitelock, eight ministers of religion and two
City aldermen as treasurers.

Morland had been told to stay at Geneva for a year from November
1655, but by the following August Thurloe found it necessary to recall
him as soon as he had arranged distribution of the £5,000 with his
'wonted care and circumspection' and with 'what speed you may'. The
final accounts of the fund, audited by a subcommittee after his return,
show that Cromwell personally subscribed £2,000 and that a further
£36,000 was collected from the parishes of England and Wales. After
several more sums had been remitted during 1657, the balance remaining when Morland's book went to press was over £16,000.[42] It is remarkable and quite revealing that the country was prepared to give these
substantial sums for voluntary relief of distress when it was chronically
unable to raise sufficient by taxation to keep up regular payments to its
own soldiers and sailors.

There was peace between the cantons of Switzerland by March 1656,
though earlier that year Thurloe had been telling Monck that Berne and
Zürich had nearly fifteen thousand men in the field and wanted money
from His Highness. Cromwell would 'strain himself', he wrote, though it
could not easily be spared. He had decided, in fact, to lend £20,000 to
Zürich and Berne, sending £5,000 at once and the rest in monthly
instalments. Thurloe authorized Pell to return to Zürich to discover what
security would be given for the loan. News of the peace meant that the

balance of the money need not be sent. Thurloe expressed a hope that the peace would not be modelled on the Savoy agreement, which had been severely criticized. 'Those of our religion had never good luck at treaties', he sadly observed.[43]

On receipt in August 1655 of the Duke of Savoy's satisfactory reassurances, the long-delayed French negotiations were resumed and an understanding was reached before the end of October. Thurloe had complained that Bordeaux was behaving 'more like a wrangling lawyer than an ambassador' in quibbles over the wording, but the intervention of Nieuport, the Dutch ambassador, was decisive in securing in agreement. Under it England was to send six thousand troops to serve under Turenne against the Spanish in Flanders and would be allowed to keep the fortified towns of Mardyke and Dunkirk upon their expected capture. Bordeaux's long and wearisome task was over. He left Dover on board the frigate *Bristol* on 7 December, though he was soon ordered back for a further spell as ambassador.[44]

In the following year (1656) Cromwell decided to send an ambassador to France and selected William Lockhart, a Scottish colonel turned diplomat, for the post. Lockhart had served as a soldier of fortune in the Dutch, Swedish and French armies before joining the Scottish army *en route* to Preston. He had refused to command a troop of horse for Charles's march on Worcester and, after an interview with Cromwell, had been given official appointments in Scotland. His loyalty to the Protectoral regime was cemented when he married, as his second wife, Cromwell's niece Robina.

Lockhart was under instruction to stress that the French had no firmer friend than the Protector, and that not of necessity but from choice. He was to urge that the time was right for the two to work together against Spain and that neither country should make peace without the consent of the other. Lockhart was to draw attention to the miserable condition of the Protestant people of Piedmont and to say that the Protector expected the French king to uphold the recent treaty by the addition as secretary of William Swift, who had gained valuable experience in Sweden with Whitelock and had since been in eastern Europe. By November Lockhart had reached agreement with Mazarin that English troops would be sent to Flanders for the following season, the French providing half the costs of transport and all their pay and victuals while on service. Lockhart now looked forward to his recall, which had in fact been authorized in October, but he still had a great deal more to do for the Protectorate in France and Flanders. He was, however, able to sail from Dieppe on 4 December just in time to rejoin his wife before her lying-in.[45]

Another member of Thurloe's staff, Philip Meadow, was selected in

March 1656 to go to Lisbon to hasten ratification of the Anglo–Portuguese treaty signed in such distressing circumstances in July 1654. An anonymous informant of the royalist Duke of Ormonde, no doubt considering the envoys to foreign courts should be drawn from the nobility, contemptuously referred to the despatch of 'this fellow (who is a kind of secretary)'.[46] Meadow sailed from Portsmouth on board the *Phoenix*, commanded by Thomas Whetstone, a nephew of the Protector, whose family came from the fens.

Meadow's arrival at Lisbon was followed in May by the anchoring of a powerful English fleet in the Tagus, an early example of gunboat diplomacy. Meadow had earlier reported no hope of agreement and the Council had responded by resolving to intercept incoming Portuguese convoys from east and west. But the show of force off Lisbon achieved its ends, and Meadow brought off his first diplomatic success with an exchange of ratifications at the end of the month. He also extracted compensation of £50,000 for the help that had been given to Rupert's squadron in 1650. Thurloe had mentioned this sum in Blake's instructions in the previous July, when he first advised Cromwell to send an envoy to the King of Portugal.[47]

Before leaving Portugal Meadow was wounded in the left hand when shot at by two horsemen as he was going to his lodging in a horse litter. His head was resting on his hand, and his narrow escape was attested by singed hair and powder spattered on his face. But he returned safely to England in November, again on board the *Phoenix*, with forty-four chests of Portuguese money, and was awarded £1,000 compensation for his injury. Nobody was arrested for the attempt on his life. Thurloe and others believed it to have been an act of reprisal for the execution of the ambassador's brother in London. When officials at the Tower counted the contents of the chests shipped home in the *Phoenix* and another frigate they found three hundred and forty counterfeit coins and a shortfall of one hundred and eight pieces of eight.[48]

Thurloe had kept up a regular correspondence with Admiral Edward Montagu since the principal English fleet had put to sea in March 1656, thanking God when he heard that it was still safe in Torbay after the spring storms. However, naval questions were hindered by ironic financial difficulties as the government explored various means of raising cash. Thurloe could find no easy solution, but he assured Montague that 'all agree [that] whatever else is neglected, you who are at the head of our greatest affairs must not [be].' He added that all receipts from customs and excise had been earmarked for the navy. 'Sometimes we think we are in sight of money, other times it is out of sight', he wrote bitterly on 3 May.[49]

A few days earlier the Protector had despatched an important letter to the admirals in which he suggested that if Cadiz was too strong to be attacked, some other place might be attainable, mentioning especially the town and castle of Gibraltar. If taken and made tenable, the Rock would be both an advantage to English trade and an annoyance to the Spaniard. With a secure base for half a dozen frigates, it would no longer be necessary to keep a fleet off the coast.[50] The copy of this piece of strategic foresight amongst the Thurloe papers is in his own handwriting, giving rise to speculation about how it and others like it were prepared. Were they the outcome of discussion between the Protector and his close advisers, their conclusions merely noted on paper by the Secretary of State? Alternatively, was it virtually Thurloe's own work, copied by Malyn for the Protector's signature and returned to him for filing? Or did Cromwell despatch such missives without formal reference to anybody, such secrecy accounting for the copy in Thurloe's hand rather than that of one of the clerks?

From what is known of Thurloe it seems unlikely that he would, at such an early stage of the Protectorate, have taken charge of foreign affairs and strategic direction to the extent of dictating policy. A couple of years later his authority had grown and the result is obvious in his correspondence. It is, of course, the role of a principal Secretary to be so in tune with the thoughts of the head of state that he can put them into words or translate them into instructions for action. It is almost impossible, at a later date, to discern which of a commander-in-chief's dispositions and directives were made on his own initiative and which at the prompting of his chief of staff. But whatever happens, the man at the top must take praise or blame, and the adviser stand in his shadow.

Cromwell was not alone in recognizing the importance of control of the Straits of Gibraltar. Monck wrote to Thurloe in September 1657 to suggest that Tangier would prove a useful base from which half a dozen frigates could stop all enemy trade. The Portuguese, he said, made little use of it.[51] By then, though, most English eyes were turned towards Dunkirk and the Straits of Dover, the government was about to detach a squadron to cruise inside the Mediterranean, and the use of a port in the Straits does not seem to have been seriously contemplated at any time.

After Meadow had obtained ratification of the Anglo–Portuguese treaty the fleet resumed its blockade of Cadiz in spring 1656 and was subsequently rewarded by the capture of plate and bullion, a significant and welcome contribution to the nation's finances. The two senior officers, Blake and Montagu, who shared a flagship, were away taking water at Lisbon when the Spanish fleet from Havana was intercepted by the rest of the English squadron under Richard Stayner in the *Speaker*. It consisted, as Stayner reported, of four warships, three merchant vessels and a Portuguese prize. The Spanish flagship (a relatively small vessel) and her prize managed to reach harbour, but the vice-admiral's ship and another were sunk, two more ships burnt and two captured. Among the casualties were the Governor of Lima, returning to Spain after twenty-three years in South America, his wife, and two of his children.

This successful action is largely forgotten today, and Edmund Waller's descriptive poem, *Of a war with Spain and a fight at sea,* is little known. At the time, however, interest was intense and centred on the huge prize of bullion – between seven and eight hundred bars of silver weighing sixteen tons or thereabouts, according to Stayner's initial report – landed at Portsmouth and carried to the Tower in one hundred and sixty-five boxes loaded in twenty-two carts and wagons. The small size of the escort – ten foot soldiers – evoked some surprise. Plunder and embezzlement had deprived the state of about three-quarters of the original haul, but at a value of over £250,000 the remaining plunder was still considerable. Thurloe pronounced it 'a renewed testimony of God's presence, and some witness of his acceptance of the present engagement against Spain', but he did not conceal his disappointment on learning that individual seamen had got away with up to £10,000 each, most of it impossible to recover.[52]

Meanwhile Cardeñas, thwarted in London, was actively negotiating with Charles Stuart at Bruges (or Bridges, as the English insisted on rendering it). Thurloe was soon to learn of the resulting treaty by which Charles would be permitted to reside incognito at Bruges, and Spain would supply him with six thousand troops to accompany him to England once his English supporters had secured a port. It was an agreement which neither side was ever able to honour, but its existence posed a continuing threat.

Thurloe was sometimes forced to turn his attention to affairs remote from Europe. In summer 1655 the East India Company, which had been awarded restoration of an island and £85,000 in compensation under article 30 of the peace treaty with the Dutch, referred to the Protector their dispute about the distribution of the money. Thurloe, on Cromwell's direction, consulted the Council, and wrangling over English arbitration went on for several months. Meanwhile two trustees holding the money agreed to Cromwell's request to lend it to the Commonwealth.

In September 1655 Thurloe received a curious approach from one Richard Wylde, who had gone to India in 1624 as a factor at Surat at £100 a year, risen to be president there by 1628 and sailed home in 1630. There was strong backing for a proposal that he should return as president three years later, but the Company could not overlook his past delinquencies. Among the many charges brought against him alleging peculation whilst at Surat was one 'that he gave presents to excess'.

Harbouring a very long-standing grudge, in July 1655 he blamed the company for neglect in a petition to the Protector about the island restored by the Dutch. He followed this up by making a barefaced attempt to corrupt the Secretary of State by offering him £500, 'besides a share of the pearl fishery formerly promised', in return for appointment as consul at Surat entitled to a percentage of the value of goods shipped. As soon as Wylde embarked, Mrs Thurloe was to receive a fine jewel set with eighteen facet and three pendant diamonds. If the Protector would recommend him to the Company as president the rewards would be even better. It is not known whether Thurloe was tempted by this offer. At all events, Wylde did not return to India, though another Richard Wylde, possibly his son, was one of the six writers of the Company at Surat early in 1658. He was listed as absent or dead before the end of the year.[53]

Throughout the long French negotiations Thurloe was wrestling with problems concerning two other states, Sweden and the United Provinces. Christer Bonde, the Swedish ambassador representing the new King Carl X, spoke good English – at their first meeting in August 1655, Cromwell expressed his regrets that he scarcely understood any other language. Only Thurloe and Strickland were present at that audience at the Banqueting House, and they withdrew before the serious discussions began. Bonde was aware that several Councillors, including Strickland, were firm allies of Holland, though he reported that both Thurloe and Cromwell – a great admirer of the late King Gustav Adolf and his championing of the Protestant cause – were well disposed to Sweden.

The Swedes feared above all else the possibility of the Dutch fleet entering the Baltic and Bonde lost no opportunity to lobby English support, on one occasion approaching Thurloe in St James's Park and offering England a share in the Baltic trade if she would supply ships against the Dutch. But little progress had been made when, in late September, Bonde again met Cromwell, with Thurloe also in attendance. Bonde wanted the Protector to warn the Dutch, via their ambassador Nieuport, that an expedition to the Baltic would be viewed with displeasure by both Sweden and England. Thurloe assured him that all his requests would be debated in Council and that he would hear from the three commissioners – Lisle, Whitelock and Strickland – appointed to deal with him. Little was achieved, however, and a further audience with Cromwell in mid-December was largely given over to the Protector's grand plans for a united Protestant cause in Europe, a scheme for which neither the Dutch nor the Swedes showed great enthusiasm. Instead, both wished to air complaints about interference with their trade arising from the Anglo–Spanish war. The Dutch were also pressing for a maritime treaty, to undo some of the unfavourable conditions imposed under the earlier peace treaty.[54]

In summer 1655 the new Swedish king was fighting a successful campaign in Poland. Edward Rolt was sent by Cromwell, to whom he was related by marriage, with orders to find the king's camp, ratify the Anglo–Swedish treaty concluded by his predecessor Queen Christina, and ensure that Carl then observed it. Reaching Hamburg in mid-August, Rolt travelled eastwards to Stettin and, after a wretched journey, found the Swedish headquarters before Warsaw. Hampered by bad weather and the slow and insecure postal service back to Thurloe in London, Rolt had to wait a further seven weeks before finally securing an audience with the king on 6 November. By then the Poles and Tatars had been defeated and the Swedes were preparing a move to Prussia and the victorious Swedish king accorded the English envoy a warm if be-lated welcome, dining him well and inviting him to travel in the royal coach. The treaty ratified, Rolt prepared to return home, sending his assistant William Swift – formerly assistant secretary to Whitelock in Sweden and later one of Thurloe's own clerks – to travel on ahead to Hamburg to arrange passage to England. In the event, the frigate sent to fetch them was diverted to escort duties in the Sound. Rolt and Swift had to kick their heels in Hamburg for over a month and did not return to England until late March 1656.[55]

Rolt was not the only English envoy in eastern Europe at this time. Thurloe was also receiving reports from William Prideaux, who had left Archangel in September 1654 to deliver a letter from Cromwell to the czar. It was a tedious journey, and not until the following year was he able to present the missive. When he saw the czar a month later he was told he might not return to England by way of Riga as he had been instructed from London, but must take ship again from Archangel. Detained as a virtual prisoner in Moscow and deprived of his own cook and scullion, he eventually obtained permission to depart at the begin-ning of July, following a further meeting with the czar at which he received a number of specious excuses for his ill-treatment. He reached Archangel on 7 August and was at last allowed to sail on 5 September.[56]

To the west Carl X had met almost no opposition in Prussia and an alliance with the Elector of Brandenburg had placed another eight thousand troops at Sweden's disposal as the 1656 campaigning season approached.[57] The Dutch became alarmed, particularly at the prospect of allied dominance of the Baltic, and hastily despatched ambassadors to Sweden and Brandenburg. In London, ambassador Nieuport had a meeting with Cromwell at which he sought the Protector's views and intentions. In the presence of Lambert, Pickering and Thurloe, Cromwell declared that he welcomed the Swedish successes against the Poles but was dismayed by their attacks upon Protestant states. The Dutch soon looked to more tangible reassurance and by March they were preparing a fleet of forty-eight ships for the Baltic. Thurloe's excellent intelligence network provided him in due course with a copy of the Dutch admiral's orders.

The Dutch also maintained their protests to England about interference with their shipping as a result of the Anglo–Spanish war and Thurloe, Strickland, Wolseley and Philip Jones met Nieuport towards the end of March in an effort to halt the complaints. He could not believe, Thurloe began, that the Dutch would wish to discourage the English in a war on behalf of the Protestant religion. They all met again on 5 April, when Nieuport bluntly rejected as quite unacceptable nine articles of a draft maritime treaty.[58]

A petition from the Eastland Company, referred by Thurloe to the Committee of Trade on 4 January, possibly prompted the government to try to reach a closer agreement with the Swedes. Cromwell sent for Bonde in January and received him in the presence of Thurloe, Fleetwood and Lambert. On the 28th the Council appointed a trio of commissioners to treat with Bonde and three days later they met Thurloe, who warned them of the ambassador's growing impatience. At Cromwell's insistence Thurloe attempted to persuade Whitelock, one of the commissioners, to return to the Swedish court, but without success. The next day Bonde made his position clear: he had no authority to treat about relations with the United Provinces, thought it would be difficult to unite the Protestant interest, and deemed it unlikely that Sweden would attack the emperor, though the English were free to approach his king on this subject. Once again the grandiose vision of Cromwell, shared by Thurloe, was rejected in favour of a down-to-earth agreement on mundane aspects of trade and commerce. Thurloe had prepared heads of a treaty for an offensive and defensive confederacy between England and Sweden, to which the United Provinces and all Protestant states would in due course be invited to join so as to fight Spain and the whole house of Austria. It remained a dead letter and an undated copy was filed among the papers of January 1656.[59]

There was some interruption to business in February when Cromwell and Thurloe both fell ill and several Councillors were absent from London. The commissioners and Secretary of State eventually met on 5 March to review progress, and a month later Bonde was received by the Protector and consulted at length with Whitelock. Cromwell was out when Whitelock came to Whitehall in the afternoon to report back. Meeting Fiennes, another commissioner, in the lobby outside the Council chamber, Whitelock took him along to Thurloe and the three of them had a detailed discussion. The other two were in favour of compromise; Thurloe found himself alone in arguing strongly for defending the government's designation of pitch, tar, hemp and flax as contraband goods during the war with Spain, and requiring the use of passes for merchant vessels.

On the afternoon of 8 April the commissioners went with Jessop to Bonde's house and read over the articles approved by the Council. Bonde asked for a copy for the text in Latin, a somewhat embarrassing request as Meadow, the Council's Latin secretary, had just departed on diplomatic business. The Swedish ambassador complained that the work had been given to 'one Mr Milton, a blind man'. He had spotted the article about naval stores being considered contraband and replied bluntly that Sweden would never agree, reminding Whitelock that there had been disagreement at Uppsala on precisely the same point. Fiennes, Stickland and Thurloe conferred repeatedly during 8 May, the deadlock was broken and a commercial treaty was eventually concluded in July. Cromwell insisted that Whitelock postpone his departure to the country in order to be present.[60]

During the summer the Swedish army attempted to capture Danzig, but the arrival there in July of Opdam's powerful Dutch fleet raised the siege and freed the shipping held there. Thurloe, who knew all about this intended fleet movement and informed Admiral Montagu of it in April, prophesied that the Swedes were 'likely to have a hot summer' in the face of opposition by Poles, Cossacks and Muscovites. The Dutch, like the English, were principally interested in freedom of trade in the Baltic, and this they secured from Sweden by the Treaty of Elbing in September.[61] Hitherto England had remained neutral and largely aloof, but the campaigns of 1657 were to lead to vigorous diplomatic intervention in an effort to prevent the Protestant states of northern Europe destroying each other.

The continued occupation of Jamaica gave rise to considerable work and correspondence throughout 1656. A relief commissioner, James Sedgewick, had been sent out and produced a depressing report on his arrival. He found Goodson and Fortescue in command of the sea and land forces, and put ashore a welcome supply of provisions and stores. But there was dreadful sickness among the soldiers, who refused to help themselves by raising crops or cattle. He was worried about his own wife and five children left in England, and asked Thurloe to receive his wife and give her his salary. Later reports continued to paint a gloomy picture of sickness and indolence. Although health and morale improved a little and the seamen eventually began constructing a fort at the harbour entrance, there was little sign that planters were willing to move to Jamaica from other islands. Thurloe, who had no experience of life on an undeveloped tropical island subject to fevers for which medical science then offered no prevention or cure, thought that things out to have turned out better, and wrote to Henry Cromwell blaming the bad conduct and unspeakable negligence of those entrusted with management.[62]

All through autumn 1655 plans had been maturing for shipping young Irish men and girls to Jamaica. Henry Cromwell, by then commander-in-chief in the absence of Lord Deputy Fleetwood, reported in September that he could recruit a thousand to fifteen hundred men and 'take up' as many girls as desired. It is evident that a forced, not voluntary migration was envisaged. Henry subsequently offered to send up to two thousand boys of twelve to fourteen years of age. It might be 'a means to make them Englishmen, I mean rather, Christians', he wrote. Broghill in Scotland was also approached and recommended recruiting a regiment for service in Jamaica and rounding up vagabond women. Rather optimistically, he assured Thurloe that recruits would be attracted by the conditions, but he received no further encouragement. Thurloe was ill at the end of September, but even when he recovered he was unable to force a decision from Cromwell and the Council. 'You know we are slow in all our business', he confessed to Henry, who had maintained a regiment due for disbandment in expectation of orders. He was finally told that shipping for the girls would be sent to Galway at the end of December, with new clothes for them on board, but the whole project seems to have fizzled out for lack of drive from central government.[63]

The government showed far greater energy in halting the migration of Scots into northern Ireland. The influx had begun on a large scale under Elizabeth I and, after a slight decline in the early seventeenth century, resumed afresh in the wake of the civil wars. Thurloe, warned by Henry Cromwell, at once recognized the danger. The influx of Scots was, he wrote in November 1655, 'a matter of very great consideration, and is certainly a growing evil, and ought to have a fitting remedy applied thereunto in time; and orders will be sent to General Monck therein'. The Scots in the north, wrote Henry in a letter which crossed Thurloe's, were a pack of knaves. On Christmas Day Broghill reported from Edinburgh that he was about to publish a proclamation forbidding the movement of Scots to Ulster. Neither he, Thurloe, nor Henry Cromwell could have foreseen that the seeds of three centuries or more of trouble had already been sown.[64]

4

POLITICAL AND PARLIAMENTARY AFFAIRS, 1654–1657

If these the Times, then this must be the Man *(Andrew Marvell)*

With such a man the meanest nation blessed,
Might hope to lift her head above the rest *(Edmund Waller)*

For the first few months of the Protectorate, with no parliament in session, Protector and Council were free to enact a series of ordinances, eighty-two in printed form and more than double that number altogether, some of them advancing their reforming policies in matters of law, religion and manners. They remodelled the law of treason, set up a new High Court of thirty-two commissioners including three judges, and regulated the jurisdiction and fees of the Chancery courts; they appointed 'triers' to approve incumbents presented by patrons of livings and 'ejectors' in every county to remove unsuitable clergy and schoolmasters, together with commissioners to visit the universities and schools (Eton, Winchester, Merchant Taylors and Westminster). Thurloe was one of the visitors nominated for Cambridge University. Other ordinances extended religious liberty to Presbyterians, Baptists and Independents, but not to advocates or prelacy or popery, use of the prayer book being prohibited under the heading of scandalous behaviour. They also suppressed cockfighting, duelling, drunkenness and horse racing, though games in Hyde Park were permitted on May Day.

In the ordinance of 28 August 1654 for ejecting scandalous, ignorant and insufficient ministers and schoolmasters, commissioners were nominated to oversee the work of each county. In the list of Cambridgeshire, Huntingdonshire and the Isle of Ely, Thurloe found himself in the distinguished company of Henry Cromwell, President Henry Lawrence, John Desborough and Edward Montagu, as well as of several more local gentry. William Codwell, minister at Wisbech, was one of the assistant commissioners.

Two further ordinances issued in 1654 were of particular interest to Thurloe. The first, of 26 May, concerned the preservation of the works in the Great Level of the fens. It confirmed the earlier Act of Parliament granting the adventurers ninety-five thousand acres once the level had been drained and adjudged. It encouraged every owner of five hundred acres to make repairs to banks, dams and sluices. It covered cases of malicious damage and, significantly, laid down that foreigners, if Protestant, could become free denizens of the Commonwealth upon purchasing or farming any of the reclaimed land.

The second ordinance, about postage of letters, was one of many measures hurried through on the day before the new parliament assembled. It confirmed Manley in his office until 30 July 1655, with sole care of letters and packets entrusted to the foreign and inland post. The rates were laid down and Manley was required to maintain a weekly service by packet boats on the Milford–Waterford and Chester–Dublin routes, as well as providing packet boats for foreign post. Four horses were to be available at each stage and were not to be ridden over more than one stage. To assist the public services, particularly the navy, weekly posts were to be run between Dover and Portsmouth, Portsmouth and Salisbury, London and Yarmouth, Lancaster and Carlisle.[1]

Royalists were again in arms in Scotland. Charles had appointed Lord Glencairn to command there and in January 1654 sent General Middleton from the Low Countries. His departure with three hundred officers was quickly known to Thurloe through an intercepted Dutch diplomatic despatch. In the previous November he had seen, amongst intercepted correspondence, Middleton's licence to export significant quantities of firelocks, muskets, carbines, pistols, armour, saddles, powder, match and bullets. A cavalier from Paris named Edward Wogan rode the length of England picking up volunteers on the way, eventually joining Glencairn with over a hundred men. Faulty intelligence led to Thurloe's failure to intercept this little band.[2] Monck, released from his successful naval posting in the Dutch war, was sent north to raise men, money and ships for the Protector. Arriving at Dalkeith at the beginning of May, he proclaimed the Protectorate and Union, promising Scotland thirty members in the parliament at Westminster. He then marched through the Highlands and defeated Glencairn. Middleton's men were routed in July, though Middleton himself escaped and returned to the Continent.

The new parliament summoned under the Instrument of Government differed in several ways from previous assemblies. The number of members representing the English counties was much increased and the borough representation correspondingly reduced. On 12 July Thurloe was elected for the Isle of Ely in the county of Cambridgeshire. Six weeks later a petition from his supporters and others who had assembled at Wisbech for the election alleged malpractice in the election of the second member, George Glapthorne. Despite a cross-petition from the candidate and his own supporters, Glapthorne was probably excluded following a Council enquiry. Under the terms of the Instrument the Scottish and Irish seats were to be arranged by Protector and Council, but after some delay and uncertainty elections proceeded there, too. From Ireland, Fleetwood complained that all the ablest men had been chosen for parliament and queried whether they should be permitted to attend, only to become alarmed when told to detain six of them.[3]

Why did Thurloe choose to enter parliament at this stage of his career? St. John's influence had certainly waned, but it had been supplanted in even stronger measure by that of the Protector himself. After the notable failure of the Nominated Assembly it may be that Cromwell wanted to be sure of some members who could be relied upon to forward his own will, and for this Thurloe was an obvious choice. In any event, Cromwell required a spokesman to explain to members the decisions of the executive and to lay information before them. Again Thurloe, with his hand on every aspect of government (except those in the province of the Attorney- and Solicitor-General) was the right person to fill such a role.

Thurloe's predecessors as Principal Secretary under Elizabeth I and the first two Stuarts had all sat in parliament either in the Commons or the Lords, and now that he had been raised to that office it was no doubt expected of him by political friend and foe alike that he should enter parliament at this, the first opportunity. While most of his early legal work had been that of a notary, in later years he had acquired limited experience as an advocate in the courts, which gave him some confidence in speaking in debates. His work for the Council had brought him into frequent contact with members of the Rump and Nominated Assembly and had given him some knowledge of the way in which the Commons handled their business. Nevertheless it was a big step for him to take when he was already so hard-pressed to keep pace with the day-to-day burden of his office.

Although it was a Sunday, the members assembled on 3 September as arranged. After they listened in the Abbey to a sermon about the arrival in the promised land after years in the wilderness, their election of a Speaker was interrupted by the Protector's summons to the Painted Chamber to hear a short speech. He returned the next day in state, escorted by liveried foot guards with halberts, the captains of his foot guards and horse guards walking on either side of his coach, to address the members again. In a major speech, bitterly denouncing Levellers, Sectaries and other enemies of good order, Cromwell praised the re-establishment of good order over the previous nine months and called upon members of parliament to continue the sound policies put in train by his Council since December 1653. Parliament quickly re-elected as Speaker William Lenthall, who as Speaker from 1649 to 1653 had been head of state in the new republican Commonwealth.

Members then spent several days debating whether to approve 'a single person and parliament' as set out in the Instrument of Government. The right of 'private persons' to draw up a constitution was immediately queried. On 12 September they were summoned again by Cromwell, who spoke for an hour and a half. He was firm that government was to be by a single person and a parliament and that he was that single person. He had received office from God and the people and was resolved never to part with it until God and the people should take it from him. It would perhaps have been more honest to have said 'God and the army'. He was equally firm that certain fundamentals be preserved: that parliaments should not perpetuate themselves, that there should be liberty of conscience and that neither parliament nor Protector should have absolute power over the militia. The remaining lesser parts of the Instrument could be altered, Cromwell declared, if members wished to pursue constitutional revision.

Although one of the first acts of the Protector and Council had been to abolish by ordinance an earlier requirement for taking an engagement to be loyal to the constitution, Cromwell now insisted that members should do so, and about a hundred complied before nightfall. About ninety others, republicans and vehement opponents of the Protectorate, failed to sign this Recognition – that government be in the hands of a single person and parliament – and excluded themselves from the House. From Ireland, Fleetwood wrote to Thurloe deploring the introduction of 'a dividing spirit' by the use of this test, whilst at the court of Charles Stuart in Cologne it was commonly supposed at this time, as Thurloe was informed by one of his agents there, that Cromwell would shortly become the first emperor of Great Britain.[4]

There were those who wanted to demonstrate more violently their opposition to the new regime. For the most part they were Fifth Monarchy men, but they were generally described as Anabaptists. Cromwell had not hesitated to have Major-General Thomas Harrison, their leader in the army, arrested early in September, though he invited him to dinner and released him a few days later. Nevertheless discontent persisted in the army and elsewhere. The Leveller John Wildman, for example, was active in preparing a petition against the Instrument of Government.[5]

In a letter to Monck in Scotland, Thurloe gave a clear description of Cromwell's handling of these difficult men. Some of them came to the Protector and demanded the liberation of 'prisoners of the Lord'. Cromwell told them that nobody in England was in prison for the Lord; they were there for stirring up people to arms. A couple of days later he sent for Harrison and some others, but they refused to come and declined a second time when summoned by a warrant in writing. He therefore had them arrested and brought before him. When asked why they had disobeyed the summons they said that they refused to acknowledge the government and feared the wrath of God should they do so. The government, they said, was against the will of God and in opposition to the Kingdom of Christ. Asked to promise to live peaceably, they declined and were committed to prison to prevent their exploitation by royalists or Levellers.[6] Three were dispersed to provincial prisons, though a fourth was permitted to go to his dying wife in the country.

The most dangerous leader of the radical opposition was Edward Sexby, a man of Thurloe's age who had fought in Cromwell's regiment but had later been deprived of his commission. He had escaped arrest in 1654 and got away to Brussels, where he made contact with the Spanish governor of the Netherlands and revealed what he knew of the plans for Penn's voyage to the West Indies. Later he went to Madrid, where he laid the foundations of an agreement between Charles Stuart and the Spanish king, before returning to seek common cause with the royalists at the exiled court at Bruges. He was back in England by February 1655 to dabble in assassination plots, but he then escaped again to the Continent.

For three months or more after Cromwell's speech on 12 September the first Protectorate parliament ran fairly smoothly. Grievances were aired, injustices corrected and a small but useful programme of public and private legislation was advanced. Members devoted much of their time to constitutional revision, examining the Instrument clause by clause and drawing up their own Government Bill. The principal points of the Protectoral system, the so-called fundamentals of Cromwell's speech, were quickly accepted but the mass of secondary details took much longer to settle.

After occasionally heated debates it was resolved that the office of Protector should be elective, not hereditary, and that the choice of a new head of state should rest with the parliament (if sitting) or the Council. Lambert had spoken in favour of the hereditary principle but had been outvoted by two hundred to sixty. Commenting on the decision, Bordeaux reported that 'the nation is no-wise affected' to Cromwell's family 'nor much to himself', an assessment which may have shocked Thurloe as much as the outcome of the debate. Despite opposition from Thurloe's friends and conciliar colleagues, the House also decided that all future appointees to the Council would require parliamentary approval. The Government Bill redefined the powers of the Protector and shared between Protector and parliament or Protector and Council the command of the regular armed forces, the declaration of war and peace and other vital functions.

By the end of November most of the Bill had been debated and agreed in Grand Committee and was about to be reconsidered on the floor of the House. In all this, Thurloe had apparently taken no part. His record for the session as a whole suggests that he played a minor and inconspicuous role in this parliament – he was nominated to just five committees and never served as a teller in divisions. Moreover, his committee record indicates that he was absent from parliament for over two months, from late September (when he was injured in the coach accident) until early December.[7]

Thurloe was present in the chamber from time to time during the last six weeks of the session and witnessed at first hand the growing rifts. The religious settlement, the extent of the Protectoral veto, the revised franchise and other vital areas of the constitution all raised some disquiet, but the parliament and its Government Bill were ultimately wrecked by new provisions concerning the command and financing of the armed forces. Members decided to all but halve the size of the army to thirty thousand men and set a military budget – £700,000 per year – barely adequate to support that number. The fleets and coastal forts were to receive £400,000 per year. Cromwell was given joint command over the regular forces for life, but after his death sole control was to pass to parliament, to be disposed of as it 'shall think fit'.

Finally members came to the old bone of contention between king and parliament: the control of the local militia forces. In the closing days of the session, members not only pressed ahead with the disbanding of all regular troops over and above the thirty thousand, but also added a clause to the Government Bill giving parliament sole control over the militia; present and future protectors would have no voice in their command. In response Cromwell quickly brought the session to an end. He dissolved it on Monday 22 January 1656, the earliest possible date available under the Instrument, which required the session to last a minimum of five months. The Government Bill and all the other proposed legislation was lost.

Cromwell's dissolution speech ranged over a number of topics: from his hopes of the previous autumn to the shortcomings of the parliament; from the threats to the regime at home and abroad to evidence of divine support for his actions; it reflected the Protector's acute anger, disappointment and frustration. Thurloe added his own gloss on the parliament and its members four days later:

> The truth is, there was so little consistency and agreement amongst themselves, and so violent and strong parties contradicting each other,

that it was scarce possible for them to come to any resolution among themselves that might be for the public good. In all the time they sat they prepared not one act to present to His Highness, nor not so much as for raising money for paying the army.[8]

In March 1655 Thurloe's salary was continued at £800 a year and in the following month a lucrative new source of income was opened to him when the Council, reviewing the administration of the Post Office in the light of a report from the Solicitor-General, ordered that management of all post, inland and foreign, should rest with the Secretary of State after Manley's two-year contract expired in July. Thurloe gave security for payment of the existing rent of £10,000 a year and undertook to keep the same conditions. The Venetian resident estimated that he would make a profit of £6,000 a year.[9]

In August the Council approved the Protector's orders for the postal service. 'To ensure security and expedition our chief Secretary of State is to have charge of the postage and carriage of all letters and packets, both foreign and inland', they read. Posts were to travel from stage to stage at seven miles an hour from April to September, and at five miles an hour for the rest of the year. Mail was to be carried in leather bags, and the horn was to be sounded on meeting company and four times a mile. Mails to and from London were to operate three times a week. Persons riding post were to change horses only at a post house and were to pay threepence a mile, and a groat (a fourpenny silver coin) to the guide if riding 'horse and guide'. Less than a week later the Navy Office complained to the Admiralty commissioners that the Post Office had refused to accept their letters free of charge in spite of Thurloe's instructions, and had thrown them into the yard.[10]

Almost another two years elapsed before the second Protectorate Parliament put a Postage Act on the statute book. It made no bones about the intention of government to intercept mail. 'A post office', it began, 'is the best means to maintain trade, convey despatches, and discover dangerous designs.' There was to be a single, comprehensive Post Office under Thurloe as Postmaster-General, who was to have the horsing of all who rode by post. London postal charges were to be twopence a letter within eighty miles, threepence to English addresses beyond that distance, fourpence to Scotland and sixpence to Ireland.[11] No reliable figures are available for the profits made by Thurloe over the four years – from August 1655 to December 1659 – during which he was in charge of the post. They may have been considerable, as the Venetian resident had forecast. They were sufficient later for Thurloe to raise the rent voluntarily by £4,000 a year, but the figures for the penultimate quarter, quoted later, suggest that there was by then little gain.

Rules for the regulation of printing followed from Thurloe's pen. On

21 September 1655 the Council directed that no one was 'to presume to publish in print any matter of public news without leave of the Secretary of State'. In July of that year he was also directed to review the instructions for the old Trade Committee and prepare a brief for a new committee. Needless to say, he was added to that committee in December.[12]

Cromwell, who has been credited with introducing the English weekend, had for some time been travelling on Saturdays to Hampton Court in order to escape the confines of Whitehall. In June 1655 he stayed longer and summoned the Council to transact its business there during the week. Thurloe, who had accompanied him to Hampton Court on the 20th, was back in London two days later. Indisposed, he was let blood, not for the first time. Blood-letting was the universal remedy for ills during most of the seventeenth and eighteenth centuries. It seldom did much good and on occasions must have done considerable harm. Four weeks elapsed before Thurloe was able to write that he had some strength again.[13]

Realizing his friend's condition, St John applied to Cromwell on his behalf and begged him to make use of leave of absence for two or three weeks in August, approved by the Protector. St John himself would be at Longthorpe about the middle of the month and suggested that they might meet if Thurloe's travels brought him that way. He wrote again anxiously from Bury St Edmunds on 2 August: 'Let me know when you intend for the country, and do that right to your health, which God and nature requires.'[14] It seems that Thurloe may have taken a week off from 2 to 9 August and a few days more later in the month, but it is not clear whether he went to the fen district.

After dissolving parliament in January 1655 Cromwell had continued his efforts to behave constitutionally in accordance with the Instrument of Government. It was not long, however, before lawyers and judges remarked how ill-suited were its provisions to existing statutes based on the existence of a monarch and two Houses of Parliament. Moreover, its very validity continued to be questioned. A new establishment of the army was approved in July. There were to be seven regiments of horse and five of foot for England, seven of horse and thirteen of foot for Scotland. With the addition of some dragoons, the artillery train and garrison troops, and the forces deployed in Ireland, the total represented a substantial reduction, though it was still far in excess of the thirty thousand approved by parliament. Simultaneously the militia had been expanded since mid-February, and Desborough's commission of 28 May to supervise the south-west of England marked the beginning of the rule of the major-generals. By August, largely perhaps at Lambert's prompting, a militia of six thousand had been embodied and ten (later eleven) major-generals appointed to supervise the districts. The action is still regarded today as an example of military despotism, but Cromwell himself did not see his major-generals as instruments of oppression.

The finalization of the new system was held up during August and September when Cromwell suffered a long illness, but by early autumn the major-generals were in place, each assisted by a body of local commissioners. Thurloe and the Council had worked long and hard drawing up two sets of detailed instructions for the major-generals and their commissioners.[15] They were not only to police their districts, but also to encourage virtue and suppress vice. Charles Worsley, for example, a former colonel of Cromwell's regiment, reported cheerfully to Thurloe from Chester that he had closed down almost two hundred alehouses, many inn-holders and brewers. A number of couples married contrary to Act of Parliament, together with those who had married them, were in gaol, as were many suspicious, idle and loose persons, common tipplers and Sabbath-breakers.Whalley proposed to clear the gaols of Lincolnshire and Northamptonshire by means of mass transportation.[16] The effect on the population of such measures can well be imagined, but not surprisingly, perhaps, the impact of the major-generals' presence varied widely between districts. Whatever their individual records, they certainly added to the burden of Thurloe's regular correspondence.

One of the tasks allotted to them was to assess and collect the so-called Decimation Tax, imposed on royalist sympathizers and designed to make the militia scheme financially self-supporting. It was in fact a tax of ten per cent on incomes of over £100 a year from landed property, and a wealth tax of £10 on every £1,500 of personal property. The rate on land was regarded as penal at the time. The major-generals found that the most dangerous of the royalists had incomes of less than £100 a year and were exempt. They were therefore authorized to require all who had borne arms against the Commonwealth to furnish bonds for peaceable behaviour, the sum fixed at the major-generals' discretion. Enforcement varied enormously, from over a thousand cases in Worsley's district to under ten in another.[17]

Another matter occupying the attention of the government was a proposal to readmit Jews, legally excluded from England since the reign of Edward I. The Jewish leader Manasseh ben Israel had asked Cromwell in November 1655 to take the Hebrew nation under his protection, to permit them the use of a synagogue and cemetery, and to grant them trade and legal concessions. There were immediate objections from Londoners: lawyers and divines, merchants and citizens. Reporting the dispute to Henry Cromwell on 17 December, Thurloe noted that there were deep differences of opinion among divines and indeed throughout society, and added that he was 'apt to think that nothing will be done'. In this he proved largely correct. Although the Jewish community in London undoubtedly grew and was permitted certain privileges, Cromwell allowed proposals for legislation to lapse because, contemporaries thought, of the strength of opposition from London magistrates and others.[18]

Occasionally Thurloe's busy life at Whitehall was enlivened by reception of lady visitors. (Those of Whitelock's and Sedgewick's wives have already been mentioned.) He presented Katherine Bradshaw, wife of the Hamburg resident, to His Highness when she called in March 1655; when she wrote to thank him she excused herself for not waiting on Mrs Thurloe. Later correspondence shows that she was a friend of Ann Thurloe and of her mother, Lady Lytcott. In August the wife of a colonel imprisoned for ten months came personally to present a petition, and Mrs Dendy called to discuss lands in Ireland for her husband, the Council's sergeant. Later Thurloe's own friend Broghill, who had recently fulsomely signed himself his 'faithful affectionate servant, and one who is obliged to be so by too strong ties ever to be broken', sent a Mrs Villiers to intercede about an allowance for her brother.[19]

Although in April 1965 the Secretary managed to get away for a week or more to see to his property in the country, there was no let-up in the crushing volume of his Council business. Ever since his appointment as Secretary of State there has seemed no limit to the number of committees to which he was added or which he was detailed to assist. Besides trade and foreign affairs, he was concerned with the disposal of lands in Ireland and the adjudication of adventurers' claims for land there, with approval of the accounts of the nation, with the revenue a few months later, and later still the import of bullion. Much of his work was probably highly secret and was deliberately omitted from the official record. More prosaically, he was even instructed to assist the committee dealing with errors in the translation of the Bible.

Sometimes, particularly when parliament was in session, it was difficult to get a committee together. On such occasions Thurloe was not above short-circuiting the system by obtaining a personal decision from the Protector alone. It fell naturally to him to deal with a postal complaint, but he was also saddled with a committee on the prevention of the spread of plague from the Netherlands and a petition for the relief of the Vaudois refugees.[20] Many more tasks were to follow in 1657 and 1658, and there were also increasingly complex political crises to be faced.

In spite of voting a regular income for the government, the Long Parliament, its Rump and the Nominated Assembly had not made sufficient provision for raising the revenue. For some years the state had been living very largely on capital sums obtained first from the sequestration of royalist lands, then from fines for composition, and lastly from the sale of church property. Large amounts had been raised from all these sources but they had been improvidently spent and there was little more to come from any of them.

In the years 1646 to 1656 the sale of bishops' lands, for example, raised the £200,000 paid to the Scots to remove their army from northern England in 1646. The surveyors had received their fees and expenses, but the clerks craved £300 from the balance of £306 – they had been given no salary for six years. The sale of lands of deans and chapters produced almost £517,000 in all up to the end of 1659. Of this the Council took £35,000 and the navy £164,000.[21] The Protectorate had inherited large debts, the parliament of 1654–5 had voted not a penny more and, despite the attempt to review the military budget and other costs, by the mid-1650s the regime was facing a financial crisis.

The desperate shortage of cash was brought home to Thurloe when the Council's under-clerks, messengers and sergeant's deputies of his office presented a petition in April 1656 for prompt payment of their wages, which had hitherto been paid fitfully and only after repeated requests. Mr Frost, they asserted, had so many warrants, and some so pressing, that he was unable to honour them. It is to be hoped that the Councillors were rather ashamed as they ordered the treasury to pay Frost £3,000 to make good two quarters' salary outstanding for the inferior officers. It suggests poor supervision on Thurloe's part that he had permitted things to go so far. Two months later the Council approved salaries of £150 a year for Nutley and three other Clerks of the Signet in recognition of the withdrawal of the income from fees formerly enjoyed by holders of those offices.[22]

It was shortage of money that forced Cromwell to call another parliament to assembly on 17 September 1656. He had summoned the major-generals to confer in London during May and the meeting reassured him both that the system was working well and that elections could safely proceed. According to Thurloe, they had 'much conduced to the safety of the country and the satisfaction of honest men'. The occasion was marred by the sudden death of Worsley. Secrecy about the approaching parliament was removed at the end of June, and thereafter Thurloe had much correspondence with major-generals concerning the forthcoming elections, and particularly with Major-General Haynes regarding the choice of candidates for the Isle of Ely.

Haynes thought that as the election of 1654 had been held at Wisbech it should on this occasion take place at Ely, with polling on 20 August. A few days earlier he reported good support for Thurloe; the second member should, he thought, be a local man. But on the day of the election he wrote of 'a clear combination to bring in persons of apparent contrary principles to the government', and later that he could not prevent the election of William Fisher, the town bailiff of Wisbech. Although here and elsewhere the election had released some of the public distaste for them, most of the major-generals somehow contrived to be elected. With Lambert, Fleetwood and several other newly-elected Councillors, Thurloe was nobly entertained by the Lord Mayor of London at the Mansion House on 29 August.[23]

On 17 September the Protector and Council, who had as usual observed 3 September as a solemn day of thanksgiving, drove to Westminster in procession from Whitehall with an escort of three hundred officers. Lambert went with Cromwell, and Thurloe followed in the second coach. They met the members of parliament at the Abbey to hear a sermon before withdrawing to the Painted Chamber, where Cromwell made a long opening speech. In it he emphasized that 'your great enemy is the Spaniard' and warned of papal involvements, but against a background of internal threats and recent attempts on his life, he also justified the appointment of the major-generals. For the settlement of the three nations, he recommended two remedies: security and reformation. The war against Spain must be prosecuted either with vigour or not at all, and there must be an end to religious intolerance (except, of course, of Catholics and Episcopalians), best secured by a broad national church supported by tithes. The characteristically involved statement of policy concluded with quotations from the Psalms.[24]

When the session opened almost a hundred members of the four hundred and sixty found themselves excluded from the House, denied certificates from the Clerk of Commonwealth in Chancery stating that they were returned to serve in parliament and approved by the Council. Under pressure perhaps from the military members of the Council, Thurloe and his clerks must have been working on the list of members of parliament ever since the election returns had started to come in, providing evidence about the newly elected members and implementing the Council's decisions to bar political undesirables from the House. Over fifty more members did not take their seats in protest.

Thurloe, a committed Cromwellian, must have found very distasteful the declaration prepared in the name of the excluded members and partially suppressed by the government. They had been turned out, the declaration complained, for endeavouring to put some limitation on the power of the Protector. 'The truth is,' it continued, 'his demerits make him fear and hate all people of any principles, and therefore he imprisoneth men upon bare suspicions, contrary to law.' It concluded by urging the destruction of 'this devourer of all our security and happiness'. Henry Cromwell, though committed to his father's government, did not agree with the exclusions and told Thurloe so. Sir Thomas

Widdrington was elected Speaker by those who remained. Of the Scottish members, Monck told Thurloe on 30 August, fifteen were Englishmen, including Broghill (in reality an Irishman), Clarges (Monck's own brother-in-law) and Downing. The rest were 'honest and peaceable Scotchmen' whom he had thought fit to nominate for approval by the Council.[25]

A shrewd appraisal of Thurloe's place in the government at this time appears in a satirical pamphlet issued in January 1656 and circulating during the year. Called *A Game of Picquet*, it featured most of the leading political figures of the day. Thurloe, who like all whose names appear in it is made to speak only once, reveals himself as the perfect civil servant or staff officer. 'My Lord,' he says, 'it will not be well for me to play, but I will stand behind the chair and make and shuffle the cards with which you are to play the next game.'[26]

A seat in the new parliament, in fact, ensured for Thurloe a much more active role than simply shuffling the cards. The House met at 8 a.m. every weekday and usually rose at noon. If adjourned for dinner it rose before dark unless a motion was passed that 'candles be brought'. Thurloe soon reported that the purged parliament was in a very good temper, quickly passing bills for the exclusion of Charles Stuart and for the creation of a High Court which he believed would be 'a great terror to designing men'. Before long he found himself the natural vehicle for reporting Council affairs to parliament and parliamentary proceedings to the Council. His first assignment was a happy one – to tell the House on 2 October of the successful outcome of Stayner's interception of the Spanish treasure fleet from the West Indies. The House chose the symbolic date of 5 November, anniversary of the frustration of the Gunpowder Plot, for thanksgiving. Montagu conveniently arrived at Portsmouth in the *Naseby* with the prizes and the bullion a week beforehand.[27]

Thurloe was also busy maintaining the morale of two of the Protector's key representatives. Henry Cromwell was dispirited by the criticism and obstruction of his every decision in Ireland and confided that he would like to resign and return to private life. In the previous January (1656) Thurloe had counselled him that 'hard sayings, yea reproaches, and worse, is the portion of the best men in these uncertain and giddy times, and you must not think to go shot [*sic*] free." Now in July Thurloe comforted Henry by reminding him that his father would have quitted his service to the public long ago if he had paid any attention to the opposition he had aroused. 'Everybody can keep his place', he admonished the Protector's son, 'when all men applaud him, speak well of him; but not to faint in a day of adversity is the matter.' His own position, he added, gave him a better opportunity 'to understand the bottom of things' than was accorded those more remote from the centre. Almost simultaneously Lockhart, dismayed by Cardinal Mazarin's apparent initial disregard of him, was protesting his unsuitability for his job, but he, too, was soon in better fettle.[28]

Thurloe still contrived to maintain his interest in Lincoln's Inn. In August he referred to the Council a petition with six sheets of signatures from members of the Society and 'persons of quality' residing in the neighbourhood, asking the Protector to order a stay on building in Lincoln's Inn Fields, 'being now the only place left unbuilt all thereabouts'. Cromwell ordered a stay ten days later, earning the gratitude of later generations who still have the largest square in London for their recreation. But there was trouble over the appointment of a preacher for the Inn. Dr Reeves, who had succeeded Ussher, former archbishop of Armagh, on his retirement in February 1654, had offended Cromwell in some way.

Early in September 1656 the Society of Lincoln's Inn received an order from the Lord Protector and the Council to elect a new preacher in his place. On 18 November the Society postponed consideration of the matter to their next meeting, and when that took place nine days later postponed it again until the next term because of the weight of business and the shortage of time before the term's end. They thought it wise to depute two of their number to inform the Secretary of State, 'one of the members of the Bench', of their reasons so as to prevent any misinterpretation.[29] This incident gives an indication of the awe in which the executive arm of government was held, but the Society demonstrated its independence by paying off Reeves generously and waiting a year before appointing a successor.

A new piece of parliamentary ceremony was introduced on 27 November when members were summoned to the Painted Chamber by the Council's sergeant-at-arms. Preceded by the House's own sergeant with the mace and followed by its clerk with bills for approval, the Speaker led the members to find His Highness attended by his Council, the Commissioners of the Great Seal, the Treasury Commissioners, the Lords Chief Justice of the Upper Bench (which had replaced the King's Bench) and Common Pleas, the Master of the Rolls and the rest of the judges. Five completed bills were read and passed by Cromwell. Scorning the customary Norman French, they became law with the words 'the Lord Protector doth consent'.[30]

Much of parliament's time in December 1656 was taken up debating the case of James Nayler, a Quaker preacher, who had apparently claimed divine inspiration by re-enacting in Bristol Christ's entry into Jerusalem. The House, sitting as the High Court of Parliament to decide if he was guilty of 'horrid blasphemy' and to pass sentence, claimed judicial powers formerly held by the House of Lords. Thurloe, pleading for leniency, said that he knew of no law currently in force against blasphemy, unless it was an Act of 1650 under which the maximum sentence was imprisonment for six months or banishment. Many members of parliament, opposed to the broad religious toleration favoured by Cromwell and fearful of the apparently revolutionary fervour of burgeoning Quakerism, sought a more severe punishment, but a proposal for the death sentence was defeated by ninety-six votes to eighty-two.

Even so, the final sentence was savage enough. Nayler was to stand in the pillory at Palace yard, to be whipped from there to the Exchange, and on a subsequent day to be pilloried again, branded with a 'B' (for blasphemy), and his tongue bored through; then he was to be sent to Bristol, where his alleged crime had taken place, to be whipped again. The legality of the sentence was immediately challenged in a petition from Londoners, and Cromwell himself was seriously concerned at the lack of appeal provisions in the one-chamber constitution. Their protests were considered by the members of parliament, but no conclusion was reached and the matter was dropped. Poor Nayler earned no more than a two-day postponement of the second part of his punishment. It was all carried through, and he returned from Bristol to imprisonment in the Bridewell.

In between the sentence and the final debates, parliament sat on Christmas Day. The House was poorly attended and a member complained that from the Tower to Westminster not a shop was open. Londoners were not giving up their holiday, even if it were no longer recognized as a holy day. Thurloe was present in the Chamber, and spoke in favour of continuation of the decimation tax on delinquents of the cavalier party in order to maintain the militia system headed by the major-generals. The bill itself introduced by the major-generals, was read by eighty-eight votes to sixty-three and the House rose at two o'clock.[31]

A draft prepared by Thurloe for a speech on this bill has survived amongst his papers. If it was delivered at all, it appears from internal evidence to belong to mid-January 1657. As the only example of Thurloe's declamatory style it is worth quoting at some length. He planned to introduce the bill as one for an extraordinary tax on the old delinquent party. Addressing the Speaker, he continued:

> You know, sir, much better than I, and so most here what the design was before the Long Parliament. It was to alter our religion, and to subvert the fundamental laws. The bishops, so they might enslave our consciences, and have us at their will to impose their ceremonies, . . . were content we should be at the king's will for our persons and

estates. I remember myself, and many here remember much better, how many were banished into foreign parts, that they might serve God without fear, which they could not do here. Many good ministers were imprisoned, others silenced.

'And so in the state the prerogative was very high,' he went on, 'but the people's liberty was very low.' a little later he reminded members:

> Parliaments were set aside, . . . they had got a way to govern without parliaments, and the laws of Westminster Hall began to be of little use. The judges, that were honest and true to the people's liberties, were either removed or discountenanced, . . . other courts flourished.

Here he referred to the Star Chamber, the Court of High Commission (which had been the centre of Laud's efforts to impose religious ortho-doxy) and others, including Chancery.

> In this conjuncture of affairs the long parliament comes, . . . under-takes the cause of the nation, and advises the king. Instead of listening to them, he takes the advantage of raising an army in prosecution of his former design, and to defend those who were the instruments thereof. A great part of the nation . . . adhere to him, take up arms with him, and in his cause; and I believe nobody here hath forgot how much blood and treasure this course hath cost this nation. These are the men, sir, this is the old delinquent that we have to do with in this bill.

After referring to divisions in their own ranks, both in church and state, he returned to

> the old enemy, men that would bring in the hierarchy again, and with it popery, persecution for conscience sake, bring in tyranny over our persons and estates. We did all once agree against them, and I hope we shall do so again so long as they retain their old principles.

The bill, he explained, was to make these men pay an extraordinary tax for the support of the public charge. It was true that they had already compounded for past wrongs and had been pardoned by the Act of Oblivion for past offences, but it was proposed that they should pay 'somewhat more' than those of the other party, though exceptions would be made for those who could provide evidence of having forsaken their former interest. 'This I would say in general,' he concluded,

> that the old delinquent party have not only the same intentions that they had when they were in open arms, . . . but they do retain their old principles, and still adhere to their former interest . . . and have been all along hatching new disturbances to trouble the peace of the state.[32]

This speech reveals Thurloe at his most virulent in condemning the cavaliers still in evidence, unchanged in their allegiance, after nearly eight years of republican government. It also shows that Thurloe, though considered by some historians as somewhat out of his depth as a parliamentarian, could be an eloquent advocate of policy that had his personal backing. He admitted in a letter to Henry Cromwell that the decimation tax met very sharp opposition and he was doubtful whether it would pass. In another he confessed that antagonism was based on the fear that the bill would establish the major-generals. Towards the end of January he spoke at length in favour of the bill, only to see it rejected by one hundred and twenty-four votes to eighty-eight. Successful passage would indeed have legitimized the rule of the major-generals, and its rejection was not unexpected. Though it was introduced by Desborough, it had been opposed by Cromwell's son-in-law John Claypole and by his son and heir Richard Cromwell, as well as by Broghill, who over other issues was an effective leader of the House on behalf of the government.[33]

A proposal to congratulate His Highness on his escape from another murder attempt led to serious consideration of the succession should he die, whether naturally or by violence. The question had first been raised by William Jephson, one of the Irish members, in the previous October, but no motion had then been put to the House. The public thanksgiving for Cromwell's deliverance took place at St Margaret's on Friday 20 February. The Protector invited all members to dine with him at the Banqueting House. (A month earlier part of a staircase had collapsed there as some members were ascending; Richard Cromwell hurt his shoulder and the Solicitor-General broke a leg.) After dinner Cromwell withdrew to the Cockpit and entertained the company with music, both instrumental and vocal.[34] This interlude of levity amidst a rather troubled period proved something of a last fling before all concerned were plunged into a new and prolonged constitutional controversy.

On the following Monday a rather obscure member, a City alderman named Sir Christopher Pack, introduced a humble address and remonstrance, later to be called the Humble Petition and Advice. It outlined a new and improved constitution, with a king and two Houses of Parliament. According to a correspondent of Henry Cromwell, Pack confessed to the member sitting next to him that he had not read it. There were immediate calls for a committee to discover its origin, but the motion that it be read was carried by a majority of almost three to one. Sir Charles Firth has ascribed authorship to Broghill and Chief Justice Glynne, assisted by other lawyers, but its origins never became completely clear.

Next day it was decided to discuss the paper clause by clause. Summing up the initial divisions, Henry's informant pointed to Lambert as being violently against the measure, with several members of the Council in his camp, while Thurloe and another six or seven Councillors were highly in favour of it. All the lawyers – those 'of the long robe', as they are termed by many contemporaries – were in favour, as were all but three of the Irish, whilst all but one from Yorkshire were against. Thurloe himself assured a correspondent that His Highness had no prior knowledge of the remonstrance. His own initial reaction was to emphasize that the Protector would reject it unless the security of 'the good people' and their cause were fully safeguarded. His first anxiety was that 'some unquiet spirits or other will take this or any other occasion to put the army into discontent by false reports.'[35]

Led by Lambert, the army officers soon voiced their concern at the new turn of events. When they complained about events in parliament, Cromwell retorted that they had admitted and kept out whom they pleased and so could have no grounds for objection now. He felt compelled to tell a gathering of one hundred officers that he would not countenance any further military interference with parliament. But he also criticized members and, citing the case of Nayler as an example of the danger of unbridled parliamentary power, supported the sort of check or balance on the House envisaged in Pack's paper.[36]

Parliament debated the measure in detail, leaving to the last consideration of the clause inviting His Highness to accept the kingly title. The rest of the draft constitution was agreed with remarkably little bitterness or hostility. The House was unanimous that Cromwell should nominate his successor in his lifetime and, somewhat to Thurloe's surprise, approved without a division the institution of an upper House with members nominated by the Protector and approved by the Commons. 'Some think', he wrote to Monck, 'that this will be very good to preserve the good interest against the uncertainty of the Commons house which is to be chosen by the people', an argument for bicameral government still advanced over three centuries later. He was particularly satisfied with the vote (largely reiterating the Instrument of Government) that parliaments should be called once in three years at the furthest and more often if necessary. The debates, as Thurloe had feared, were very long. In parliament all day, he had little time for his correspondence. Yet, realizing the importance of reassuring Cardinal Mazarin, he managed to send a series of progress reports to Lockhart who, newly knighted, had recently returned as ambassador to Paris.[37]

When the matter of religion was reached on 18 March the House resolved that

the true Protestant Christian religion, as it is contained in the Holy
Scripture of the Old and New Testaments, and no other, to be held
forth and asserted for the public profession of these nations; and that
a Confession of Faith, to be agreed upon by His Highness and the
Parliament, be recommended to the people.

It was a resolution remarkable for putting responsibility for the content
of the people's religious belief into exclusively lay hands. Like many
other decisions of this period, it was a resolution that bore no fruit. But
Thurloe, at least, was satisfied. 'I think', he wrote to Lockhart in his
fourth letter in nine days, 'the matters of religion are better settled for
the liberty of conscience than ever they were in England, and much
beyond whatever any man did expect this Parliament would have
done.'[38]

On the same day Morland, back from Switzerland three months earlier and restored to Thurloe's staff, wrote to Pell, still at Zürich, that the
Secretary was 'hardly at leisure to read or think of anything else, but the
business of kingly government, which the Parliament has already very
far advanced'.[39] Besides attending daily debates in the House, Thurloe
was reporting progress to the Council at its meetings and thus had less
time to supervise foreign affairs and other facets of administration for
which he was responsible.

Most of the new constitution was settled during March. The Humble
Petition retained the overall structure established by the Instrument of
Government, though the balance of power shifted slightly and procedures were amended. Government was to be shared between a single
person, now a king rather than a Lord Protector, regular parliaments
and a permanent executive Council. The system of checks and balances
was retained, denying any one officer or body excessive or absolute
power and ensuring that the three principal elements of central government would co-operate and restrain each other. The vital functions of
controlling finance, commanding the regular armed forces or the local
militias and appointing to senior military, civil and judicial offices were
shared between the single person and parliament (if sitting) and between
the single person and a Council in the intervals. The Council would
possess certain executive and supervisory functions at all times, even
when parliament was sitting. The new Council of State, more often
known simply as the Council or even – echoing the old regal system – as
the Privy Council, was to comprise up to twenty-one members 'of known
piety and undoubted affection to the rights of these nations', who were
to hold office for life. Cromwell was apparently free to nominate the
founder members of his new Privy Council.

The clause asking His Highness to assume the 'name, style, title, dignity and office of King' was eventually carried, though it was decided to leave the final word blank when the constitution was initially engrossed. 'There were several bitter speeches made last night in Parliament against the business,' Morland told Pell, 'but they could not carry it, there being almost two to one against them, and for it.' The whole document, read on the afternoon of Friday 27 March, contained a proviso that Cromwell should accept the entire constitution – including kingship – or nothing.[40]

On the following Tuesday the House rose at 11 a.m. and members repaired to the Banqueting House for audience with the Protector. Speaker Widdrington's address to Cromwell was 'flowery' in all sense. He was, he said, 'not unlike a gardener, who gathers flowers in his master's garden, and out of them composeth a nosegay. I shall offer nothing', he added, 'but what I have collected in the garden of Parliament.' He went on to discuss the title of king, urging it on Cromwell with scriptural precedents and a quotation from Aristotle. After going through the whole document he asked His Highness to take an oath to govern according to law and to accept the new constitution *in toto*. The assembled members can scarcely have expected Cromwell to give his immediate consent, and in a short speech he asked for time to consider.[41]

He gave his reply on 3 April to the small committee headed by Whitelock, nominated by parliament to treat with him. He praised much in this Humble Petition and Advice, but said that he could not take the title of king. Therefore all fell. The Commons promptly decided to resubmit their constitution without amendment, and the outcome was tossed to and fro between Westminster and Whitehall throughout the rest of April and the first half of May. On 13 April Cromwell told the committee that he doubted whether the title mattered, that of Protector having already been accepted by the judges, albeit after some hesitation. Later he was presented with a list of weighty reasons in favour of kingship, but he maintained several detailed scruples about the content of this and other clauses.

Reporting progress to Henry Cromwell on 21 April, Thurloe said that Cromwell had held three or four meetings with the committee but was still keeping everybody in suspense as to his acceptance of the Petition and Advice. 'Certainly', he went on, 'His Highness hath very great difficulties in his own mind, although he hath had the clearest call that ever man had.' Parliament would not be persuaded that settlement could be attained any other way. 'The title is not the question, but it's the office, which is known to the laws and the people.' He admitted that Fleetwood and Desborough were much opposed to the title. Henry himself, after studying the copy of the Advice sent to him by Thurloe, was not convinced that the title of king was necessary. But Oliver was not looking for counsel, keeping himself reserved, as Thurloe remarked in a subsequent letter, 'from everybody that I know of'. One who did see him was Sir Francis Russell, Henry's father-in-law, who remarked on 27 April that the Protector was beginning to come 'out of the clouds' and that his troubled thoughts seemed to be over.[42]

Meanwhile Thurloe was taking a prominent part in parliamentary debates. His role in the 1656–7 parliament was altogether larger than the one he had played in the first Protectorate parliament. Thomas Burton's diary of the session shows that he frequently spoke in debates, acted as teller in several divisions, and was nominated to a large number of committees over the nine-month session. Even when the major issues – the Nayler case, decimation and the major-generals, the constitution and kingship – had been concluded, Thurloe continued to play a leading role, and during April and May 1657 he orchestrated efforts to have the Acts and ordinances passed since the break with Charles I in 1642 confirmed by members of parliament. He saw no harm in parliament announcing that it confirmed them all until repealed. Speaking as Principal Secretary to His Highness, he asked for as much precision as possible; to leave things doubtful would have them all 'at blindman's buff'.

Not until the end of April was it finally decided to ratify and confirm all laws passed since the dissolution of the Long Parliament and to inform His Highness that the House conceived no need for declaration or confirmation of Acts and ordinances passed between 1 April 1642 and 20 April 1653. In order to avoid any difficulties, however, Thurloe seconded a proviso, moved by Desborough and passed by the House, that this should not be construed to confirm anything contrary to the Petition and Advice.[43]

After all his scruples had apparently been met, Cromwell asked to see the committee in the Banqueting House on 8 May. On the 6th he walked with his brother-in-law Desborough in St James's Park and was told quite firmly that Desborough would never work with him again should he accept the kingly title. Lambert and Fleetwood agreed, and army officers presented a petition saying that since they had hazarded their lives against a monarchy, they humbly desired parliament to discountenance all endeavours to press 'their general' to become king. In the face of this opposition and after a great deal of thought and prayer, Cromwell finally answered, apologizing for the time taken by parliament and the committees, but announcing that he could 'not undertake this government with the title of a king'.[44] The deciding factor was undoubtedly his desire to act, in this as in all things, in conformity with God's will. The guiding hand of Providence had been seen in the victories obtained by the army on the field of battle. Now it seemed to be manifest in the army's opposition to the title.[45]

When the Speaker reported Cromwell's decision to the House, members altered their stance and it was resolved to offer the title of Lord Protector. By 22 May the exact style, as recommended by a committee, had been accepted. Three days later, while members were debating whether to present completed bills before the adoption of the Petition and Advice, Downing spotted the Protector's coach passing the parliament House. Shortly afterwards, with the House still undecided what to do, members were summoned to the Painted Chamber, and there Cromwell assented to the new constitution.[46] A formal investiture, at which the Protector would take an oath and the new constitution would be ceremonially inaugurated, was expected to follow in due course.

Faced with Cromwell's intention to prorogue parliament on 20 June until the beginning of the Michaelmas term, Thurloe reminded the House on 30 May of the necessity to secure a constant revenue over and above that already approved in the April constitutional debates. Subsequently there were long discussions about the assessments for revenue from the English and Welsh counties, as well as from Scotland and Ireland; an Act for raising £60,000 a month for three months from England was passed on 6 June. Thurloe, along with Richard Cromwell, Claypole, Desborough, Sir Francis Russell and others, was a commissioner for raising the assessment from the Isle of Ely. With government business still unfinished, Thurloe had to propose on 15 June the exclusion of all private bills, which were time-consuming and delayed public business, and that the House should sit afternoon as well as morning. Later he persuaded the Protector to allow two more days, but even so a further extension had to be given.[47]

Before the imposition of the ban on private business Thurloe had been able to do good turns for two of his friends. He spoke in favour of settling the castle of Blarney on Broghill. 'This noble person', he said, 'well deserves your favour, much more your justice.' In the other case the Earl of Bedford had incurred penalties under the Act specifying a fine of a year's rent on any new building erected since 1620 in the suburbs within ten miles of London. Using designs made by Inigo Jones, the earl had developed the three sides of the piazza of Covent Garden, and a member now proposed that his liability should be abated by £5,000 because he had built and endowed a church on the fourth side. Thurloe said that this was hardly enough and his proposal of a reduction of £7,000 was accepted.[48]

The session ended with a flurry of votes on the forms of oath to be taken by His Highness, Councillors and members of parliament under the new constitution. Thurloe argued against the inclusion of the words 'disadvantage' and 'interest' in these oaths. They were not legal terms, he said, and nobody could tell how far they reached. The Commons, surprisingly, agreed to leave the choice of members of 'the other House' to the Protector without their approbation. When a member suggested that as part of the ceremony of investiture Cromwell should be presented with a robe instead of a sword, some heard the word as 'rope' and laughed. But these were earnest men and such occasions of levity, particularly at the expense of the head of state, were rare. At last, on 25 June, Thurloe got the explanatory additional Petition and Advice read and a resolution passed that the Protector's oath should be recorded in parliament and in the four courts of Westminster – Chancery, Upper Bench, Common Pleas and Exchequer.[49]

For the investiture next day 'the chair of Scotland' was brought from the Abbey and placed on a dais at one end of Westminster Hall under a canopy of state. The chair had been used at coronations for centuries, with the Stone of Scone lodged beneath the seat and gilt lions guarding each leg. In front of it and below stood a table covered with pink velvet fringed with gold. On it were a Bible, a sceptre and a sword, with pens, ink, sand, wax and paper. Seats for the members rose as in a theatre on either side. Members came in pairs in procession from the Council room adjoining the Lords' House, and the Speaker took his place before the table. Councillors were already assembled, with Cromwell's son Richard and his two sons-in-law, Fleetwood and Claypole, behind the Protectoral throne. The aldermen of London and others filled the body of the hall.

When the heralds commanded silence Speaker Widdrington presented in turn a purple robe lined with ermine, the Bible, sceptre and sword, with a brief comment on each, emphasizing for instance that the sword was a civil sword for the defence of the Protector and his people. After the Speaker had administered the oath to the Protector there was a prayer, then a fanfare and proclamation by the heralds. The investiture closed with the cry 'Long live His Highness' repeated three times, followed by three cheers. In spite of Cromwell's use of the coronation chair, the ceremony lacked the sanctity, while preserving much of the formality, of the crowning of a monarch. Only the oath and prayer marked it as a religious occasion, investing the head of state of a Christian Protectorate. The rest emphasized his authority under a written constitution approved by the elected agents of the people, for whom the Speaker stood as representative. The Protector then departed by coach to Whitehall and members walked back in pairs to the parliament House.[50]

The Commons sat again in the afternoon. First they ordered that His Highness be pleased to encourage endeavours for uniting Christian churches abroad; four members of the Council, plus Thurloe, were to present this vote. They also recommended to His Highness and the Council that they reform the government of the Inns of Court, place godly and able ministers there, provide sufficient maintenance for them and revive readings. They then adjourned till 20 January 1658.[51]

It had been a hard session for Thurloe, trying to push through the government business. He had at first been optimistic that Cromwell would take the crown. Sir Francis Russell wrote on 25 May that 'the little secretary's' optimism had infected many others,[52] and he described Thurloe and some of the Councillors as 'too grave and wise for this quick mercurial age'. Writing on 4 July, he rejoiced that Cromwell and his Council rode 'but one horse, I mean he counsels himself. Were it not so, I well know what would become of things.'[53] This is one of the few contemporary views to come down to us of Cromwell's strength of mind in relation to Thurloe's influence and advice. It puts the Secretary back to the role seen for him by the author of *The Game of Picquet:* as a shuffler of cards, not a player of a strong hand. The author of a narrative of the 1656–7 parliament saw Thurloe in a very different light. 'He may justly be said', he wrote, 'to have a great hand in bringing all this abominable wickedness, slavery and oppression that hath been for above these three years to this day upon the nation.'[54]

In the passage quoted Russell seems to characterize Cromwell's closest advisers as too conservative, and the Protector himself as more in tune with the progressive, even experimental, ideas of government to which the nation had turned through its elected representatives. He applauds Cromwell's personal government and disregard of his Councillors' opinions. It is necessary to draw a sharp distinction between Council and parliament. Cromwell could afford to ride roughshod over the one, but could never quite gainsay the other except by turning it out. In the second quotation Thurloe is blamed not only for the late excesses of some of the major-generals, but for all the oppressive Acts and ordinances of the first three and a half years of the Protectorate. It was fair comment only in so far as the instructions to sheriffs and justices were issued over his signature, and warrants for detention and transportation were prepared in his office. But he would have had a ready answer to any criticism of his actions in suppressing sedition and even subversion by removing their practitioners from the scene for an indefinite period, while he could have denied any major role in framing the legislative instruments.

The new Council, of which Thurloe was a full member, was sworn on 17 July. In addition to his work in Council and Council committees, Thurloe remained Secretary of State, with heavy duties in the realm of foreign affairs. At least he would be spared time-consuming duties in parliament for six months. But Thurloe was still required to maintain constant care of intelligence, watching foreign powers and containing recurring threats to the regime at home and abroad. This side of his work, hitherto largely neglected in these pages, is the aspect for which Thurloe is best known and calls for detailed examination.

5

CONTROL OF INTELLIGENCE, 1652–1660

> Cromwell carried the secrets of all the princes of Europe at his girdle *(John Birch)*

> Really it is a wonder that you can pick as many locks leading into the hearts of the wicked men as you do, and it is a mercy that God has made your labours therein so successful *(Henry Cromwell)*

Thurloe may have been introduced to foreign intelligence and first acquired his taste for it through seeing a series of reports from Paris carrying political and military information received by Oliver St John in the winter of 1645–6.[1] At all events his flair was recognized soon after he became Secretary to the Council of State. He had been there sixteen months when he took over George Bishop's duties. These related only to foreign intelligence, but as 'the enemy', Charles Stuart, was abroad, they covered affairs at his court and his future plans. Thurloe's total control of the apparatus of state security was never formally assigned to him. It merely evolved from his exploitation of foreign intelligence, from his control of the Post Office and of censorship, and from the traditional role of the principal Secretary of State. The crucial difference, in the words of a modern historian, was that 'genius had replaced mere competence'.[2] Thurloe's recruiting of agents to penetrate the various subversive movements and royalist plots followed naturally from his inheritance of sources reporting from abroad. He did not have to look far for them; mostly they volunteered their services, usually in return for money.

One such was Joseph Bampfield. Formerly a colonel in the royalist army during the civil war, he was really a professional intelligence agent. Charles I employed him in 1644 'to penetrate the designs of the two parties in Parliament' and in April 1648 he was sent by the king to organize the flight of his second son, James, Duke of York, from St James's. Arrested after Charles I's death, he escaped from the Gatehouse prison to Holland, but returned to England in 1652. It must have been then that he was recruited to report on the man parliamentary correspondents often referred to as the King of Scots (for Charles had been crowned in Scotland before the disastrous march to Worcester) or as R.C. (Rex Carolus). Others, including Thurloe himself, called him C.S., the initials of a mere Charles Stuart.

In August 1652 Bampfield was arrested and ordered by the Council to leave the country, a normal procedure when Thurloe wished to infiltrate an agent into royalist circles abroad. He was then sent by Charles to Scotland, whence he returned with two Scots. According to intercepted royalist letters read by Thurloe, he had been sent to deliver commissions to Argyll and others, but his return journey to Paris took over five months from April to mid-September 1653, thus exciting royalist suspicions. On 21 July the royalist Robert Phelips reported, under a pseudonym, that the arch-villain Bampfield had been lately with Cromwell. This, too, Thurloe saw, together with reports of Bampfield's arrival at the royal court with the two Scots and of his discomfiture at his reception by Charles. In December another intercepted letter exposed Bampfield's treachery to Charles 'by counterfeiting the king's hand and seal, and getting the secrets of the lords' designs in the highlands'. Bampfield, 'looked on as a knave', retired for a while from the intelligence scene, to reappear in 1654.[3]

Phelips, who was among those who had helped Charles to evade capture during his flight after the Battle of Worcester, was a member of a Dorset family of landed gentry and was himself engaged in a royalist conspiracy to seize several southern ports, among them Poole, Portland and Weymouth. Examined on 12 August 1653, he denied any subversive intent.[4] With no continental backing, the plan had no hope of success; the interrogation of Phelips and one other was sufficient to kill it.

Another – and potentially far more significant – royalist grouping was being formed towards the end of 1653. Later known as the Sealed Knot, it was to consist of but six members. Their influence was small and geographically not well spread, being concentrated too much in the eastern counties which, as the forcing ground of Puritanism, were hardly a promising area for raising royalist support. They agreed not to engage in any absurd or hopeless ventures, but would certainly take the first reasonable opportunity to renew the fight for the monarchy. They would report to Hyde at the exiled court; only he and Ormonde, a member of Charles's Privy Council, were to know of the secret correspondence.

The members of the Knot were Lords Bellasis and Loughborough, Sir William Compton, Colonels John Russell and Edward Villiers, and Sir Richard Willys. Of these it is the last-named who is of greatest interest to this story. Willys was the second son of Richard Willys of Fen Ditton, a village on the Cam just outside the university city. He went up to Christ's College, Cambridge in 1631 and was admitted to Gray's Inn in the same year. Apparently he soon decided that his future lay with the sword rather than the pen, for he saw active service under Monck in the Netherlands in the 1630s and was in Charles I's army for the Scottish campaigns of 1639 and 1640. He joined the king's life guard in the following year. Captured at the end of 1642, he broke parole and rejoined the royalist army, rewarded with a knighthood and the rank of major-general. Taken prisoner a second time and exchanged in 1644, he became Governor of Newark at a critical juncture, was made a baronet in April 1646 and went into voluntary exile after the surrender at Oxford. According to his own statement of 1660 he returned to England from Italy about midsummer 1652 and went to stay with his brothers in Cambridgeshire.[5]

In February 1654 eleven men were arrested and sent to the Tower for interrogation. They had quarrelled about contributions to the cost of sending two emissaries to Charles Stuart. None was put on trial and all were later released, but Thurloe was now aware of the existence, and to some extent the composition, of the Sealed Knot. In the same month he saw at least two intercepts referring to its meetings and to a specific member.[6]

On 10 August 1654 Willys sent a petition to the Protector. He had been a prisoner since 26 May and in the Tower since 2 June. Seeking bail, he added: 'I will express my gratitude by obedience'. He went on to beg a licence to lead a force of Irishmen in Venetian service against the Turks. Cromwell referred the document to the Council and Willys was released on 25 September on a bond of £5,000 to appear before them within three days if summoned and to do nothing against His Highness or the state. As it happened, the Council had on 31 July reviewed the cases of forty-five prisoners in the Tower and had decided that Willys should be banished on security neither to act to the state's prejudice nor to return without leave.[7] But far from giving obedience to the Protector or leaving the country, he seems to have renewed his contact with the Sealed Knot and was active early in 1655 trying to prevent royal approval of what turned out to be a disastrous and rather farcical 'national' rising.

There is something odd about Willys's imprisonment. First, his name was included on a list of conspirators at Whitsuntide 1654, which at least accounts for his arrest. Secondly, one of the ringleaders of that conspiracy named him as 'in the plot', though only on the flimsy evidence of having heard his brother say so. Thirdly, in all the records of examinations of suspects in this, the so-called Gerard Plot, neatly bound up together, there is no report of an examination of Willys, even though he was in custody for a considerable time. In royalist circles Willys was believed to have attributed his arrest to betrayal by Lord John Bellasis, whom he knew to be friendly with Lambert.[8] All this suggests that as early as 1654 Thurloe may have attempted to recruit Willys as an agent within the Sealed Knot and that Willys may have been sufficiently tempted to give him a hearing even if not yet disposed to agree to work for him. Against this is a later allegation by Willys that up to 1656 he had never seen Cromwell or Thurloe. Most historians of the period place his recruitment in 1656; certainly there is no evidence of the receipt before that time of intelligence of the kind Willys could supply.

Willys had been one of several royalists arrested at Whitsuntide 1654 in the light of the discovery of a plot to murder Cromwell. It made the Protector very sensitive about his personal security – it is revealing that he was carrying a primed pistol in his pocket at the time of the coach accident in the following September. He is also said to have worn breast and back armour under his civilian clothes and to have varied his movements, even his bed, so as to avoid a regular observable pattern.

Thurloe first got wind of the plot in February when one Roger Coates gave under interrogation the names of several conspirators, including John Gerard. A week later another man gave full details to Colonel John Barkstead, Lieutenant of the Tower. Thurloe was warned on 9 March that the plot was still in train in spite of the disclosures already made. Gerard's plan was to fall on Cromwell with his escort with thirty mounted troopers as they were on their way to Hampton Court on Saturday 13 May. Instead of starting by road from Whitehall, Cromwell went by water as far as Chelsea, thus frustrating the design. The conspirators did not get a second chance. The Council issued warrants for their arrest on 21 May, the day on which they had planned a surprise attack on Whitehall chapel.[9]

There is evidence that Thomas Henshaw and John Wildman acted as *agents provocateurs* among the conspirators. They were denounced that June in a letter which Desborough passed on to Thurloe. In it they were described as brothers-in-law, though in fact they were stepbrothers (Wildman's father having married Henshaw's mother). Examination of those arrested revealed that the conspirators planned to seize all horses in and around London and, when Cromwell had been assassinated, to fall on the guards at the Mews, at St James's and Whitehall. About eight hundred men were involved but there was no widespread backing amongst the gentry. From a report despatched in early June from Brussels, Thurloe learned that Lambert and possibly he himself were also targets for assassination. Lambert and two other members of the Council were mentioned as proposed victims in another interrogation. Gerard himself, examined by Thurloe on 5 June, denied all knowledge of the plot. Wildman, examined a fortnight later by Barkstead, alleged that Peter Vowell, a schoolmaster of Islington who had also disclaimed knowledge of any of the conspirators when interrogated on 6 June, had thought that the plot could still go forward despite the arrest of Gerard's men.[10]

In a series of letters to Pell at Zürich Thurloe was unusually outspoken about those taking part in the Gerard plot. At first they were "some desperate people of the king's party', but he added: 'the scum and faeces of that party were engaged in it, and none else that I can hear of.' A week later he enlarged on the plotters as 'some desperate fellows come from France', who had enlisted 'several people here of desperate fortunes'. No persons of honour or interest were involved. Those having neither conscience nor estates, he concluded, could hope to achieve nothing more by it than to put things into a sudden confusion and disorder, out of which some advantage might arise to the party.[11] It is difficult to see how even the assassination of Cromwell at this stage could have led to a general uprising in favour of a Stuart restoration. Thurloe was plainly correct in dismissing as futile or impractical a popular rebellion unsupported by 'persons of honour or interest'. The ringleaders were tried before a new High Court of Justice, which had come into existence in May. Conviction was made easy by the way in which those arrested talked under interrogation. Gerard and Vowell were executed on 10 July; three others were transported to Barbados, where it seems they were treated in much the same manner as African slaves on the plantations. Wildman was released and Henshaw escaped, perhaps with government connivance, to France.

It was at this stage, in the wake of the Gerard Plot, that Bampfield again made contact from Paris. As usual he required money, but he hoped to come to London to discuss with Thurloe a matter of importance. Apparently he persuaded the Secretary to re-employ him, for he next appears in the records as author of a long and detailed paper submitted to the English government. It is undated but was clearly written shortly after the discovery of the Gerard Plot, of which, said Bampfield, Charles was assuredly cognizant and had given personal approval, in spite of a warning of Henshaw's doubtful loyalty and some misgivings about the wisdom of assassination. Bampfield went on to identify royalist supporters in England and Scotland, naming amongst others those who had provided money for the cause, some of those currently planning risings in the west and north, and several ladies in England who were keeping up correspondence with people at court. It would appear that Bampfield had given Thurloe details of the membership of the Sealed Knot, for he mentioned Bellasis, Russell and Compton, saying that he and others believed them to be 'engaged in the king's business'.[12]

There was another scare towards the end of 1654 when Thurloe heard of the purchase and distribution of arms in London. Just before

Christmas Cromwell authorized Barkstead at the Tower to raise an extra four companies of troops, nine hundred men in all, and on Christmas Day increased the number to twelve hundred in six companies. Several arrests were made and on 1 January 1655 Thurloe began to examine the suspects and gunsmiths concerning recent arms deals and the despatch of chests and hampers from London to the provinces. The conspirators had a good cover story, claiming that they were collecting arms to ship to Virginia, but the seizure of trunks full of weapons in Staffordshire and Derbyshire revealed the true state of affairs. Reporting to Pell, Thurloe recounted the capture of great quantities of arms at gentlemen's houses in the country, and as usual gave the credit to divine intervention: 'Thus God is still pleased to disappoint the purposes and intentions of enemies of all sorts.'[13]

Interrogations by Thurloe, assisted by William Jessop and George Firbank, continued throughout January. One Rowland Thomas was committed to the Tower on a charge of high treason, but in this as in later plots there was seldom sufficient evidence to sustain a trial and obtain a conviction by a jury. In these circumstances Cromwell and Thurloe resorted to a practice common in times of civil unrest – detention without trial. In the case of Rowland Thomas and seven others, they went still further. On 18 May Cromwell signed a warrant authorizing their transportation to Barbados. The propriety of this neat way of disposing of undesirable citizens, which had already been used for some members of the Gerard Plot, was to be questioned some years afterwards.[14]

There was discontent in the army at this time too, and a mutiny was planned. According to a report reaching Monck, Robert Overton was to replace him in command in Scotland, and the army was to march for England with the support of the extreme republicans John Bradshaw and Sir Arthur Heselrige. Overton, arrested by Monck and sent south by sea from Leith, was safely secured in the Tower on 17 January, and other senior officers were also placed under arrest. Like Thomas, Overton was to return to haunt Thurloe. The Secretary had first learnt of the plot when examining a suspect on 21 December 1654, but obtained fuller details only when Wildman was rearrested in February 1655.[15] Wildman, something of a professional conspirator with a gift for presenting an argument with clarity and skill, had been active in army circles for some years.

The royalist rising foreseen by Bampfield took place in early March 1655 and was a incoherent affair from start to finish. Its failure came as much from its own inadequacies of scale and preparation as from the vigilance of Thurloe and the authorities. Members of the Sealed Knot were firmly opposed to it and warned Charles accordingly, but he approved it in spite of their protest and in mid-February moved from Cologne to Middelburg at the mouth of the Scheldt, so as to be in readiness to cross the sea to England. He had sent Rochester ahead to command his forces.

Henry Wilmot, first Earl of Rochester, had fought for Charles I at Edgehill and had won a convincing victory over Sir William Waller at Roundway Down in July 1643. Though at odds with other royalist military leaders, he was always popular with his own officers, and his position at court was greatly strengthened when he shared with Charles Stuart the flight after Worcester and the successful escape to the Continent. Charles ennobled him at the end of 1652 and employed him thereafter on several diplomatic missions to raise money in Germany, all of them reported to Thurloe by his regular sources there. His companion on this trip to England was Sir Joseph Wagstaffe, a soldier of fortune who had changed sides after capture by the royalists early in 1643. The pair landed at Margate from Dunkirk about 22 February and went to lodgings in Aldersgate Street, London, just outside the City wall. Two previous emissaries, David O'Neill and Nicholas Armorer, had been stopped at Dover by the clerk of the passage, but to Thurloe's disgust had been allowed to return to the Continent.[16]

The plan envisaged co-ordinated risings in many different parts of the country. Rochester decided to go north and sent Wagstaffe to the west. In the event the promised support failed to materialize. At Marston Moor in Yorkshire, in Northumberland, the Midlands and on the Welsh border it was the same story: the few horsemen who assembled dispersed with nothing achieved. In Cheshire Colonel Robert Werden, a former agent of Scott, became involved, Though arrested, he was soon released upon giving a £1,000 bond not to act against the government, and resumed his intelligence career. Thurloe instructed Barkstead to seize all horses in London, but the Tower was too small to stable them all and he was unable to search Islington and Southwark. Only in the West Country, where Wagstaffe joined the force raised by John Penruddock, was there a real rising. But John Pendruddock, after briefly holding Salisbury, rode hard through Blandford to north Devon, towards Bristol or Cornwall. His tired and depleted force was surprised at night at South Molton and obliged to surrender. Penruddock and others were executed. Both Rochester and Wagstaffe got away to the Continent, the former after a narrow escape at Aylesbury when his disguise was penetrated at an inn. In the aftermath of the rising the local militias were strengthened and reorganized in many areas. Thurloe was appointed one of nine commissioners for the militia of the Isle of Ely, charged with securing arms, enquiring into conspiracies and suppressing rebellion. In fact his appointment was largely honorific, for he had far too much work in London to have paid much heed to this assignment.[17]

John Reynolds, later the commander of Protectorate troops in Flanders, compared the plot to 'a rat running behind stools, which although seen plainly, yet a full blow cannot be made at him'. It might have been neater if a large and recognizable royalist force had been raised and crushed in battle. Nevertheless, the number of persons in custody was to keep Thurloe busy for some time to come. First he had to order dispositions to prevent escape by sea. Then he despatched James Nutley, one of his clerks, to report to him from the courts held at Salisbury and Exeter. A few successful charges of treason were preferred, but most of those held were prosecuted on charges of levying war or on various accusations of theft.

Thurloe saw several advantages arising from this abortive rebellion. First, it had confirmed the accuracy of the recurring reports of plots which had reached him over the preceding months. Secondly, it seemed to have served to unite army and the people behind Cromwell. Thirdly, it had demonstrated that active and committed support for Charles was numerically, socially and geographically very limited. To these considerations he added two more practical results: the people would more willingly pay taxes, and there could be more confiscations of cavalier estates.[18] But the unity of which he boasted was more imaginary than real. Frequent escapes from custody and the almost unhindered movement of royalists to and from the Continent argued a strong residual sympathy for Charles, even if support fell far short of actual insurrection.

According to Hyde, Charles returned to Cologne with the realization that Cromwell had 'perfect intelligence of whatsoever His Majesty resolved to do, and of all he said himself'.[19] Thurloe had in fact made use of three sources at court. The first, Sir John Henderson, a Scot, reported accurately for several months, obtaining much of his information from Charles's Latin secretary, Peter Massonet. Henderson had been recruited by Bradshaw at Hamburg at Thurloe's request. Having spent over thirty years in Germany, Sweden and Denmark, he was a useful and experienced contact at court. Neither Thurloe nor Bradshaw was discouraged by his frank admission that his son was fighting with Middleton's rebels in Scotland. This and the fact that he had no recent connection with London undoubtedly helped to save him from royalist suspicion.

In September 1654 he supplied Thurloe with a list of fifteen English, three Irish and five Scots royalists then with Charles at Aachen, and from Massonet he learned details of the royalists' difficulties and delays in raising money from German princes. He visited London briefly in

March 1655, when he asked Thurloe to meet him 'rather when it is dark than in the day'. After a final visit to court he was back at Hamburg by the end of May, submitting accounts for eleven months' work and recommending that Massonet should be kept on at around £10 a month. He then resigned. His work for Thurloe was not exposed, but when he offered the Protectorate his services again at the end of 1655 after a spell at the Émperor's court, Thurloe declined them and allowed him to join the King of Sweden's retinue.[20] John Adams, who was reporting concurrently with Henderson, at first from court and later from Holland, had dropped out a little earlier. His reports, signed 'yours really', were mainly concerned with movements of royalists.[21]

The third agent, Henry Manning, was not of the same calibre and did not fare so well, paying the penalty for the successes of Henderson and Adams. He was raised a Catholic and during the civil war he was at Alresford, where his father was killed and he himself was wounded. Recruited by Thurloe, he reached the court at Cologne shortly before Charles left for Middelburg, offering to serve Charles in a military capacity and giving out that he had sufficient means to do so out of his father's estate.

Manning started to report in May 1655, and was soon writing regularly in cypher and using a pseudonym. Historians as well as contemporaries have occasionally accused him of indulgence in what is now known as 'confection' – that is, invention of intelligence – and the repeated exaggeration of his closeness to the person and policies of Charles Stuart. But he certainly did identify many royalist sympathizers travelling between England and the Continent, frequently drawing attention to the ease with which they passed through Dover, as well as others resident in London and the provinces. One of his reports led to a search of Covent Garden in May 1655 and a roundup of royalists including William Rumbold, secretary of the Sealed Knot. His chief source in royalist circles seems to have been Rochester, who recounted the tale already mentioned that Willys had been suspicious of Bellasis because of his intimacy with Lambert.

Hyde, who distrusted Manning (or so he later claimed) from the start, began checking on his antecedents. He found that Manning was not, as he had claimed, in the trust of the Earl of Pembroke. Moreover, he was corresponding through an accommodation address in Antwerp and receiving funds through letters of credit. Charles ordered the interception of this traffic and was rewarded with incoming letters from Thurloe and three outgoing letters full of mainly fabricated intelligence. Two servants sent to arrest Manning on 25 November found him writing, with cyphers on his desk. Manning seems to have been careless about his use of cyphers, since a colonel examined in London on 11 December revealed that when sharing lodgings two months previously, he had two or three times found Manning working with them.[22]

Under interrogation Manning admitted that though he was still a Catholic, he was in the pay of Thurloe, and further asserted that he intended later to confess to Charles and ask for pardon. He would never have reported the truth, he said, and saw no harm in telling lies for money. Hyde concludes his account of this episode with the remark that 'the wretch soon after received the reward due to his treason'. Unable to carry out a death sentence on him in the bishopric of Cologne, the royalists obtained the consent of the neighbouring Count Palatine of Neuburg to settle the affair in his territory. Manning was shot in a wood in December by two senior royalists. Several others, including a servant of the Duke of Gloucester, were forbidden the court because of their intimacy with Manning, but there was still fear of a 'great spy not yet discovered among us'.[23] Thurloe had achieved a feeling of helplessness in the enemy camp.

One story bearing out Cromwell's knowledge of all Charles said and did was first related by James Welwood in his memoirs published in 1700 and amplified in further statements. Welwood alleges that the Duke of Richmond was given leave by the Protectorate government to go abroad, but only on condition that he did not see his cousin Charles Stuart. In order to keep his undertaking, their meeting took place in the dark. When, on his return, he told Cromwell that he had not seen Charles, the Protector exclaimed that it was no wonder, since the candles had been put out.

Worried that he had thus exposed the Protectorate's source at the exiled court, Cromwell went late the same night to Thurloe's chamber to tell him what had occurred. Walking up and down in his agitation, Cromwell suddenly became aware of the recumbent form of Morland, apparently asleep at his desk in a little closet off the end of the room. According to Welwood's account, as related to him by Morland, Cromwell would have despatched Morland with a dagger he carried had not Thurloe pleaded that his clerk had been up several nights running and was certainly asleep. Morland feigned continuing sleep, though he averred years later that he had in fact overhead the name of Thurloe's agent. If it was indeed Manning, as later writers have assumed, the incident must have taken place almost as soon as he began to report and shortly before Morland was sent abroad.[24]

Much was made in later years, particularly by political opponents, of the amount of money used by Thurloe to maintain his network of agents and informants. Most allegations, in fact, grossly exaggerated the sums involved. As it happens the receipts for the years from April 1654 to March 1658 have all survived in a complete and apparently accurate form. They show that a proportion of the expenditure was devoted to general expenses such as conveyance of prisoners to the capital from the country, 'bringing of letters out of Holland' and settling printers' bills. Nevertheless Thurloe was not niggardly in paying for intelligence and expenses. Reimbursements of £20, £50, and £100 frequently occur. One source, known as Captain Holland, seems to have received sums of £125 on at least two occasions in 1654 and 1655, though the first is entered as a quarterly payment. The name concealed the identity of a valuable source of access to the deliberations of the Dutch cabinet. He had been worth a high price during the Dutch war, but his usefulness and value must have been greatly reduced in time of peace.

Even casual informants were well rewarded for their trouble. When Mary Jenkins came in February 1658 with information about the cavalier party, Thurloe minuted Firbank: 'Give this poor woman £5 for her journey hither'. Of course these accounts do not tell the whole story. Many sources were recruited in Scotland and abroad; the expenditure for these would appear elsewhere. Lockhart, for example, reported his acquisition of two agents in July 1656. One, a messenger between Queen Henrietta Maria and the cardinal, had little access to secret information. Lockhart considered him worth £50. The second, however, at £200, was one of Mazarin's secretaries, an Italian completely in his confidence.[25]

In this activity, as in all others, the Protectorate government was perpetually embarrassed by the lack of ready cash. The records are full of pleas from agents for advances of money, a common enough experience in any intelligence organization. More significantly, they contain complaints of failure to pay over what had already been agreed. On one occasion Thurloe addressed a note to an assistant, Firbank, praying him to pay the bearer 'out of the first money you receive'. It was dated 24 September 1656, but the payment was not made until 14 November.[26]

Mention has already been made of the use of figure substitution codes in diplomatic and in agents' correspondence. There are also references in the records to the use of secret writing or 'white ink'. 'I hope my ink will be good,' wrote one agent in 1655, 'but here is no lemons to be got, which makes the best.' When in Sweden Whitelock left 'water' for treatment of his secret writing. The royalists also made use of 'white ink'. When a letter using this technique was 'developed' for Thurloe it meant, of course, that it could not be forwarded to its destination. Even without the Secretary's interference, letters could become unreadable. In October 1653, for example, a writer told his correspondent that the last letter received in white ink was largely illegible and urged him to use more powder. The third method of disguise was to make use of plain language codes by substituting fictitious names for personalities and places and alternative words for objects and actions. Thus Charles appears in extant examples as Mr Cross, Tom Giles, Mr Knox and your mistress. Substitutions such as Normandy for Scotland, Swedish for Scottish, Essex for France and Denmark for England tended to make these communications difficult to understand without a key, though like all missives based on a system of substitution they became more vulnerable the more they were used.[27]

Measures to control the royalist threat continued. The instructions issued in 1655 to the major-generals directed them to disarm 'all papists and others' who had assisted the royalist cause in the civil wars or since, together with 'all others' deemed to be 'dangerous to the peace of the Nation'. Most of those arrested in the early summer were released by the end of November. On 20 October the Protector and Council issued an order for a registry of the movements of all delinquents to be kept in each district. The London office opened on 1 February 1656 in the house of a silk-stocking-seller at the back of the Old Exchange.

From the surviving records it can be established that the Sealed Knot member Lord Bellasis and a servant left lodgings in Martin's Lane on 15 February for Dover or Rye on their way to France with the Council's warrant. Sir Richard Willys, who had been held a prisoner at Lyme since mid-June of the previous year, was in London from 5 February, lodging at the White Horse in Russell Street until 14 March, when he went to the family home at Fen Ditton. As on the previous occasion there is confusion about the terms of his release from prison. In December 1655 Cromwell had consented to Willys going abroad on two reliable sureties of £10,000 on condition he left within a month of release and did not return without leave. No doubt that sureties were not forthcoming.[28]

Sir William Compton, another member of the Sealed Knot from Cambridgeshire, was in lodgings near Charing Cross for a few days at the beginning of April 1656. Willys was back in London for much of May, but on the 23rd he returned to Fen Ditton with his younger brother William, who had been in town since 7 May. The brothers had been staying at different lodgings at Holborn. Richard paid further visits to London from mid-June to early September and again from 13 November to 12 December. These were crucial times for Willys. Thurloe could generally ascertain through the registers kept by the major-generals the whereabouts of most potential enemies of the state or counter-revolutionaries, since each major-general was kept informed of movements in and out of the counties for which he was responsible. All arrivals from abroad were also carefully reported when they came through the usual ports. Royalist emissaries could contrive to come and go clandestinely, but it appears that this measure put a stop to the easy passage of royalists through the port of Dover to which Manning had drawn attention. Dorislaus had earlier investigated the abuse for Thurloe, and an agent reported from the Low Countries that royalists might pass unhindered through the Kent port for as little as twenty shillings.[29]

The failure of the rising in March 1655 had left the royalists with two alternatives: either to create an exploitable political crisis by the assassination of Cromwell, or to employ foreign troops to seize power for Charles Stuart. Not all the assassination plots posed a real threat to Cromwell's person, but every one had to be treated seriously. As will be seen, on one occasion when Thurloe disregarded an unsolicited report he was caught out and reprimanded by Cromwell. Not all royalists approved of political terrorism of this nature. Sir Philip Monckton, a Yorkshire cavalier who had survived Marston Moor and Naseby, unequivocally condemned it. Thurloe interviewed Monckton in April 1656. At that time it was thought that the Pope's efforts to secure peace between France and Spain would be successful. In that event, said Monckton, Charles would attempt to obtain some help from the disbanding armies. If unable to pay them he would invite them to help themselves from the property of Englishmen who opposed them.[30]

In November 1655 Thurloe received a report that Spain would try to find 'means to help His Highness and some of his councillors out of this world', and another that Sir Joseph Wagstaffe had bought a fearsome murder weapon, an air gun firing seven shots without recharge and with little sound or smoke. He also heard of a plot hatched by two men, James Halsall and Richard Talbot, to murder the Protector. His informant was Halsall's servant, who betrayed his master for money. Both conspirators were arrested. When examined by Thurloe on 25 November Halsall admitted sending £3,000 to Charles Stuart. On 11 December Thurloe wrote that he was examining Halsall's designs and had five suspects in custody. Whilst Halsall was in the Tower he carried on a brisk correspondence with his wife, all of which was read by Thurloe. Even so, both Halsall and Talbot eventually succeeded in escaping to the Continent.[31]

In the same month Monck informed Thurloe from Scotland that he had recruited 'an intelligencer' well respected by Charles Stuart. He had advanced him £20 and suggested that Thurloe should give him more with his directions before sending him off to the royal court. There was no doubt in Monck's mind that Charles would employ him as a courier with notice of his designs upon Scotland and England. The agent was not named in surviving correspondence and it is difficult to trace his subsequent activities. It is possible that he was the John Watts who wrote to Thurloe from Antwerp in May 1656 to report his arrival two days before Charles entered the town with Ormonde and Rochester. He had visited them all, had been kindly received, and had delivered letters to Ormonde. He believed that they had designs on some towns in England

and that he would be employed 'on some of this business very shortly'. Maddeningly, this seems to be the only letter from Watts to survive, though there is a receipt for £10 initialled JW and dated 1 July 1656. In March 1658 Thurloe received a letter from the resident at The Hague describing a Captain Watts, a one-eyed veteran, as a desperate cavalier who had continually travelled to and fro between the Netherlands and England.[32]

In Lord Broghill, Lord President of the Council in Scotland in 1655–6, Thurloe had not only a personal friend but also one who shared his enthusiasm for the acquisition of intelligence. At the time of Glencairn's operations in the Highlands Broghill penetrated both his personal staff and his communications with Charles Stuart at Cologne, including those in cypher. When Glencairn was captured by Monck toward the end of 1655 it was necessary to detain Broghill's source as well, so as to allay suspicion. By May 1656 he had been released and banished from Scotland, and was writing to Thurloe from lodgings at Charing Cross offering to serve as an agent in Flanders. Thurloe apparently decided to send him to collect military intelligence in eastern Europe, for he reported from near Danzig in November. Broghill had meanwhile recruited another cavalier, the one-armed Colonel Blackadder, to join Charles's entourage and report back to Scotland.

In April 1656 Thurloe had given Broghill a further task – to find a priest who would work as an agent in Spain. Unfortunately the request reached Edinburgh just after the issue of a proclamation threatening death to any priest found in Scotland, 'which possibly may have blown away most birds of that feather', Broghill observed. He quickly suggested an alternative. Sir James MacDonnell could recruit an agent in Madrid, who would report to London – notionally to Sir James, though the letters would first pass through the hands of Thurloe and Broghill. Within a month Broghill had also obtained the services of a Jesuit who had left for Madrid and would direct his letters to the Venetian resident at Covent Garden.[33]

Thurloe saw nothing incongruous in his attempts to find agents amongst the clergy. In the context of the religious background to the struggle between king and parliament, and particularly in the necessarily underground activity of Roman Catholic priests in England and Scotland, it made sense to consider them a possibly fertile field for recruitment. In June 1657 he received a report from a priest acting as an agent in Ireland, a Jesuit whom Longland had sent to report from Rome a couple of years earlier. On a later occasion Thurloe attempted to suborn Father Thomas Talbot during a visit the priest made to England in 1658. He saw him with Sydenham, another member of the Council, who afterwards expressed surprise that Thurloe should have made such a proposition to a man in orders. Talbot was sharply told to leave the country when he refused to co-operate.[34]

In 1656 it was the turn of Edward Sexby to provide the chief menace, his plans coming to maturity early in 1657. Thurloe knew of Sexby's visit to Spain, and notified an agent at Antwerp when he returned to Brussels. 'I would you could get his papers some way or other and send them hither', he wrote on 1 December 1655, a tall order for the over-stretched agent. Though the letter was mostly in cypher, it evidently came into the hands of Ormonde. Before the end of the month Gilbert Talbot, the agent, was forced to defend himself, to report what Cromwell and Thurloe had said to him and to hand over his cypher with Thurloe's letter.[35]

Sexby had persuaded the Spaniards to advance him money for subversive purposes – 'a good part whereof is fallen through the goodness of God into our hands', Thurloe noted drily in a letter to Montagu at the end of April 1656. He went on to explain that the Levellers' treasurer in England was a seaman and a great confidant of those captains in the fleet who had been persuaded, partly by promises of Spanish gold, to desert their commands at the beginning of March. He was certain that Sexby had assured Spain that the English fleet under Blake and Montague would not sail. In the course of what he described as an 'excessive long scribble' he returned to the subject of the Levellers who, with the Fifth Monarchy men, were still active in small numbers. Earlier in the same month he told Henry Cromwell of meetings of Fifth Monarchy men in London and elsewhere.[36]

Charles Stuart had received Sexby's proposals with caution. He wanted Sexby's friends in England first to 'begin the work' by declaring themselves against the present government. At that point his own friends would intervene. But Sexby played the Spanish card with some skill and on 12 April 1656 a treaty was signed in Brussels by Ormonde and Rochester on Behalf of Charles and by Cardeñas, the former ambassador in London, and another for the king of Spain. It appears that Thurloe did not obtain the full text of this treaty, but its main provision, that Spain would put four thousand foot and two thousand horse into the field to restore Charles, was soon common knowledge. In return Charles undertook to provide, after his restoration, twelve warships to help the Spaniards against the Portuguese, to restore all conquests made since 1630 in the West Indies, and, by a secret article, to suspend the penal laws against Roman Catholics in his dominions.[37]

This strange alliance against the Protector had Thurloe somewhat perplexed. 'The Spaniards, cavaliers, papists and Levellers,' he wrote to Henry Cromwell on 20 May, 'are all come into a confederacy. What monstrous birth this womb will bring forth', he added, 'I cannot tell.' The Commonwealth men were also on the lookout for an opportunity to intervene. Anabaptist preachers had earlier hoped to stir up an insurrection. Thurloe received a warning and was able to send church leaders to frighten them off.[38]

There was a diversion at the end of June when an informant reported that Lucy Walter and two children, one of whom was a son by Charles Stuart, together with her brother and Thomas Howard, were in London, lodging near Somerset House. Lucy and Tom Howard were soon under interrogation in the Tower. Lucy maintained falsely that her son by Charles was dead, as was the father of the two children she had with her, and that she was in London to claim an inheritance from her mother. Howard said that he had left England soon after the Battle of Naseby and since that time had been Master of Horse to the Princess Royal. They had apparently broken no law and presented no threat. They soon regained their liberty and returned to the Low Countries. Lucy only had a couple of years to live, but Howard was to reappear in Thurloe's world at a later date. Lucy's son was to grow up to be Duke of Monmouth and in 1685 to raise an unsuccessful rebellion against his uncle, by then James II.[39]

Government anxiety continued throughout the summer and autumn of 1656. In London Thurloe was concerned in August by the preaching of Thomas Venner and the distribution of leaflets about the choice of members for the forthcoming parliament. Barkstead reminded him of an order made in the previous December for the recovery of arms from the officers of three regiments raised under Harrison at the time of the Battle of Worcester. The order had been found imperfect and never enforced, but now, Barkstead advised, it ought to be amended and put into immediate execution. Also in August Lockhart reported that Sexby was in Flanders negotiating with Cardeñas, and at the end of the month Thurloe was referring to 'strong combinations to put us into blood'. In an undated memorandum about the abortive rising of March 1655, the Secretary concluded that more must be expected. The cavaliers were 'men of another interest, which they can no more cease to promote than to live. Besides, they are now joined in with a foreign prince, and thereby the dangers from them is increased.' Charles Stuart was raising four regiments in Flanders from Britons already on the Continent and an Irish regiment in French service was ordered to march thither. 'I trust they will not find us asleep, nor the Lord departed from us, without whom we shall watch in vain', wrote Thurloe in September. It was encouraging to be informed in October by an agent at Bruges that Charles could depend on no more than seven hundred men in all, whose pay was too small to live on. Somewhat disingenuously Thurloe informed Pell in the same month that parliament had perfected a bill for a High Court of Justice for trying persons accused of treason, 'it being thought more safe to try them in this way than by the ordinary juries'.[40]

Though since Manning's death Thurloe had lacked a regular agent at court, he had certainly by this time acquired his most valuable source of all, Richard Willys of the Sealed Knot. The letter in which Willys offered his services, preserved in the Rawlinson manuscripts, is undated and unendorsed, and it is not clear precisely when he was recruited by the Secretary. It was clearly written while Willys was at liberty, possibly soon after his release early in 1656 and no later than his London visit beginning in mid-June.

Signed in the name John Foster, the letter opened by praising Thurloe's vigilance and singular wisdom in aborting designs before they could come 'to prosperous birth from malicious conception'. The writer confessed to a past share in promoting violence, but for the purest motives. He now acknowledged his errors, but preferred to put his proposals in writing before presenting himself. If accepted, he went on, he would betray conspiracies against His Highness's person, as well as designs by the cavalier party, the Commonwealthsmen, discontented army men, and combinations of all three. He had letters and papers to support his claim and believed that only one other man could offer the same service.

His terms were given in a businesslike manner. He wished to be known only to Cromwell and Thurloe and wanted never to be asked to bear witness against any individual since he would aim to uncover things, not persons, plots not plotters. Because no public recognition would be possible, he desired his reward in money. He wanted £500 on appointment with an advance of £50 to accompany the reply to his letter, and £500 more for revealing conspiracies against the Protector. He ended by giving precise instructions for delivery of the reply to a named apothecary near Charing Cross, at the house late of Dr Clarges, to be called for by a Mr Foster or his servant.[41]

There is no record of Thurloe's response to this remarkable document, nor how contact was made between him and Willys. There are only the notes of a discussion with 'RW' dated August 1656. Although there was another individual, Sir Richard Welsh, with the same initials and also known to have had two or three meetings with Thurloe at his own request, the August meeting is generally believed to have been between Thurloe and Willys. In his rather unconvincing defence, written in May 1660, Willys made no admission of having taken the initiative. He said that Thurloe sent for him and proposed to use him for reconciliation with Charles Stuart, in reality a notion most unlikely to have been entertained by Thurloe in the winter of 1656 – 7. Willys and his friend

Edward Villiers had been active since early May trying to revive the Knot. They had renewed contact with Hyde and had recruited a new secretary, Alan Broderick, and a courier. Their attempts to bring in Sir Robert Shirley – a young baronet who had been corresponding with Charles and had written a series of papers in the Tower proposing a reconstructed royalist party based on the organization of the Church of England – were thwarted when he died of smallpox in November.[42]

Sexby's plans for the assassination of Cromwell began to take shape towards the end of 1656. The first clue reached Thurloe from Willys, who, writing as Thomas Barret, had opened correspondence on 15 November, the day after he reached London. He denounced a man who had gone to Calais to act as guide for a proposed landing near Lynn; the royalists planned to seize the Isle of Ely. He thought Charles might be willing to risk such a venture because he was short of money and his military force was dwindling. Another report three days later, though initialled 'PM', seems to be from the same source. It again talks of the Ely project, but adds that Kent was also to be taken. It goes on to forecast an assassination attempt to be made with gunpowder in the rooms below those of the Protector at Whitehall. The writer closes by suggesting a meeting, weather permitting, at which he could name in person the chief royalist agents in the country.[43]

Willys, who had evidently been engaged in some legal business in London, sent Thurloe a further note on 24 November. Now that the term had ended he was anxious to bring the Secretary up to date before returning to the country, 'that I may preserve myself free from suspicion and yet . . . continue to serve you'. He suggested a meeting opposite the smith's shop – its precise location was apparently known to Thurloe – at five o'clock that evening or the next. Thurloe failed to reply, so he sent a further note two days later emphasizing his anxiety to depart and to report before he left.

It appears that a meeting was arranged for Saturday the 29th but did not take place. Willys waited in appalling weather until nearly seven o'clock before concluding that it was pointless to stay longer. By then he claimed to have very important intelligence to impart because a messenger had recently arrived from Charles Stuart with information Thurloe was unlikely to receive from any other source. There is an undated note from Morland to Thurloe stating that Mr Barret 'is now in my chamber', expecting to see the Secretary. It was then seven o'clock in the evening. The paper is filed out of place, but it may refer to one of the proposed meetings of November and December 1656. By 9 December Thurloe was able to boast to Henry Cromwell that he knew of the plan to murder His Highness 'with as much certainty as that your lordship is in Ireland'. Next day Willys at last departed to the country after despatching a letter to Hyde, and on 13 December was writing to Thurloe from Bury St Edmunds that he had achieved little in Suffolk.[44]

Another pointer to the plot came from a Swiss agent, Jean Baptiste Stoupe, later described by Gilbert Burnet as 'a man of intrigue and without virtue', who had earlier served in Savoy and France. Since 1654 Stoupe had been providing Thurloe with regular political reports, mainly from Paris but also from Switzerland and Holland, in return for large if irregular payments. In 1656 he received a letter alleging that an Irish assassin was lodging in King Street, between Whitehall and Westminster, and promptly sent a message to the Protector in Council that he had something of importance to divulge. Cromwell asked Thurloe to leave the Council table to interview Stoupe. Somewhat embarrassed, Stoupe showed him the letter and was both surprised and hurt when Thurloe made light of it, saying that such reports were often received. To his suggestion that the houses in King Street might be searched, Thurloe indicated that he would not make the authorities a laughing stock by undertaking pointless investigations. He advised Stoupe to write to Brussels for more precise information.[45]

Sexby's chosen instrument, Miles Sindercombe, disbanded from the army after a mutiny in Scotland, had in fact rented a shop in King Street. However, he was forced to abandon his plan for firing at the Protector as he passed when he discovered that the property had no back door by which to make his escape. He had earlier recruited John Cecil, a former trooper, and John Toope, a member of the Protector's life guard, which had recently been strengthened. Cecil had bought reliable horses for Sindercombe and himself.

Alerted by Toope when Cromwell was about to go out, they made several attempts to approach him, hoping to surprise him as he was changing between horse and coach. Foiled in this mode of attack, they next tried an ambush, first in King Street, then at a house next to a door of the Abbey, hoping to shoot Cromwell with a special screw gun supplied from Flanders as he walked from the service to the parliament House. But they found this site far too public, with people standing on either side of the path. Next Sindercombe rented a house at Hammersmith that had a room overlooking the road to Hampton Court. The Flanders gun, which fired twelve bullets in one discharge, ought to have been well placed there, but this mode of attack was also abandoned untried in favour of an attempt to burn down the Palace of Whitehall by setting fire to the chapel.

Although Thurloe was aware of some details of the plots through reports from Wildman and George Cokayne, the Independent minister who had formerly served as chaplain to Whitelock, he initially made no arrests and on the night of 8 January 1657 the conspirators were able to put the plan into action. Sindercombe entered the chapel while the other two conspirators kept guard at the door. He placed a basket of incendiary materials in one of the pews and lit a fuse. However, an alert officer of the guard smelt the smouldering match and gave the alarm. Thurloe reckoned from the length of the fuse that it was discovered some three hours before the fire would have started.

All three plotters were apprehended, and the next day Thurloe personally carried out the examination. Sindercombe refused to talk, but from the testimony of the other two it was deduced that the plan was to attack Cromwell and then escape through the smoke and confusion of the fire. Cecil also admitted to riding in Hyde Park seeking an opportunity to kill the Protector, trusting to the speed and endurance of his horse to make good his escape. He had been told that he would be able to go overseas, where Sexby would look after him. Toope, on the other hand, had received £19 in cash and had been promised £1,500 and his own troop of horse upon successfully completing his mission.[46]

On 12 January the Council appointed the 15th as a day to return praises to God for his mercy in preserving the person of His Highness. Thurloe was instructed to engage three preachers for the occasion. He rose in the House on 19 January 'to acquaint you with the discovery of a late heinous plot'. It had been hatched in Flanders, he said, by malignants and Levellers, and he named Sexby as the originator. He went on to describe a paper, issued from Blackfriars and found in early December at the Tower, alleging that Charles Stuart's plans had been put back two or three months by lack of shipping, but that he would act at once should the assassination attempt be successful. The examinations of Cecil, Toope and the two Tower witnesses were read to the House. Two days later the Speaker reported that he had received from the Council a printed acount of 'the late bloody and inhuman conspiracy against His Highness'. It would appear that Toope was successfully turned in his allegiance and became a Protectoral agent: Thurloe's papers contain a receipt signed by John Toope on 2 December 1657 and record of another payment on 26 May 1659 'for the public service', the euphemism used throughout the Secretary's accounts for intelligence activity of one sort or another.[47]

It is always difficult to decide the right moment to break up a conspiracy by arrests. On this occasion Thurloe seems to have held back almost too long, but although he was aware that some sort of plot was in train, he may not have known in advance the details of the Whitehall venture, nor the identity of the three protagonists. He could be and certainly was criticized for dismissing Stoupe's earlier warning that Sindercombe was involved. Told of this incident, the Protector sent for Stoupe and upbraided him, but the Swiss defended himself by describing Thurloe's reception of his intelligence. Thurloe, summoned by Cromwell, did not attempt to deny Stoupe's account but pointed out that he had received several similar reports, all false. Cromwell nevertheless argued that he should himself have been the one to judge the importance of Stoupe's report. Thurloe was forced to defend his record of vigilance and fidelity, and ended by appeasing Cromwell's wrath. Stoupe subsequently alleged that because he had embarrassed the Secretary of State, he was never completely trusted again.[48]

Sindercombe went on trial in February before the Upper Bench. Condemned to death, he committed suicide by poison on the morning set for his execution. The alarm caused by the plot was genuine enough, though by late February Thurloe was able to write that fears 'doth somewhat cool', the Spanish not yet being in a position to make good their promises of supplies to the royalists.[49]

The Fifth Monarchy men planned one last attempt at insurrection in April 1657, still hoping to exploit discontent in the army. Thurloe moved in good time by promptly seizing the ringleaders with their arms and ammunition. On 11 April he reported to the House and produced a copy of a printed book, *A Standard,* and a painted standard showing a red lion couchant with the motto 'Who shall rouse him up?'. The conspiracy, he said, had started in the winter of 1655–6 with initial cells of twenty-five men in and around London. It was led by Thomas Venner, a wine cooper who had been dismissed from his employment at the Tower a couple of years previously as a fellow of desperate and bloody spirit. 'Settle what you will in this nation,' Thurloe declared, 'there are more than one sort of man who will never rest, especially whilst they see troubled waters and things unsettled, till they can set up their principles.'

Having attempted to win the support of the Commonwealthsmen, including some senior army officers, they planned a first rally at Mile End Green. Although only eighty were expected there, it was confidently assumed that thousands more would soon flock to join them from the city and suburbs. Hearing of a preliminary meeting at Shoreditch and of a gathering of twenty ringleaders led to orders for arrests. Six trunks and four chests of arms and ammunition were found in the searches which followed. Venner and five others were in the Tower by 9 April, the day fixed for the rising.

The Commons, absorbed by the kingship question, were informed of the conspiracy and acknowledged the importance of the subject by resolving that Thurloe receive the public and hearty thanks of the House. Standing in his place, he was addressed by the Speaker in these words:

Mr Secretary, I am commanded to return you the hearty thanks, in the name of the Parliament, for your great care and pains in discovering

this business, and the great services done by you to the Commonwealth, and to the Parliament, both in this and many other particulars.

The committee under Whitelock conferring with Cromwell over kingship was ordered to inform His Highness that Parliament was very
sensible of the great consequence of Mr Secretary's report and had set a
date to consider it. But the debate, thrice postponed, never took place.[50]
The ringleaders were not brought to trial but were detained in prison.

At the end of the following month copies of Sexby's pamphlet entitled
Killing No Murder, printed in the Netherlands, were shipped to London.
Seven parcels of them, made up like bales of silk, were seized in a house
at St Katharine's dock, and Barkstead was soon interrogating suspects at
the Tower. Morland thought this the most dangerous pamphlet printed
during the Protectorate. When Sexby came to London in June, Thurloe
found that the best way to apprehend him was 'to lay for him as he went
back'. He was arrested as he tried to leave the country 'under a very great
disguise' on 24 July, and died in the Tower six months later without
being brought to trial. When he was examined in October he admitted
sending Sindercombe to assassinate Cromwell and authorship of *Killing
No Murder,* though he implied that the situation had changed because
parliament itself had since settled the government on the Protector.
Soon after Sexby's death Thurloe received a detailed account of his
subversive activities from a man who had been his servant but had
become disillusioned by his master's disloyalty to England in espousing
the cause of Spain and making contact with cavaliers. He had spent many
months imprisoned in the Spanish Netherlands as a result of his break
with Sexby.[51]

Not all the murder plots amounted to very much. When Lady Gen-
nings, an Englishwoman born in Flanders, landed on the Isle of Sheppey
from Dunkirk, she described in detail a plan hatched by Rochester and
others to send over a major and three men. They were to report to a
papist tailor in Lincoln's Inn Fields upon arrival and await an opportunity to attack Cromwell as he went to Hampton Court, virtually the only
regular occasion on which he was outside the well-guarded palaces of
Whitehall and Hampton Court. A force of fifty men was to be sought to
secure the assassins' retreat.

Nothing more was heard of this plan, but in August there was another
one-man plot. Thomas Gardiner was arrested as he walked through
Whitehall with two loaded pistols in his pockets. Examined by Jessop, he
said that he was armed for his own protection and had come to see a
kinswoman who happened to be a servant of Richard Cromwell's wife,
Dorothy. It was not this coincidence, however, that proved his undoing,
but his own extreme indiscretion in the presence of fellow-lodgers at
Hampton Court and in London. Alarmed at his interest in the Protector,

coupled with his possession of pistols, two of them reported their suspicions to the authorities. Later another witness testified that Gardiner had taken part in preparations for a royalist rising some five years earlier. The Venetian resident's allegation that torture was used on Gardiner can be safely discounted. Thurloe also received several reports of attempts to use poison, including one emanating from one of Queen Henrietta Maria's ladies in Paris. Some reports reached him direct, others via Lockhart in Paris.[52]

Since May 1657 Bampfield had been pestering Thurloe with letters from Paris and Saint-Germain-en-Laye. He complained that he had written fourteen times without acknowledgement, that Lockhart had levelled false accusations against him and he had received no money. He wrote that he would go to Calais but changed his mind upon receiving no encouragement or guidance from Thurloe, and subsequently decided to go instead to Germany, where he would report on political developments. During this time in Paris he had provided a regular flow of reports of variable quality, sometimes employing lemon juice for secret writing and frequently using cypher. At one time he used sources of his own in Madrid and Turin. At the beginning of June he produced a short account of royalist negotiations with the King of Spain; the contents suggest that he was 'with circumspection' able to intercept correspondence passing to and from Charles Stuart's court at Bruges. He suggested to Thurloe the suborning of a Calais merchant, whom he named and who was allegedly receiving weekly despatches by the hands of seamen in the packet boats.

It seems that the Secretary was at last persuaded, perhaps after a personal meeting, that Bampfield might be of some use in Germany, but he took the precaution of obtaining from him a written understanding not to return to any part of the Commonwealth without prior leave. At all events Bampfield, who in urging his case had indulged in a good deal of name-dropping, wrote on 19 August that he was leaving for Frankfurt and hoped to be there in twelve days. Swearing innocence of any breach of trust, he acknowledged receipt of money and asked for a further £50 to be sent to Frankfurt. Once there he continued for several months to send detailed reports on the political and military affairs of the empire. But by March 1658 he was back in London, despite his undertaking, asking for a meeting with Thurloe and boasting of his exceptional access to political information in Germany and ability to negotiate leagues of the small duchies. 'Modesty is folly in those who are starving', he excused himself.[53]

Before leaving Bampfield, mention must be made of a curious approach he made to Thurloe in autumn 1656. Bampfield had observed that the price of tin was a great deal higher in France than in England.

He therefore proposed a takeover of the entire output of the Cornish mines to the great profit of himself, his French partner and Thurloe, who was to carry through the arrangements. It is possible that Bampfield's objective was to obtain written recognition of his plan from the Secretary so that he might acquire some hold over him. There is no evidence of Thurloe's response, though Bampfield reverted more than once to the subject. He subsequently admitted that he appeared to have aroused Thurloe's distaste, but brazenly went on to assert that the best way to obtain pardon was not to ask for it.[54]

In September 1657 there occurred an example of a practice which is still the mark of successful intelligence organizations: the care of agents whose usefulness has been exhausted. Monck sent Colonel Henry Blackadder and Major James Borthwich, both of whom had proved invaluable sources on royalist intentions, to Thurloe in London with a recommendation for employment in the Portuguese service.[55]

By that time Spain was at last showing signs of being ready to carry out long-standing promises made to Charles Stuart. To keep his royal master's side of the bargain Hyde wanted a seaport secured by mid-January 1658. In March Lockhart had reported from his sources in Paris that Charles was still planning to land in the west of England. Though he considered this plan very improbable, he repeated the rumours at the end of the month, naming Plymouth as the port of entry and September as the date. The information was in essence correct, for the latest royalist plot centred on Bristol and Gloucester, and reports of a Spanish invasion force had been rife ever since Charles had obtained 'all his desires' from the King of Spain in July 1656.[56]

Although the conspirators were far from ready, moves against them started in December 1657 with warnings to the authorities at Gloucester and Bristol, and strengthened guards at the Tower. On Christmas Day soldiers intimidated church congregations meeting illegally in private and arrested several preachers. Thurloe was now relying on Willys, who copied for him a letter he had received from Charles, asking him to see a man named William Rolleston. Willys subsequently gave an account of this meeting when he saw Thurloe on Christmas Day.[57]

Charles, uncertain of the support he could expect, sent Ormonde and Daniel O'Neill to London. In James Butler, twelfth Earl of Ormonde, Charles possessed an adherent whose loyalty never wavered. Strong, good-looking and always carefully attired, he had been Lord Lieutenant of Ireland from 1644 to 1647. He had proclaimed Charles II there on the death of his father, but Cromwell's victorious campaign of 1649 had forced him to flee to France at the end of the year. Later a member of Charles's Privy Council, he had been employed in preventing the conversion of Catholicism of the Duke of Gloucester, Charles's youngest

brother, and in negotiations with German princes. His companion, also
an Irishman, had fought for Charles I in the English civil war, in Ireland
(where, as a Protestant, he was widely distrusted) and in Scotland. He
had made a similar visit to England three years before.

The pair arrived at the end of January 1658 and Thurloe, though far
from well, attempted to effect their capture. Willys, in spite of an offer
(according to his own statement) £1,000 in gold and strong pressure
from Morland, refused 'so perfidious an action' and kept the hunt a day
or two behind. Ormonde received no encouragement from his meetings
with the Knot members Russell and Willys. Nobody in England seemed
prepared to move before Charles landed, yet Charles could not obtain
Spanish help without the promise of a secure port. After nine days of
narrow escapes, Ormonde and O'Neill managed to return to the Continent. The editor of Broghill's state letters relates that Broghill had been
directed by Cromwell to warn Ormonde that his presence in London was
known to the Protector.[58]

At the end of February 1658 the English fleet established a blockade of
the coast of Flanders, and the invasion project was quickly abandoned.
Nevertheless the Knot leaders were sent back to the Tower – Russell in
March, Compton and Willys in April, the latter for his own protection.
Villiers managed to escape the net by leaving London. All papists and
royalists were ordered out of the capital and confined to within five miles
of their residences.

Thurloe had meanwhile acquired a new and prolific source in Francis
Corker, a former vicar of Bradford. Since Morland's return to Thurloe's
staff, he had become invaluable for conducting clandestine meetings
with agents as well as in copying letters intercepted by Dorislaus. Encouraged by Morland, Corker produced a great deal of information about
active cavaliers, particularly in Sussex and Yorkshire, though most of his
reports are undated and it is difficult to reconstruct the precise extent
and duration of his work. He was certainly in touch during spring 1658
with two prominent royalists, William Deane and John Hewit, the latter
the divine alleged to have conducted marriage services by prayer book
for one or more of Cromwell's own daughters after the legal civil ceremonies had been completed.

By mid-April Thurloe was able to write that it had 'pleased God to give
us great light into their affairs and designs, both as to persons and
things'. In May Corker gave warning late on a Friday that a rising was
planned for the following night. Cavaliers would come into the city from
the suburbs and it was hoped to secure Windsor, where the Duke of
Buckingham was confined, on the Sunday. Thurloe was able to nip the
conspiracy in the bud by searching the alehouses on Saturday evening

and making a show of military preparedness with a force under Barkstead from the Tower.[59]

Hewit, named by another conspirator, refused to plead before the
High Court of Justice, claiming the right to be tried by jury. Whitelock
and Thurloe had indeed recommended trial by jury but had been
overruled by Cromwell, a rare recorded instance of Thurloe opposing
Cromwell's view. Hewit met his end by execution on 10 June at the same
time as another royalist, Sir Henry Slingsby, who had been held in prison
at Hull for a couple of years before his fate was sealed when an *agent
provocateur* persuaded him to offer a royalist commission in the presence
of a witness. Three others were hanged, drawn and quartered. The
nausea induced by these bloody spectacles caused Cromwell to reprieve
the others condemned to die for participation in the conspiracy. Fortunate to escape at this time was John Mordaunt, second son of the Earl of
Peterborough. After his wife had been extremely active in his support,
the High Court divided equally on his guilt, with nineteen votes on
either side. He was freed by the casting vote of the president and lived to
organize what was known as the Great Trust in favour of Charles
Stuart.[60]

Corker, whose family had been installed by Thurloe at the dowager
Countess of Mulgrave's house in Kensington, continued to send reports
to the Secretary. At one point, he alleged that Ann Thurloe had warned
the countess that her son was implicated in a murder plot against her
(Ann's) husband. The plotters were reportedly trying to trace Thurloe's
movements, particularly the times of his journeys between Kensington
and Whitehall. Later, Corker named Gregory Palden – mentioned already in other reports as a royalist courier expected in England from
Flanders – as 'one of the greatest enemies to Mr Secretary's person'.
Corker also claimed that the plot against Cromwell was still alive despite
Sexby's arrest and the flight of Deane, who had earlier proposed to
murder him when he dined in the city. This conspiracy was not sanc-
tioned by Charles Stuart or the cavalier party, but the plotters were said
to be very confident.[61]

In July 1658 the Knot leaders were released from the Tower with
warnings that they could expect no mercy should they again plot against
the Protectorate. The arrest of Willys with the others successfully de-
ceived Hyde, who knew that Monck had warned Thurloe that Dick
Willys was the most dangerous man in the nation. This warning accounted, Hyde still thought in spring 1659, for Willys being held among
the first whenever there was a roundup of royalist suspects.[62]

After being held without time limit in the Tower as a close prisoner
since December 1657, Gregory Palden, named by Corker as a threat to

Thurloe's person, was evidently quietly released in February 1659. By June he was again active as a courier between Charles Stuart and John Barwick, one of his sources in London. Barwick, a Cambridge graduate, had been charged with high treason in 1650 but released over two years later for lack of evidence. He was now living at the house of a younger brother in St Paul's churchyard and Thurloe was intercepting some of his correspondence with Charles. Bampfield, another long-serving but troublesome source of foreign political intelligence, continued to press his merits. Unabashed by a reproof from Thurloe for offering advice instead of reporting facts, he emphasized how much he could achieve in Frankfurt, particularly if he was recommended to the Elector Palatine and the Landgrave of Hesse. Thurloe saw him in London in April.[63]

In the early months of 1659 the royalist threat appeared temporarily quiescent. Mordaunt was now leader of the Great Trust, formed in March and including five members of the Knot, while Thurloe still relied on postal interception and on Willys to keep him informed. He had earlier seen a letter from Charles Stuart in a form of plain language code. It was not difficult to gather the true meaning when he wrote that he and his brother James had been at Ghent treating with the Spanish merchants and had agreed that all commodities should be sent over and everything read in about six weeks' time. Although twice that time had elapsed without any action, Thurloe remained apprehensive as winter gave way to spring. So it was that, in the midst of a constitutional crisis, parliament debated on 19 April a declaration requiring all cavaliers to leave London and Westminster and to stay at least twenty miles away.[64] Some thought Thurloe prone to exaggerate the threat for his own ends but there seems little doubt that he based all his precautions on intelligence reaching him, though not all of it proved reliable. The reported plots were usually in train, but their authors were often unable or unwilling to carry them through.

But by mid-May 1659 the Protectorate was at an end, Thurloe was out of office, and control of intelligence reverted to John Scot. Worse was soon to follow. Thurloe must have been perturbed when a notice was posted at the Old Exchange in early July exposing Sir Richard Willys as a traitor, and detailing his meetings with the former Secretary and the manner of their communications. It appeared on the very day that Mordaunt arrived in London for final decisions on a proposed rising. His initial reaction was to condemn it as a scandalous libel. A regular royalist correspondent in London at once despatched a copy of the denunciation to Nicholas, at the royal court.[65] Sadly, Thurloe had tardily succumbed to the chief danger facing all heads of intelligence organizations – penetration by the opposing side. The weak link appears to have been his former assistant, Samuel Morland. Morland had been Thurloe's trusted helper, hiring rooms in London under false names to provide safe meeting places, helping to run agents and assisting Dorislaus in the interception of letters. Now Morland turned against his former master and betrayed his system.

How Morland was turned in his allegiance was related in a letter from George Paul addressed to Charles II in 1663. Paul himself had been a seaman and merchant in the Mediterranean area and became a citizen of the republic of Ragusa, but he returned to his native England after six years of captivity in Algeria. Paul alleged that he had first won over Morland's servants so that he could gain access to the office and Morland's study, enabling him to identify the writer of letters signed 'Barret' as Sir Richard Willys. Before long Morland himself had changed allegiance. His wife, who was the decisive influence in turning him, had been rewarded by Paul with a present of a cabinet bought in Antwerp for £50. When Morland equivocated and wanted £10,000 for his defection she deftly 'beat him off that gimcrack'.

On the fall of Richard Cromwell, Paul's account continued, Morland was persuaded to quit Thurloe (though in fact all the clerks were dismissed at the same time as the Secretary in May) and work for John Bradshaw, now Lord President, at Wallingford House. From there he reported to Paul the names of active royalists known to the government, who were then alerted to their danger.[66] It may be true that Paul persuaded Morland to work at Wallingford House. Morland's first thought on losing his job was to take refuge with his wife's family in France, but just when Paul made public Sir Richard's treachery by means of a notice at the Exchange, Morland received notification of the glittering rewards promised him by Charles.

Gilbert Burnet later gave a different version of how Willys was uncovered. According to Burnet, Morland noted where Thurloe kept the secret papers, borrowed the key on the pretext of wishing to use the seal hanging from it, took a wax impression and had a duplicate made. In this way he was able to find letters in Willys's hand and so identify Thurloe's principal royalist source. However, this story does not stand up to scrutiny. There is plenty of evidence that Morland had long been assisting Thurloe in the control of Willys, as of other agents. It may, on the other hand, be a true account of how Morland extracted the evidence he needed to convince Charles.

Morland himself, writing many years later, gives no credence to Paul's influence or his wife's, but attributes his change of heart to disgust at the manner in which Dr Hewit was 'trepanned', a surgical term used figuratively to denote the encouragement of treachery by an *agent provocateur*, in Hewit's case the versatile Corker. Morland protested that he had not acted out of a desire for more money; had he wanted cash he could have made away with over £20,000 at Geneva or, for Spanish gold, betrayed the objective of Cromwell's expedition to the West Indies. Nor had he succumbed to a desire for titles; the restoration of Charles was at that time but a remote possibility.[67]

Yet the inference to be drawn from Morland's own representations to Thurloe at the time is that financial considerations predominated. It was almost as if he were pleading with his superior to prevent him from surrendering to the lure of easy money in return for treachery – from practising himself what he had witnessed in others. He was insensitive enough to ask Thurloe for the post known as Clerk of the Pells in the treasury, vacated only the day before, in the midst of the disturbances and distractions caused by Cromwell's terminal illness. He first started to plead poverty in October 1658, when he told Thurloe that all his fees as Clerk of the Signet – about £8 a quarter – went on wages for his own writing clerk and on parchment. He had been promised half of Marchamont Needham's profits from publishing the official newspapers, but nothing had reached him. Next to Providence, he pleaded, Thurloe's favour was his only refuge, one in which he was resolved to live or die.

In the following January (1659) Thurloe recommended Morland for a seat in parliament, but was disappointed to learn that the sheriff had already secured the election of two others for the borough concerned. A month later Morland again applied for more money. He had been forced to mortgage his London house and half his furniture to provide a country house for his wife. The final blow fell in May 1659 when, in common with Thurloe, he lost his job. It appears that although his salary had recently been increased, he was already £100 in arrears and was owed £20 more for expenses incurred in corresponding with Pell and Piedmont, and for personal purchases for Thurloe including locks, keys and even a hat. In asking for an advance, he emphasized the difficulty of finding fresh employment after such a long and close association with Thurloe. This letter was written on 17 May. If he had not already broken faith with his employer he must have done so immediately afterwards. Thurloe's accounts presented in the following November show payments to Morland of £300 on 25 April, £20 on 26 May and £50 on 15 June.[68]

Morland evidently possessed a highly developed capacity for intrigue. He admitted to receiving £150 from an unnamed foreign ambassador in London for one letter lifted from Thurloe's desk. By the time he sent Charles Stuart what was accepted at the time as proof of Willys's treachery – a batch of letters in Sir Richard's distinctive handwriting – Thurloe was no longer in office. It seems to have been on 15 June that Morland, using Henshaw as a courier, despatched his damning evidence. Acknowledging its receipt on 27 June, Charles promised Morland the

Garter and something else to make him wear it with delight. Clearly regarding Morland as now safely on his side, Charles asked for political intelligence about the peacemaking activities of the English government and instructed him to do what he could to obstruct them.[69]

Morland's well-known ability to copy handwriting without detection has led to suggestions that the Willys letters were forgeries. Indeed they may have been, for Morland would have had to extract originals before leaving the Secretary's office some time earlier. However, their veracity is in some ways immaterial, since it is certain that Willys did betray his royalist trust and that Morland in turn uncovered his treachery. The first report was received in royalist circles with dismay and incredulity. Initially Mordaunt had spoken highly of the Knot and particularly of Willys himself, stressing how impossible it was that he should be guilty of treachery. Charles, considering that the best course would be to send for Willys, did so on 18 July, while Hyde instructed Broderick to press him to comply. Broderick, who shared meals and lodgings with Willys over a considerable period, had never noted anything suspicious in his conduct. He admitted, however, that his handwriting was distinctive and that the letters appeared genuine and damning proof of guilt. Noting Willys's reluctance to approve any plans, to obey Charles Stuart's summons, or to appear in arms, Hyde forbade any further communication with him. Charles was convinced by mid-October – and probably even earlier – that Willys had long been false and had betrayed his affairs to Thurloe.[70]

Despite the public exposure of Willys's treachery, and repeated warnings by Hyde against trusting him with any further information, members of the Knot were not inclined to accept the allegations levelled against their colleague. Mordaunt, conducting royalist affairs from Calais, complained to Hyde on 19 October that they 'stickle fiercely in the vindication of Sir Richard Willys, and will have him still a very fine gentleman, extremely honest and brave beyond expression'. He warned Hyde not to give the Knot any information that should be kept from Willys. 'Lord have mercy on us', he concluded, should Willys again be trusted. Three days later he complained to the king that Russell and Compton, displaying a typical reluctance to believe ill of their colleague, had disregarded Hyde's instructions. Thurloe, of course, was equally trusting of Morland. The latter seems to have provided Mordaunt with intelligence from early 1659, though he may not have been that 'great intimate' of Thurloe on whose statements Mordaunt based his reports to Charles. There is, after all, evidence that Broderick was making use of a source in Thurloe's office as early as March 1657.[71]

Morland is the only source for the unlikely story of a Westonhanger Plot. At the time of Booth's rising in August 1659, it was said, Willys had

taken over a house in this Kentish hamlet close to the sea at Hythe and
had invited Charles Stuart and the Duke of York to land there with the
supposed object of having both assassinated. Morland is alleged to have
sent Henshaw to warn Charles, the message reaching him just as he was
pulling on his boots to depart.[72] It seems totally out of character for
Willys to have considered such an idea, but of course he may told this
story to Morland as a cover whilst scheming in earnest to provide
military support for the two royal brothers on landing. When two double
agents are in contact there is scarcely any limit to the possible deceptions
and double-crossings.

Morland is not an altogether credible witness. When he claimed that
by betraying Thurloe he risked having 'his flesh pulled off his bones with
red hot pincers', one may doubt the source and veracity of such threats.
Perhaps, like many intelligence agents, he merely liked to exaggerate his
own importance and the risks he ran. In the following March he furnished Willys with a letter to help him refute a libel. It was drawn in
palpably false terms, denying that he knew 'so much as your name', that
he had ever been present at any private conversation between Willys and
Thurloe, or that he had shown to Charles any letters or receipts signed
by Willys. Anyone capable of such deceit could hardly inspire confidence
in his word.[73]

From June 1659, onwards Morland reported regularly to Hyde, sending extracts of Thurloe's correspondence and copies of his cyphers. He
identified Corker as an agent who had been paid £400 a year for almost
four years and announced the arrest in September of Malcolm Smith,
who under the pseudonym of Blanc Marshall had long been one of
Thurloe's sources at Bruges. As for Willys, Morland said that he and
Thurloe remained in touch, though Morland had prevented several
meetings between them. By October Willys was alleging that he had been
threatened by other royalists.[74]

Scot, replaced on Thurloe's recall to office in February 1660, had been
equally successful in providing the Council with intelligence, and was
critical of the value and expense of Thurloe's sources. It is no surprise to
find that Bampfield was still reporting. There had been another leak
from the Council in Scot's time. Henry Darell, one of its principal clerks,
had passed information through his wife to his brother-in-law Roger
Palmer, husband of the notorious Barbara, later Countess of Castle-
maine and Duchess of Cleveland, favourite mistress of Charles II. Palmer in turn passed everything on to Broderick, who was able to inform
Charles.[75]

Charles Stuart's arrival at Breda early in May 1660, as an obvious
preliminary to his return and restoration, caused a number of people to
rally to his side. Willys was there and on 9 May presented an abject

petition. If he were as spotless as innocence itself, he began, it was no diminution to the clearest virtue to beg pardon either of God or the king, since neither could be served as exactly as he ought to be. 'Being the most disconsolate and afflicted person alive by lying under Your Majesty's displeasure', he went on, he had purposely come over to cast himself upon His Majesty's gracious pardon and clemency. He prayed that the royal charity and forgiveness would extend to the frailties of the king's friends as well as to the malice of his enemies. On the same day he addressed a letter to Hyde begging his intercession with the king 'to pull this sharp thorn of grief out of my breast'.[76]

Charles replied on 13 May. He was in a singularly benign mood. Vengeance was a passion largely alien to his nature, and he had publicly declared in the previous July that he would pardon all except those responsible for his father's death. Although he noted that Willys had not acknowledged his great offence and breach of trust, and that further evidence of his intrigues was still to come to light, he was 'graciously pleased in compassion to the petitioner and in such a time of public joy to grant the petitioner his full and general pardon'. Even so Willys was forbidden to come into the king's presence or within the verge of the court until the Attorney-General had prepared a bill for signature.[77]

Morland had also come to court, to claim his reward. Samuel Pepys, who had known him as a Fellow of Magdalene College and his tutor at Cambridge, noted on 13 May that he had been knighted that week, the king saying openly that it was for giving him intelligence all the time he was clerk to Thurloe. 'Nobody respects Sir S. Morland on board,' he remarked sourly a couple of days later, 'he being looked on by all men as a knave.' Intelligence agents often inspire great interest and curiosity about their motives and admiration of their skill when successful, but they seldom command respect, regardless of the risks to which they expose themselves.

Another long-standing servant of the Commonwealth and Protectorate had also made a satisfactory transition: George Downing, knighted at Breda on 21 May. In March he had sought the help of Tom Howard, brother of the Earl of Suffolk and Master of Horse to the Queen of Bohemia, still the Princess Royal of England. In August 1658 Downing had seized an opportunity to blackmail Howard into becoming a royalist source for Thurloe, taking possession of secret papers which Howard had left with a whore at The Hague. Howard's indiscretion never came to the ears of the court, though he fell under suspicion when named by Morland. He was now able to repay Downing by making sure of a good reception for him from the new ruler of England, Scotland and Ireland.[78]

In spite of his knighthood and a baronetcy which followed in August

1660, Morland remained an unhappy man. Writing in November to Nicholas, the new Secretary of State, he complained bitterly that after private and public acknowledgement of his services and 'so many large promises of honourable, profitable and exemplary preferments' he had been forgotten and 'laid aside as a useless thing'. He referred to the letter in the king's own hand promising him the Garter and admitted that although he had returned the original, as advised by Hyde, copies had been taken and were now in France. He alleged that Henshaw had brought him an oral promise that he would be made second Secretary of State, a post for which his experience surely fitted him, and ended by praising his wife, who had stood by him in danger when she chould have gone to France to be made heiress to her uncle.

In an intemperate petition he named sixteen individuals who had received money from Thurloe and others 'during the late usurped governments', betraying His Majesty's councils or at least the persons, liberties and estates of his loyal subjects. According to Morland, these people were a danger to his own life. He pleaded for them to be brought before the king's Council. He was quite ready, he declared, to undergo the penalty for slander should they be found innocent. Willys, Bampfield, Corker and Howard were among the sixteen he wanted branded on their foreheads for treachery. No doubt it was to mollify Morland at this time that the king gave him a gold medal with leave to wear it as an honourable badge of his signal loyalty, referring to 'the great and important services Sir Samuel Morland did His Majesty from time to time, during the late usurper's power, by the faithful intelligence he so constantly gave him'. But it was far from the end of Morland's discontent. Seventeen years later he wrote a narrative of his services to the crown and begged an income of £500 a year to leave to his family.[79]

It seems that the Attorney-General never found time to rescind the prohibition against Willys's appearance at court, for in due course Sir Richard had to petition to have it removed so that he might defend himself in several lawsuits. He claimed that although induced to 'become an intelligencer' he had expected thereby to benefit rather than to injure the royal party. He went on to repeat a boast of Morland's that he and a Mrs Russell had actually poisoned Cromwell and that Thurloe had 'a lick' of it and was laid up. The story lacks credibility and probably appears in no other sources, though an intercepted letter from Antwerp in March 1658 did claim that Cromwell was dangerously ill and that Thurloe was 'distracted' and had to be carried to an apothecary's premises in the Old Bailey. Finally Willys alleged that Thurloe intended to live in Normandy. This, at least, had some foundation, for before Thurloe's arrest in May 1660 Morland had written to his father-in-law asking him to facilitate Thurloe's residence in France and had even arranged for the shipping of his effects.[80]

Willys had married a wealthy widow in 1659, escaping the poverty which had dogged his earlier years and proved his main motive in becoming a double agent. Morland alleged that Willys had asked Charles Stuart to send him £50 or £60 with his monthly instructions, at the same time as Morland was passing him larger sums at clandestine meetings in a Holborn tavern and in hackney coaches. Ignored by the court, Willys retired to Fen Ditton and died there in 1690.

In August 1661 Morland was granted an annuity of £500 on surrender of letters patent for a like annuity from the profits of the office of Postmaster-General. The new annuity continued to come from the Post Office. Shortly before the Restoration, Dr Benjamin Worsley had taken over the farm of the Post Office from Thurloe, paying a rent of £20,000 instead of the former one of £14,000. His contract was set to run for seven years but he was soon turned out, suffering a loss which he put at £1,600 when petitioning for restitution a few years later. Detailed accounts for Thurloe's penultimate quarter as farmer, from 25 March to 23 June 1659, show receipts and expenditure nearly in balance at around £7,450. Far from making a profit on his quarter's rent, Thurloe had been forced to make up from his own pocket a small deficit of just over £31. Nine months later there were debts of almost £1,700 outstanding on the postage account, which must represent the sum Worsley wanted repaid. It was not only the farmer of revenues who suffered at this time of political upheaval. In June 1660 a great many petitions were received from local postmasters begging to be continued in their places or restored to them.[81]

Although Thurloe was in retirement, and control of the Post Office had passed to Henry Wilson at an increased rental of £21,000 a year, Dorislaus still exercised his skills there. Shortly after the Restoration he was visited by Dr John Wallis, who had been so successful in breaking the substitution codes used in royalist and diplomatic correspondence. He told Wallis under great secrecy that letters could be opened, copied and shut again, and all hands imitated 'without the least umbrage of discovery'. This technique, which in fact had been developed by Morland, was attributed to Thurloe.

About 1664 Henry Bennet, Lord Arlington, who had succeeded Nicholas as Secretary of State, told Morland that the Spanish had a way of sealing letters to that it was impossible to open them without leaving a trace of the work. Morland was, however, able to demonstrate his own ability to deal successfully even with letters sealed in the Spanish fashion. When the king was informed he went late one night in a private gentleman's coach to the Post Office and there witnessed the opening of seals in wafers and wax and the resealing of letters without trace. He permitted the practice to continue, but there was no pressure to resume it after all the equipment had been destroyed in the Fire of London two years later. Morland wrote an account of these techniques for King William III in 1689. To a proposal that this art ought to be put in practice in the general post offices of England, Scotland and Ireland, the Secretary of State of the day noted that the king thought the secret was too dangerous to be encouraged, and ought to die with Sir Samuel.[82]

The government of Charles II, like its predecessors, had trouble with the Fifth Monarchy men, who staged what became known as Venner's Insurrection in January 1661. Thurloe, who was still in London at that time, must have watched its suppression with a critical eye. Less well informed than when he was at the helm, the administration failed to arrest the leaders of the conspiracy as he had done in 1657. As a result there was more bloodshed and a final battle with the trained bands in the streets around Cripplegate. The king welcomed an excuse to retain one regiment of horse and one of foot for internal security duties. The disbandment of the standing army had been approved by parliament at the end of the previous August.

Thurloe could continue to enjoy his retirement in the knowledge that he had made a significant contribution to the security of the Protectorate throughout its lifespan. Though he may not have known it, he had also left his mark on the manner in which intelligence would be sought, gathered and disseminated in his own and in other countries for generations to come.

6

POLITICAL AND PARLIAMENTARY AFFAIRS, 1657–1660

His name is and will be precious to all generations and is now
even to those who murmured at him in his life time
(*John Thurloe*)

Cease now our griefs, calme peace succeeds a war,
Rainbows to storms, Richard to Oliver (*Andrew Marvell*)

A fortnight after Cromwell's second investiture, his new Privy Council
met for the first time. There were minor changes in personnel, though
most of those appointed during 1653–4 under the Instrument of Government
reappeared in the Council established under the Humble Petition.
Thurloe's exact status between 1653 and 1657 was a little
ambiguous, for although he had a very influential voice at the Council
table he appears not to have been a full Councillor. Such doubts were
swept away in July 1657 when 'His Highness nominated John Thurloe,
Esq., Secretary of State, to be one of his Highness's Council, which was by
vote of the Council upon the question consented unto." Thus on 13 July
Thurloe took the prescribed oath – swearing not to do anything against
His Highness, to preserve the secrecy of Council business and faithfully
to perform the trust imposed upon him – and became a full member of
the new Council, henceforth appearing in all official and unofficial lists
of Councillors.

Although a second new member, Cromwell's eldest son Richard, was
added a little later, the only other changes to take place at this time
concerned the removal of former Councillors. Anthony Ashley Cooper
and Richard Major, two of the founder members of December 1653,
had long since ceased to attend meetings and their removal in summer
1657 was a mere formality. Much more significantly, John Lambert, the
architect of the Instrument of Government and for a long time the most
powerful member of the Council, had broken with Cromwell over the
kingship proposals and other aspects of the new constitution. He was
dropped from the Council and forced by the Protector to surrender his
commission as a major-general and all other offices. Lambert promptly

complied and retired to Wimbledon, Fleetwood succeeded him as the most influential military leader (after Cromwell himself), and by the end of July Thurloe was able to assure Lockhart that all was quiet in the army.[1]

With parliament prorogued and a pause in the succession of plots against the new regime, Thurloe was able to pass a relatively calm late summer and autumn concentrating on foreign affairs and his voluminous correspondence. Even so, he still had to spend time serving on the Council and its numerous committees, handling mundane matters: the preservation of wood in Epping and other forests, the cost of His Highness's new sceptre, and – important – the raising of revenue and the ejection of scandalous ministers. Thurloe also had onerous duties to perform as head of the conciliar secretariat and as principal Secretary of State. It was, perhaps, as well that business was relatively slack at this time, for Thurloe was deprived of the services of Morland for well over two months when he went to Normandy to get married and was then delayed for six weeks awaiting ship at Dieppe to carry him back.[2]

Council meetings were both infrequent and poorly attended during July and August, for in the wake of a long parliamentary session and with disease rife in London over the summer, many Councillors returned for a time to their country estates. Cromwell, too, spent over a fortnight at Hampton Court and then continued to pay weekend and slightly longer visits to his Thames-side retreat. His eldest surviving son, Richard, who had taken almost no part in affairs of state beyond rather inactive membership of the two Protectorate parliaments, was seriously hurt during the summer when he fell while hunting on his Hampshire estate. He broke a thigh and dislocated a knee, though by late August Thurloe reported that both were mending well and that Richard was in no danger. At about the same time Thurloe, too, managed to take one of his rare holidays in the country.[3]

With two other Privy Councillors, John Desborough and Philip Jones, the Protector's brother-in-law and the Controller of his Household respectively, Thurloe drew up the marriage settlement for Cromwell's daughter Frances to Robert Rich, grandson and heir of the Earl of Warwick. Cromwell had expressed some disappointment with the earl's proposed provision for the marriage. Thurloe's failure to keep an engagement with Nieuport to discuss the maritime treaty gives an indication of the priority given to this matrimonial matter over his other commitments. In the end Frances received a jointure of £2,000 a year for life, together with Warwick House.

On 11 November the wedding took place at Whitehall and on the following day there was a great feast. An orchestra of forty-eight violins and fifty trumpets provided music for dancing until early morning. We may be sure that John and Ann Thurloe were of the company, though Ann was three months pregnant. Cromwell had entertained in similar almost royal fashion as long before as February 1656 when his niece Lavinia Whetstone, daughter of his sister Catherine, had married Major Richard Beke.

A week after Frances's wedding, her sister Mary was married with less ostentation at Hampton Court to Viscount Falconbridge. Andrew Marvell composed two songs to be sung for them at their wedding. Falconbridge, Thurloe told Henry, had an income of £5,000 a year, was a person of very good abilities and seemed very sober. But the Venetian resident expressed his amazement at the match, alleging that Falconbridge and all the Bellasis family had favoured the king throughout. It was Mary, according to the Scottish divine Gilbert Burnet, who waspishly commented that of all Oliver's children those in breeches should be in petticoats and those in petticoats ought to be in breeches.[4]

Mary's two eldest brothers had long been dead, Robert in 1639 and Oliver of smallpox whilst on active service with his father's regiment in 1644. Richard, recovered from his fall, was nominated a Privy Councillor by Protector and Council, and arrived in London just before Christmas 1657. He made his first appearance at the Council on 31 December, took the oath and was added to all the standing committees. He had by that time received his writ of summons to the new upper House of parliament. His brother Henry had lived for a time in Kensington and had married Elizabeth Russell there in 1653, but since July 1655 had been in Ireland as commander-in-chief of the army and, in Fleetwood's absence, virtual governor of the island.

In the following March Thurloe, who maintained a regular correspondence with Henry in Dublin, reported how difficult it was proving finding suitable men to serve as Councillors in Ireland, men 'in whome your lordship may repose perfect trust and confidence, as well for their fidelity and affection towards yourself as ability for their work'. Many had been considered, but none selected. In a letter of 20 October 1657, which he asked Henry to burn, Thurloe bemoaned the Council's inability to make progress on Irish affairs: 'I never consider that business, but I am ashamed, yea confounded; and do wonder with myself what reason will be rendered for it either to God or the nation.' But he derived some satisfaction from his own conscientious and honest labours for the public. A fortnight later Henry was at last appointed Lord Deputy, though Fleetwood, his predecessor, had left Ireland soon after Henry's arrival. Henry took the oath on 24 November, protesting in a letter next day of his unfitness 'for his burden'. Ten days later he was telling the Privy Councillors that he was ready to resign in favour of any other who could do his work without pay. According to Sir Francis

Russell, Thurloe was 'much in love' with Henry, and used to commend him to his father-in-law. Thurloe was not alone in having a high regard for Henry: Broghill told Montagu at this time of his good opinion.[5]

The Privy Council's contingency accounts for the period ending September 1657 show an expansion of Thurloe's office with the employment of one Thomas Priestly as 'usher to Mr Secretary's chamber' at a salary of £9 2s. a quarter. Since taking up his lodging in Whitehall, Thurloe had had little or no occasion to make use of his chamber at Lincoln's Inn. The council of the society, faced in November 1657 with many empty chambers, made a list of twenty-nine absentee gentlemen, ordering them to show cause why their chambers should not be seized. Not surprisingly Thurloe's name appeared on the list.[6]

As the time approached for parliament to reassemble on 20 January 1658 the Protector was busy selecting members for the new upper House. 'The Lord be with him in it', Thurloe prayed in a letter to Henry. 'A mistake here', he went on dramatically, 'will be like that of war and marriage; it admits no repentance.' A little later he clarified the difficulty his master was having in choosing between 'those who are fit and not willing to serve, and those who are willing, and expect it, and are not fit'.[7] The Protector managed to compile a list of sixty-three names, and on 11 December writs of summons under the Great Seal were issued.

The recipients included seven English peers, one Irish and one Scottish, five sons of peers and four baronets. The Cromwell family were to be represented by Oliver's sons Richard and Henry, his sons-in-law Fleetwood, Falconbridge and Claypole (the latter married since 1646 to his daughter Bettie and serving him as Master of the Horse and Groom of the Bedchamber), and his brother-in-law Desborough. The army contingent was strong and included Montagu, General-at-Sea. The Welshman Philip Jones, Controller of the Household, and several members of the 'inner cabinet' such as Wolseley, Pierrepont and Broghill, found places, as did Fiennes, St John, and Whitelock. Sir Arthur Heselrige was also summoned but declined to sit. Some of those summoned, including Henry Cromwell, Monck and Lockhart, were absent on duty, but others, such as the old peers Warwick and Wharton, simply refused to attend.

Thurloe attended a meeting of the Council on Christmas Eve before retiring to bed seriously ill. He had been ailing for some time. Broghill had written from Ireland on 23 November expressing anxiety, beseeching the Lord 'to restore you speedily both for the public, your friends' and your own sake'. It is touching to note the genuine concern shown by Thurloe's friends and correspondents when he was ill. Henry Cromwell, much distressed by news of the drowning of John Reynolds, his wife's brother-in-law, missed Thurloe's regular letters and wrote to

Falconbridge on 20 January 1658 that he was 'much in the dark' because of Mr Secretary's indisposition; again on 10 February he complained that 'the want of Mr Secretary's intelligence leaves a great dimness upon my sight of affairs'. It was not only lack of information that worried Henry for, as he told Broghill, he was concerned for 'a person whose welfare I do think myself concerned to study, both as he is a man of much worth, and has shown a particular friendship for me'.[8] Not until early February did Thurloe resume duty, and by then much had happened on the home front. When parliament met on 20 January about a hundred members, who had been excluded by the Council in the last session, were allowed to take their seats – unfortunately, as it turned out. In the new upper House forty-two members were sworn.

On 25 January Cromwell summoned both Houses to the Banqueting House to hear one of his long speeches. He spoke about the Protestant cause in Europe, deploring Denmark's attack on Sweden and the possible closure of the Baltic. He pointed to Spain as the enemy, but warned that the Dutch, too, could not be trusted. At home he lamented the division of the country by the sects and reminded the Commons that army pay was five or six months in arrears. In a final plea for unity he asserted that there had now been peace for six years. He meant, of course, peace from civil strife at home, not from war abroad, for during those six years the English had repeatedly fought and finally defeated the Dutch at sea, destroyed two Spanish treasure fleets, captured Jamaica and assisted at the siege of Montmédy and the reduction of Mardyke. In fact, even within the British Isles the army had had to suppress risings in the West Country and in the Scottish Highlands. But he did remind both Houses of their good fortune compared to the countries of continental Europe. 'You have accounted yourselves happy', he told them, 'in being environed with a great ditch from all the world beside.' Rather oddly, he made this an argument for having an army to fight on the Continent.[9]

Two days later there was a day of public humiliation when members gathered to hear very long exhortatory sermons. Then on 28 January the Commons started to debate their relationship with the other House. Thurloe, who wrote on this day that he was 'now pretty well recovered', had received enough information to give Downing a hint of the proceedings while deploring his own inability to attend. Control of the Commons quickly passed to a group of members highly critical of the regime, the so-called Commonwealthsmen or republicans, most of whom had originally been excluded in September 1656. They focused their attacks upon the role of the new 'other House', condemning it as yet another step towards the pre-war monarchical system. One of the few sensible contributions was made by Chaloner Chute, a knight of the shire for Middlesex and bencher of the Middle Temple who had acted as defence lawyer in several notable trials, including those of the bishops in 1641, Laud in 1644 and Hamilton in 1649. But on 2 February Heselrige, pleased to be back in the Commons, was still arguing for a grand committee to examine what he saw as a re-creation of the House of Lords. 'It is a matter of the highest concernment that ever was debated in a Parliament of England', he declared. They were still at it on 4 February, an icy day, when they were summoned to the chamber of the 'other House' to be told by Cromwell that this parliament was dissolved.[10]

The Protector had decided on this action in order to prevent the presentation of a critical petition concerning the control of the City of London militia. This threatened to unite the Protectorate's opponents in parliament, the City and the army. Three leading Anabaptists had been arrested on the previous day and there was serious disaffection in the army. Cromwell blamed the promotion of sedition in the City and the army on some members of the lower House, notably the Common-wealthsmen. On 6 February he addressed two hundred officers for two hours and a few days later – after a dispute in which, so Thurloe told Monck, there was no meeting of minds – he cashiered William Packer and five officers of his own regiment, all Anabaptists.[11]

In the bitter weather, with an icebound river, Thurloe got back to work. He attended Council again on 19 February, though Guavarina, the Venetian resident, reported that the Secretary was still confused and left irresolute by his long illness. It seemed to him unlikely that Thurloe would ever be able to resume his former duties. Cromwell was distressed, he wrote, for he loved the Secretary dearly and trusted him more than anyone else; a replacement would be very difficult to find.[12] Fortunately for Cromwell this gloomy prognosis proved incorrect, but it is an indication of how seriously Thurloe's illness was viewed.

In spite of the work by Thurloe and Jones in the 1656–7 parliamentary session on the monthly assessments for England, Scotland and Ireland, the government was still woefully short of cash to carry on its business. Cromwell had asked the second session for more, but had dismissed parliament before a penny more had been voted. An estimate made before the end of February 1658 showed nearly £245,000 owing to officers. Less than half of this was accounted for by outstanding assessment, leaving over £130,000 still to be raised to pay off arrears. Without parliament there was little the Council could do to secure more revenue. The capital realized from the estates of royalists, bishops, deans and chapters had nearly all gone: only a trickle was still coming in. The Council had hoped to increase income by about £100,000 a year by farming the customs and excise, with weekly payments on account. 'The great want is money,' Thurloe wrote to Henry on 16 March, 'which puts us to the wall in all our business.' At the same time Henry, desperate himself for cash for the wages of the army in Ireland, was sending a personal representative with letters to ten Privy Councillors begging for relief. Though still feeling the effects of his illness, Thurloe had already resumed his punishing schedule of meetings, correspondence, and even examinations at the Tower. The continuous cold weather and northerly winds of a late spring cannot have helped his recovery.[13]

Although Thurloe reported in several letters that the army was quiet, and expressions of loyalty continued to flow in from regiments in Scotland and Ireland, the army leaders were still restive and had formed an army committee to promote their desires. Their principal request was for a new establishment to replace that of 15 October 1655. They had submitted a fresh one in April 1658 and complained on 7 July that it had 'lain with the clerks of the Council ever since'. The Council adopted its usual practice of setting up a committee to deal with it. Mr Secretary was inevitably a member.[14]

The subject of kingship had now arisen once more and opinions in the Council were as usual divided. A committee of nine was formed to consider and recommend what the next parliament should be asked to do. The continued dominance of the army is exemplified by the composition of this committee. There were five military members, including Fleetwood and Desborough, and four civilians – Nathaniel Fiennes, Philip Jones, Thurloe and Sir Gilbert Pickering, the Lord Chamberlain. When it reported on 8 July the committee advised in favour of elective rather than hereditary succession, but until parliament decreed otherwise the procedure laid down in the Petition and Advice – that the Protector should nominate his own successor – was still in force, but time was running out. Richard Cromwell, a reluctant contender for the succession, again proved accident-prone, injured in June when his coach horses bolted and smashed the vehicle.[15]

What was called a malignant fever had been prevalent in London in the summer and autumn of 1657 and there had been a renewed outbreak in April 1658 and again at the end of July. The Cromwell family had already lost Frances's husband Robert Rich, who had died in February, only three months after his wedding. His grandfather, the Earl of Warwick, had also died in May. Now Cromwell's daughter Bettie Claypole lost her youngest son, and both Bettie and her father lay ill at Hampton Court. Oliver Cromwell was struck down again by the malaria he had picked up in Ireland and his daughter was dying of cancer. Thurloe, having returned from a visit to Hampton Court on 27 July, reported that both patients were taking water from Tunbridge Wells. (Spa water was supposed to be a sovereign remedy.) At Thurloe's request Downing had already sent dozens of bottles to Fleetwood and Thurloe until stocks of spa water at The Hague were exhausted.[16]

After 20 July the Council met on Tuesdays in London and on Thursdays at Hampton Court. Early in August both father and daughter were pronounced a little better, but Elizabeth Claypole died suddenly on the 6th. Thurloe attended her burial at Westminster Abbey six days later. At about the same time he received a report from Corker, back from a visit to the north, that his own life was threatened. His movements between Whitehall and Kensington were being studied, as were those of Barkstead between the Tower and his home in Essex.[17]

The Protector's health ebbed and flowed, and on 24 August he was moved to Whitehall during an interval between seizures. Cromwell realized the seriousness of his illness and sent for a sealed envelope addressed to Thurloe, containing his nomination for the succession. Even before Cromwell died it could not be found. But its loss seems to have been very lightly accepted and passed over without investigation by Thurloe himself or by possible beneficiaries, such as Fleetwood and Desborough. According to the editor of Broghill's state letters, one of Cromwell's daughters was responsible for removing and destroying the envelope.[18]

Thurloe attempted to obtain a decision from the Protector on 30 August but could get no definite reply. Next day His Highness was too ill to be approached again. By Thursday 2 September he was obviously dying. Thurloe tried once more and in the presence of some other Councillors was rewarded with a clear nomination of Richard Cromwell to succeed. The Protector died in the midst of a storm during the afternoon of the next day. At about eight o'clock Pickering, as Lord Chamberlain, went to Richard's lodging to inform him that the Council was about to wait on him. They arrived with the Lord President at their head to condole on his father's death and to endorse, by formal resolution, his late Highness's appointment of Richard as his successor in accordance with the Petition and Advice.[19]

There is no doubt that Thurloe was genuinely distressed by Cromwell's death. He wrote a large number of letters during the next few days, some revealing his innermost feelings. To Whetstone, Cromwell's nephew with the Mediterranean fleet at Marseilles, he wrote that the death was 'the saddest thing which could have befallen this nation', and to Downing that 'He hath died more lamented than any man in this or the generations past. His name is and will be precious to all generations, and is now even to those who murmured at him in his life time.' As a matter of course he also informed his old friend and former employer, Oliver St John. In acknowledging Thurloe's 'sad letter', St John volunteered that he would account it a great happiness if he could be of any service to any of His Highness's family. Clearly he feared storm clouds ahead, for he added a hope that the Lord would be merciful to his people. Thurloe wrote at once to Henry Cromwell and a few days later a further letter was taken to Ireland by the hand of one of Oliver's Grooms of the Bedchamber, sent by Richard to give an account of the late Protector's terminal illness. Thurloe's sense of loss was not, perhaps, widely shared. One modern historian has gone so far as to assert that Cromwell died 'hated by all save a few intimate friends and admirers such as his competent little Secretary of State'.[20]

Ever since the failure of the rising of March 1655 royalists and Anabaptists alike had been trying to contrive the Protector's death. Now it had happened from natural causes. Yet all remained calm. Downing at The Hague was candidly outspoken. The acceptance of Richard, he wrote to Thurloe, 'doth most wonderfully amaze all that hear of it, who expected nothing but confusion in England after his late Highness's death, and thereby a wide door opened for Charles Stuart'. Just as Thurloe's corresondence shows his grief at the death of Oliver, so it equally reveals his relief at Richard's smooth transition to the Protectorship.

Heralds proclaimed Richard at Whitehall and Westminster on Friday morning, 4 September, and he took the oath the same afternoon. Thurloe wrote five days later to Nicholas Lechmere, Attorney of the Duchy and formerly member of parliament for Worcestershire:

> His new Highness hath the blessing of a very easy and peaceable entrance upon the government, all parties centring in him as deserving it of himself, as also being the eldest son of the bravest man that ever this nation bred.

Since his wife was a kinswoman of Lechmere through the Overbury family, he signed himself 'your affectionate cousin'. To Whetstone he confided that the proclamation had been received with satisfaction in the City, though less so in the army. He expanded on the latter theme in a letter to Henry:

> It hath pleased God hitherto to give His Highness your brother a very easy and peaceable entrance upon his government. There is not a dog that wags his tongue so great a calm are we in. The Lord continue it. . . . But I must acquaint Your Excellency that there are some secret murmurings in the army, because His Highness was not general of the army as his father was. . . . But I am not able to say what this will come to.[21]

Plainly the army's attitude would determine the fate of the new administration, and the fact that there had already come into existence a group of senior officers of questionable loyalty, known as the Wallingford House party (after Fleetwood's residence), pointed to future difficulties.

Thurloe's attention was urgently needed in foreign affairs and in counter-subversion, but just at this time he suffered a recurrence of illness. It seems to have started about 13 September and for the rest of the month he could not write letters, though he dictated a couple of short notes to Henry. On 1 October he referred in a letter to Downing to 'my own indisposition which I cannot yet shake off', and a fortnight later, in one written in another hand and merely signed by him, he admitted 'my distemper still hangs upon me'. The nineteenth-century French historian Guizot emphasized the political results of Thurloe's indisposition, writing that 'the most trusted and able of Richard's advisers . . . was quite unable to attend to business'.[22]

Thurloe was still confined to his room on 2 November when some members of the Council and several army officers came to complain that the new Protector was led only by the advice of Philip Jones and himself. 'Having heard this,' he wrote the same day to Henry,

> and observing that it was industriously spread amongst the officers of the army that I was a very evil counsellor, I did desire of His Highness that I might have leave to retire, hoping it might be a means to quiet things and facilitate his affairs with the whole army.

Thoroughly depressed by this virulent opposition on top of his want of health, he went on to say that he did not see what opportunity there would be for 'doing further service in the station I have done, either to God or the nation',

A week later he confessed that he was more puzzled by the actions of 'some of our friends' than at any time since entering the public service. Having no political ambition, he was quite unable to understand the eternal preference of politicians for tearing each other to pieces and stirring distrust rather than working for the peace and contentment of all. 'Nothing will do', he complained; 'dissatisfactions are still retained, and many things whispered up and down to affright honest and well meaning people into a fear of His Highness and Government.' Richard told him, he wrote, that he was equally perplexed to see 'what great endeavours were used to persuade Godly men that he loved them not, and that they could not trust themselves and their concernments with him'. But on the same day Thurloe was at last able to leave his room and a fortnight later he was about the House, determined to do what he could towards his duty 'without much considering the danger'.[23]

He had been one of six Privy Councillors chosen to arrange the ceremonial for the state funeral of Oliver Cromwell, the others being Pickering, Jones, Desborough, Viscount Lisle and Montagu. His illness must have reduced his contribution to this committee to nominal proportions. On 17 November he returned again to Kensington, so that Morland had to apologize on the 20th for Thurloe's continued inability to write a letter to Downing. But he was well enough three days later to take his place in the funeral procession, and no more was heard about resignation.[24]

Cromwell's body had probably been buried some weeks earlier and it was an effigy made of carved wood with wax hands and face that had been lying in state at Somerset House under a black-fringed canopy, robed in purple velvet and bearing a sword, sceptre, orb and purple velvet cap furred with ermine. Behind its head was a gold chain and the imperial crown. A complete suit of armour lay beside the bier, which was ringed by eight silver candlesticks five feet high with three-foot wax tapers and guarded by bareheaded mourners with black wands.[25]

Whatever the state of the nation's finances, the government was determined that no expense was to be spared to make the state funeral a memorable occasion. The procession from Somerset House to Westminster Abbey was led by the Knight Marshal on horseback, his deputy and mounted escort. Then came a group of poor men of Westminster in mourning gowns and hoods with two conductors carrying black staves at front and rear. There followed groups of servants and officers, each group separated from the next by drums and trumpets with banners and black-plumed horses. The contingent from the government offices was led by three of Sergeant Dendy's men, followed by the solicitor of Admiralty Isaac Dorislaus, George Downing and three other tellers of the Exchequer, the treasurer of contingencies Gualter Frost, the Council's solicitor, and five secretaries of the French and Latin tongues, including Andew Marvell and John Milton. Then came the two clerks of the Signet, Samuel Morland and James Nutley, two clerks of the Privy Seal, the clerk of the Council William Jessop, and the clerks of the Commons and Lords. The Lord Mayor of London came next, followed by Cromwell's relatives, ministers of foreign states and Black Rod. Thurloe took his place next as Secretary of State, followed by peers of the new creation, commissioners of the Great Seal and foreign ambassadors.

Needless to say, there had been some unseemly wrangling over precedence, Bordeaux, the French ambassador, wishing to walk alone and not between the ambassadors of Portugal and the United Provinces. Behind the ambassadors came the sergeant-at-arms, the heralds and the Lord Chamberlain. The coffin was borne on a chariot escorted by pallbearers with armour carried on either side and followed by Garter King-of-Arms and finally Fleetwood as chief mourner. (Richard was excluded as the new Protector and Henry was still absent in Ireland.) The procession started late and took so long to reach the Abbey that the short November day was over, darkness was falling and there were no candles. There was no religious service, sermon or oration. The trumpets sounded and everybody dispersed.[26]

Many thousands of pounds had been spent in mourning the first Protector. At the end of August in the following year over £19,000 was still owing to drapers and mercers for cloth, velvet and fringes.[27] Now it remained to be seen how his son would fare as his successor in the face of mounting debts, army opposition, royalist and Anabaptist subversion, a continuing war with Spain and a difficult international quarrel in northern Europe. Quite inexperienced in statecraft, Richard had already demonstrated his dependence on the advice of others. Thurloe, his health recovered, stood ready to make his contribution.

Once the funeral was over, it did not take the Council long to decide on their next move. Indeed, they had already discussed it – they must call a parliament. 'I hope the Lord will give a good issue thereunto', Thurloe wrote to Downing on 3 December. 'I am sure the land hath need of it and therefore all good men should pray for a blessing upon it.' More honestly he had already confessed to Henry, whose hopes of a swift recall to England had proved unfounded, that he did not like the outlook: 'my fears are greater than my hopes', he wrote.[28]

On 17 December the burgesses of Tewkesbury wrote to Thurloe that they understood he would be pleased to honour their poor corporation by accepting their free and unanimous vote to be one of their burgesses in the next parliament and to sit as its member. This nomination he acknowledged on 31 December, but it seems that in the event he was not a candidate there. Later there were allegations that Thurloe had been instrumental in securing the election of as many as twenty-four sympathetic members, but no evidence was produced and little attention was paid. His own papers show attempts, sometimes unsuccessful, to nominate four or five Scottish and two Irish members. Thurloe himself was returned for two borough constituencies and for the University of Cambridge, where St John as Chancellor had proposed him. He decided to sit for the university and new writs for Huntingdon and Wisbech were issued on 23 February 1659.[29] After his unanimous election, he was promptly admitted by the university as a Master of Arts by proxy. The master and fellows of St John's College were also quick to contact the new member seeking a favour.

As the returns came in Thurloe told Henry that the new House would contain such a mixture that nobody could tell which way the majority would lie.[30] It was with some uncertainty and trepidation, then, that Protector and Council faced the new parliament on Thursday 27 January. The Privy Councillors attended His Highness by water in a new galley from Whitehall to the parliament stairs and walked thence first to the Lords' chamber and then to the Abbey. The text for the sermon was taken from the 85th psalm, twice quoted by Oliver Cromwell in addresses to parliament. With the 86th, it had also served Milton as a model for one of his hymns. Richard's speech, short and to the point, almost certainly owed much to Thurloe's drafting. It contained some biblical allusions, but there were none of the convoluted passages and 'seesaw sentences that defy condensation', as one writer has it, that members had heard from the late Protector. Richard confined his speech to what he wanted parliament to do: to pay arrears to the army, to prosecute the war with Spain and to support intervention in the Sound.[31] It was a model speech from the throne and tends to show the increasing dominance of Thurloe as the court's representative in parliament. In the event Richard, like Oliver, failed to control parliament. But if Thurloe's task was hopeless, it was not for want of effort.

The new House of Commons contained about fifty republicans, some seventy lawyers and nearly one hundred officers. Having elected Chaloner Chute as Speaker and set a date and nominated preachers for a fast, they fell to debating the usual petty points beloved of parliamentarians. But on 1 February, 'in a full house Mr Secretary very suddenly and abruptly stood up'. He told members that it was time now to mind other things. The hand of God had been seen in the succession, and the House should recognize this mercy by acknowledging His Highness to be the undoubted successor. He adduced precedents from the reigns of Elizabeth I and James I, both of whom had somewhat controversial claims to the throne. He had information, he said, that strong endeavours were abroad to change the government. So he now presented a Bill of Recognition to the Speaker and prayed that it might be read. As soon as he sat down Heselrige, in spite of a cold, sprang to his feet. Now was not the time for such matters, he argued; first the fast, then the committees of the House might be nominated. The bill, as Thurloe admitted to Downing, met organized opposition from Commonwealthsmen, but it was received and read a first time without a division and a date was set for second reading. It excluded Charles, James and Henry Stuart from succession and made it high treason to promote their pretended rights.[32]

Thurloe can scarcely have failed to appreciate what a hornet's nest he had stirred. When the bill was read a second time, Heselrige – called, it seems, unwittingly by the Speaker – launched into a speech lasting three hours in which he reviewed the whole history of the English government since the Norman Conquest and emphasized that parliament had won the right to speak for the people. He was not satisfied with the succession, but if the majority were in favour of a single person he would submit. On a subsequent day a member criticized the wording of the bill, which should have tied the succession to compliance with the Petition and Advice. Some members became restive and called for the question to be put, but others still wanted to speak. William Packer, deprived of his commission a year before and now MP for Hertford, expressed dislike of the words 'by the death of his father', as a phrase which seemed to admit a hereditary title.

Throughout the whole long debate the main bones of contention were the negative voice – that is, the power of veto – the status of the 'other House', and (as always) the control of the militia. The Speaker was censured for not keeping members to the point. Having twice tried unsuccessfully to sum up the sense of the House, he made two more attempts before confessing 'we are indeed in a wood, a wilderness, a labyrinth'. The next day he reminded members that the 'sun does not stand still but I think you do not go forward'. After it had been resolved to include the word 'recognize' but not 'undoubted', a motion 'that it be part of this bill to recognize and declare His Highness Richard Lord Protector and Chief Magistrate of England, Scotland and Ireland, and the dominions and territories thereunto belonging' was carried with few dissentients. A further resolution was then put declaring that additional clauses limiting the power of the Chief Magistrate would be part of the bill, but that no part would be binding until the whole bill was passed. To this Thurloe returned the sole negative vote.[33]

The parliamentary opposition was ably summarized by Marvell in a letter to Downing of 11 February. 'Mr Secretary being something tired with Parliament and other business', he began, had been asked to give an account of the week at Westminster. There had been fierce opposition to the bill. All power rested in the people, it had been argued; power had been returned to the House by the death of the old Protector and Mr Speaker was therefore 'the protector in possession'. Though they pretended that they favoured a single person, opponents of the bill would not concede the negative voice or control of the militia. A petition had been got up in the City and another was brewing in the army, but supporters of the bill outnumbered the opposition by two to one and therefore, Marvell concluded, 'our justice, our affection and our number will wear them out in the long run'.[34]

The debates dragged on. Other business intervened, but the Commons kept returning to the burning question of the constitution itself and often sat long and late. In the course of a lengthy debate on the motion that the House would transact business with 'persons now sitting in the other House as a House of Parliament', some members took great exception to the present members of the new chamber and would have had the pre-1649 Lords restored. Thurloe had to speak again on 7 March to defend the constitution set up by the Petition and Advice, arguing that the power therein given to His Highness and the 'other House' could not now be taken back. If all power was concentrated in the Commons, he told the House, 'we have anarchy or absolute tyranny'. He could not support such a motion.[35]

Next day the House managed to pass one amendment, but the Speaker was exhausted, 'ready to die in the chair', and business began to falter. On 9 March at almost noon he prayed to be excused and was escorted by the sergeant to his coach. He was not permitted to resign and Sir Lislebone Long, the member for Wells and Recorder of London, was appointed in his stead until his return. But on Monday 14 March he, too, fell ill and prayed to be dismissed. He died two days later and was replaced by Thomas Bampfield, the member for Exeter, whose severity in the chair was quickly noted: 'he behaves himself like a Busby amongst so many school-boys', Thomas Burton remarked in his diary of the session, an invaluable source. On 19 March four members who travelled to Chute's country residence at Sutton Court, Chiswick found him very infirm and weak, but grateful to be remembered by the House. He undertook to return as soon as his health permitted, but it never did, and he died in London on 14 April. Bampfield was promptly confirmed as Speaker.[36]

At length on 28 March, after the defeat of two amendments calling for the approval of the 'other House' by the Commons – Thurloe acted as teller for the 'noes' in the first – the main motion was carried by 198 to 125. In its final form it read:

> That this House will transact with the persons now sitting in the other House as a House of Parliament during this present Parliament. And that it is not hereby intended to exclude such peers as have been faithful to the Parliament from their privilege of being duly summoned to serve as members of that House.

The right of the Scottish and Irish members to sit and to vote had already been disputed but confirmed. Members, however, proceeded no further towards recognizing the constitutional position of Richard as Lord Protector.[37]

In retrospect the introduction of the recognition bill appears unwise. Thurloe may have felt that an oral nomination by a dying man lacked the force of one written whilst in good health, and that parliamentary approval was therefore necessary. None the less, the bill permitted every parliamentary opponent of the regime to have a say, producing weeks of dissent and probably hastening the death of two Speakers. During the first week of the sitting a member referred to the Protector as Richard IV, a calculated indiscretion which met with a very restrained response. Perhaps, therefore, the government would have won tacit approval without having to force the point through contentious and ultimately unsuccessful legislation. As it was, debates over the constitutional question, together with customary squabbles over precedents and privileges, absorbed much of the session, though the House of Commons did manage to devote some time to the two subjects commended to them by Richard – the revenue and foreign affairs.

It was Heselrige who first directed attention to His Highness's words about arrears of pay for the army. Thurloe, who in the absence of so many Councillors and other officials in the 'other House' was principal manager of government business in the Commons, welcomed the initiative. Instead of referring the matter to a committee, he suggested that officers of the navy and army should be directed to submit their accounts direct to the House. Members thereupon passed a series of resolutions: that the commissioners of the Treasury should deliver an account of the state of the Treasury, the committee of the army a statement of the army establishment, and the commissioners of the Admiralty and navy an account of the present charge and debt of the navy. Some time later Heselrige accused the Protector and Council of maladministration, demanding to know the size of the state's debt.

At length on 17 February the accounts of the Treasury, army, navy and Admiralty were received. On the same day Thurloe committed a tactical blunder by causing to be read a letter from His Highness to 'our House of Commons' asking members to proceed more quickly. He was forced to defend the Protector, who simply thought that members should understand the urgency of their affairs. The House disdainfully ordered the letter laid aside and asked Mr Secretary to take note that nothing so distasteful and counter to its privileges should again come from the court. None the less, some progress was made and on 12 March the commissioners and farmers of the excise were ordered to pay all monies owing within fourteen days.[38]

A parliamentary committee formed to examine the accounts had completed its work by 7 April, to be thanked by the Speaker for its exactness and speed. The report showed that Scotland and Ireland had been much less successful than England in raising revenue. Thurloe, admitting that 'my business was never to meddle with money', pointed out that the House now had the first full account for eighteen years and hoped 'we are all clear of misemploying your money'. The total debt, at about £1,384,000, was not as great as feared and Thurloe asked the Commons to find some way to pay it off.[39]

Two days later he pointed out that only £10,000 of the £200,000 expected from the excise had come in. The farmers of the excise on ale in London, Middlesex and Surrey, summoned to explain, blamed the reluctance of the brewers to pay their dues. But the House ordered them to pay £15,700 on the following Saturday and a further £20,000 on or before the first day of the next term. At the same time a committee of the company of brewers was told that the farmers must be promptly paid. On 15 April, when a committee of the House produced a declaration continuing the excise, Thurloe queried its wording and forced a division to recommit it. This was carried by 100 votes to 93, but the parliament ended before further progress was made on finance.[40]

The House had found early in its session that it contained at least two members of doubtful loyalty, one a royalist who had compounded for his estate and had sat in the 1654 parliament, the other a member of a papist family. They escaped being sent to the Tower and fined by 145 votes to 122, but were expelled and permanently disabled from sitting. In fact many more royalist sympathizers sat in this parliament, their presence and identity well known to Thurloe, who asked Downing to investigate whether any of them was in correspondence with Charles Stuart.[41]

The sensitive issue of imprisonment without trial also arose several times during the session. On 8 February the Commons resolved with little debate that Robert Overton should be brought from detention in Jersey and a frigate be sent to collect him, decisions which troubled the court of Whitehall. Overton, imprisoned in Jersey since January 1656, came before the House on 16 March. Judge Advocate Whalley justified his detention in the circumstances which then existed, a line seconded by Thurloe. Recounting how at a dangerous juncture Overton had tried to turn the army against the government, Thurloe recommended that the case be referred to a committee, and that if the House wished, Overton could be released on bail.[42]

On 4 February 1658 a number of Fifth Monarchy men had been arrested and held in the Tower. Now, just over a year later, the legality of their detention was questioned in the Commons. Although it had been carried out in accordance with a letter from the late Protector, the House resolved that it was illegal, a decision that worried Barkstead, the Governor of the Tower. The House returned to the matter on 26 February when Jessop, clerk of the Council, submitted a narrative of the arrests, particularly that of John Portman, formerly secretary to the generals-at-sea. They had arms and horses ready and were prepared to seize the Mews. The Protector was 'tender' towards them because they sought God through Christ, but he committed them to prison in order to preserve the peace. The House, noting that the crown had formerly possessed no such power and asserting that every committal warrant ought to state a specific crime, ordered the discharge of Portman, whose detention was adjudged illegal and unjust.[43]

A third instance arose when on 25 March a petition from Rowland Thomas was read, alleging that he had been committed to the Tower by

Thurloe and then sold into slavery in Barbados by Noel. Barkstead had sent warrants to Thurloe for the committal of Thomas and others and for their delivery to Noel for transportation, which had taken place on 31 May 1655. Thurloe, on the defensive, denied responsibility for committing Thomas, who was a royalist agent discovered sending several trunks of arms into the country. Moreover, he argued, the House should not have received and read a petition from an active royalist. Sir Henry Vane took the opportunity to speak up for liberty and against tyranny from any quarter, but the debate was adjourned without a vote.[44]

A few days later Thurloe returned to Thomas's petition and resulting insinuations 'as if the Secretary of State could enslave, and had enslaved, the people of England at his pleasure'. He used the occasion to rebut another calumny – that he had by his letters procured the election of many members of the Commons – and asserted that he did not know of three thus chosen. He had looked up the papers on Thomas, who had paid £150 to a merchant to conceal arms and transport them to royalists around the country. He did not know whether it was by his order that Thomas had been initially committed to the Tower. Thomas would not confess, there were insufficient witnesses to bring a charge of high treason and although he could have been sent to the Bridewell prison, it was adjudged expedient to exile him to Barbardos. Thurloe proposed that Thomas be secured and held in custody while the evidence of January 1655, all preserved and still to hand, was reconsidered.[45]

In the course of the ensuing debate, Vane alleged that threats had been used to extract information. Thurloe at once intervened, declaring 'there were no threats other than to discover the whole plot'. It was not much of a defence, but it was sufficient to secure a resolution that Thomas be taken into safe custody by the sergeant-at-arms on a Speaker's warrant. It was small wonder that by then Thomas had disappeared from the door, where he had been waiting. In royalist circles, where it was believed that in fact Thomas had been treated in Barbados very much as a gentleman, it was considered that Thurloe and others were fortunate not to have been ruined by the affair.[46]

Thurloe came out strongly against the arbitrary power of parliament when on 12 April members debated the case of Major-General Butler, who had taken over a royalist estate in Northamptonshire, the owner having fled abroad. Some were pressing for deprivation of both his office as a justice of the peace and his army commission. Mr Secretary said that Butler should be heard before sentence was passed, and was forced to speak a second time urging that parliament's actions should be founded on law. It was without precedent that judgement should be given without hearing the parties or witnesses, an argument supported by the Speaker. At length it was resolved that a committee should draw up an impeachment against Butler and consider the procedure for action in similar cases. Although Thurloe had stood firmly on principle, his concern for Butler was based in part on loyalty to the Cromwells, for he was an officer of what had formerly been Oliver's – now Richard's – regiment of horse.[47]

Thurloe was by this time caught in a three-cornered fight between army, parliament and Protector. The army had begun by appearing loyal to the new regime, but it was not long before agitation began, by petition and otherwise, for the appointment of a commander-in-chief, no discharge without trial, and devolution to the army commander of the power to grant junior commissions. On his sick-bed, Thurloe drafted an address for the Protector to deliver to the officers. 'The enemy', he pointed out, wished to sow division between the Protector and the army, and within the army itself. In response, they must strive for unity and accordingly the Protector was grateful for their loyal addresses.

The aims of the 'good old cause' were defined as liberty of the nation as men and liberty of conscience as Christians, while keeping the army in the hands of godly men and retaining a godly magistracy and a godly ministry. The Protector was devoted to all these aims. He hoped that time would improve the army's knowledge of him, since God and the nation had chosen him. He refused to surrender the nomination of officers for commissions, though he would naturally listen to advice. Although not obliged to do so, he had appointed Fleetwood commander-in-chief. Finally he hoped that he and the Council would be able to obtain for the army their arrears of pay. On 16 November 1658 Desborough presented Richard with further loyal addresses from army officers, and four days later a number of them attended and 'made large professions of obedience and faithfulness'.[48]

In fact opinion in the army at this time was divided between the Commonwealthsmen, who desired a republic, the Wallingford House party, who supported Richard in the expectation of governing through him, and Richard's own party, who stood for the existing constitution of two Houses of Parliament and a single person. 'Write very particularly what your intelligence is about our divisions here at home,' Thurloe had instructed Downing on 5 November, adding 'and this I am rather earnest in.'[49]

By mid-February 1659 it was clear to Thurloe which way the wind was blowing. There were enemies on all sides, he told Henry Cromwell, but God would bless courage and lively actions. Experience had shown him that judgements made in a melancholy frame of mind were always erroneous. 'The case is as good as ever it was,' he went on, 'and the enemies are baffled men; and if we can believe that God will be with us, he will be with us; and who can then be against us?'[50]

Early in April the officers began to show their strength by holding meetings at Wallingford House. In this they were encouraged by the republicans in parliament, who wished to revive their version of the 'good old cause' and saw no hope in carrying a resolution against the combined votes of their old cavalier and new court opponents. The parliamentary majority took fright and on 18 April passed a resolution that during the sitting of parliament no general council or meetings of officers of the army might take place without leave of His Highness and both Houses of Parliament. It was passed by 163 votes to 87, a fair indication of the relative strengths of the parties. A further resolution was passed that no person should have command in any of the armies or navies of England, Scotland or Ireland who should refuse to subscribe that he would not disturb nor interrupt free meetings in parliament or the freedom of members in debates. Another meeting of officers had been planned for the 20th, but on the same evening that the resolutions were passed in parliament Richard sent for them and dismissed them to their places of duty.[51]

The House sat on Tuesday and Wednesday, the 19th and 20th, when some officers did assemble at Wallingford House but soon adjourned. The confrontation could, however, no longer be prevented. At noon on 21 April Desborough told the Protector that if he would dissolve parliament the officers would take care of him. If he refused they would do it anyway and leave him to shift for himself.[52]

Richard, aged thirty-one at this time, still had Broghill, Jones and Thurloe to advise him. Another name mentioned at this time as a member of his 'inner cabinet' is that of John Wilkins, a cleric who had sided with parliament and taken the covenant, served for a time as chaplain to Charles Louis Elector Palatine, a cousin of Charles Stuart, but in 1656 married, as her second husband, Robina, sister of Oliver Cromwell. Apart from this family connection, Richard had been in touch with him since 1657 as Chancellor of Oxford University, where Wilkins was warden of Wadham College. However, Wilkins seems to have missed Richard's crucial consultation with Fiennes, Whitelock, Wolseley and others, on receipt of the army's stark conditions.

The House had met as usual on the 21st, adjourned for dinner and sat again until six o'clock debating control of the militia, a bone of contention since 1642. Meanwhile, after much discussion with his colleagues, Richard decided to issue a proclamation under the Great Seal dissolving parliament. Supported, it appears, only by Thurloe, the Protector had argued strongly that to dissolve parliament would spell ruin for himself and his government, but had eventually given way. Thurloe handed a copy of the dissolution order to Fleetwood and Desborough in the early hours of the morning. Fiennes, as first Commissioner of the Great Seal and leader of the 'other House', was able to dissolve it without difficulty, but the Commons, assembling on the 22nd as usual, closed their doors against Black Rod and adjourned until Monday morning at eight o'clock. Richard, on the advice of his 'inner cabinet', thereupon had the doors of the Commons House padlocked and guarded.[53] The first round of the struggle was over.

The army had recalled the leaders of the radicals such as Harrison and Packer, and hoped that by forcing the dissolution they had rid themselves of a faction that would by degrees have brought back Charles as King. Thurloe heard on 29 April that the officers would be approaching His Highness in a day or two, but it was not until 5 May that the blow fell. 'The officers have at last taken resolution what to do', Thurloe wrote to Lockhart. The Rump of the Long Parliament was to be recalled. 'His Highness is excluded from having any share in the government and must retire as a private gentleman.' It was said that he would, however, be allowed Somerset House and £20,000 a year. 'All who have been in relation to his father are much afflicted', Thurloe added; 'I am in such confusion I can scarce contain myself to write about it.

Discussion had gone on amongst Richard's closest advisers until the early hours of the morning, but when some of his supporters mentioned fighting for him, Richard thanked them for their friendship but said that rather than see a drop of blood spilt on his behalf, he would lay down the greatness which was such a burden to him.[54] His renunciation of power was not the action of a coward but rather a humane reaction to the bloodshed of the civil wars which he had witnessed in his youth.

Thurloe's world was overturned by the abrupt fall of the Cromwell dynasty. The star to which he had hitched his wagon had been giving but a pale and uncertain light since Oliver's death, for Richard lacked executive experience and was ill-suited to the greatness which had been so abruptly thrust upon him. Even so, Thurloe and his companions in the 'inner cabinet' had worked hard in Council and parliament to bolster Richard and to give the three countries firm and fair government. Now the republican element, led by Vane and Heselrige with Lambert providing military backing, was in the ascendant, though the recall of the Rump would soon prove its ruin. From Scotland Monck had independently expressed the view, in a private letter to Thurloe, that only the Long Parliament would ever be able to preserve the peace of the nation.[55]

On 6 May some officers went to Lenthall's house in Chancery Lane and delivered the resolution for the recall. The former Speaker refused to summon the members to London, saying that he was too old and infirm, though it was unkindly rumoured that he did this because he preferred to hold on to his new status as a lord of the other House. Vane and his colleagues did the job for him the next day, and about thirty members initially turned up. Realizing that a quorum of forty would soon be reached, Lenthall changed his mind and led forty-two to their seats at about noon. Those excluded in 1648 were refused admission and soon formally re-excluded. A Committee of Safety, comprising seven members of parliament and three army officers, was appointed. Thurloe, of course, no longer had a seat in parliament, but he remained active for a few days longer. Many of Richard's friends took their seats in parliament, but Fiennes had none and Falconbridge was away in the country keeping a 'low profile'. He had good reason: in June Bellasis sent Falconbridge's secretary to Flanders with a contribution to royalist funds of £1,000 from the viscount. Henry Cromwell was still in Ireland, but was forced to resign in June.[56]

'I write to you only as a private person,' Thurloe told Lockhart on 9 May, 'and as one who hath no relation at all to public affairs.' A new council of State had been chosen under John Bradshaw as Lord President, though later the presidency changed hands about twice a month. Bradshaw, whose signature had headed those on the death warrant of Charles I, had been at odds with the Protectorate and for six years had taken no part in government. The Council's thirty-one members included St John, who was making a vigorous return to political life, Heselrige, Vane and Whitelock. They took an oath 'to be true and faithful to the Commonwealth, in opposition to Charles Stuart or any single person'. They dismissed Thurloe and recalled his predecessor, Scot, to take charge of intelligence; they appointed no new Secretary of State. 'I know not yet in what order they will put their foreign affairs', Thurloe told Lockhart, and advised him to address his letters to Fleetwood, who was apparently the most powerful man in the country and was shortly to be confirmed as lieutenant-general and commander-in-chief of the land forces of England and Scotland.[57]

Members of Richard's discredited government, including Thurloe, were subjected to an avalanche of hostile comment in broadsheets and newspapers. Thurloe even had to suffer the taunts and catcalls of a hostile crowd when he was turned out of Whitehall. Guavarina, embittered by his personal losses and the frustration of his long and fruitless stay in London as resident, poured out his scorn in a report to Venice. Richard, he wrote, had been badly let down by Thurloe, who had been raised by his father from 'a mere lawyer's notary to be secretary and councillor of state, in which offices he has amassed a heap of gold, has betrayed and sold the Protector without any profit and with manifest signs of lack of respect and an utter absence of gratitude.'[58]

This was a formidable indictment, but it was utterly unfounded. Such gold as Thurloe had acquired came legitimately from his earnings as

Secretary of State and a Privy Councillor, from the profits of the Post Office, and from his rents on property. All his own writings, and those of others in a position to observe events at close quarters, show him as loyal to Richard to the end, though royalists believed that for his part Richard had lost faith in his Secretary. There is a report, dated early June, that Richard afterwards blamed Thurloe for his break with the lower House, but this is unfair because his decision to dissolve parliament was made on the collective advice of the 'cabinet'. Thurloe was not in a position to save the Protectorate; one cannot argue unarmed against a man with a sword.

Bordeaux saw Thurloe at his Kensington home on 18 May. He assured him of full French support for Richard if there was any likelihood of his restoration, and asked for information on the plans of the former Protector's supporters. Thurloe could tell him nothing, except to emphasize his antipathy to civil war, but they agreed to meet again clandestinely so that the new government would have no suspicion of their continued contact. They met once more, but Bordeaux must have appreciated that he had nothing further to gain. When in early June he met Fiennes, who had previously declined to see him, he found that Fiennes seemed to know of his talks with Thurloe. The former Secretary of State, said Fiennes, was 'not a man to enter into any warlike designes'; he accepted the fact that there was no course open other than submission to the will of Divine Providence.[59]

It has indeed been a peaceful revolution. One correspondent in London remarked, on the first sitting of the recalled Rump on 7 May, that to the astonishment of all there was 'not a broken pate'. Though none could see clearly how matters would develop, many must have realized that 'very great things are upon the wheel'.[60]

Thurloe had an early indication of moves to restore the Stuarts when he received an approach offering him safety if he 'would heartily join restoring' Charles to his throne. Two others were similarly approached, but 'they are cowards to that wretched degree', Broderick reported to Hyde on 23 May, 'they dare not think of running the hazards.' They had produced scruples about religion, he went on, and concern about security of tenure of church and crown lands. Meanwhile a friend was attempting to suborn Philip Jones.[61]

Records of Thurloe's activities during summer 1659 are sparse and it may be that he put some distance between himself and the new administration by going with his family to his fine new mansion at Wisbech castle. He certainly did not hurry away, for he found that a civil action had been brought against him claiming £10,000 for wrongful imprisonment. The case was a complicated affair about misappropriation of money from the Scottish Treasury. All the relevant papers were in Edinburgh and on 31 May Thurloe wrote to Monck requesting that the general deal with the whole matter. He was almost certainly still in London on 9 June, when he was reported to have written to Montagu. It seems that some despatches from abroad were still reaching him personally, for he told Montagu that his had been delivered to the President of the Council, read and referred to a committee which would despatch commissioners to continue the mediation process in northern Europe. Even in July Hyde had reason to believe that Thurloe was meddling as much as ever in foreign intelligence.[62]

By mid-August he was back in the capital, not at Kensington but at Hammersmith, and he obtained a pass from the Council to travel to and from London, as well as a general permit for him 'with his servants and their riding arms' to pass on their occasions without let, hindrance or molestation. He has been tentatively identified as the writer, under the pseudonym Johnston, of a letter dated 25 August to Lockhart, then at Bayonne observing the negotiations for the Treaty of the Pyrenees. If so, he had been 'several weeks under physic' when he wrote.[63]

When Paul wrote to Charles II in 1663 concerning Sir Richard Willys, he also alleged that in early summer 1659 he had despatched Thomas Whetstone, Oliver Cromwell's nephew, to Charles at Brussels bearing a suggestion that he be sent to the Sound to tempt Montagu to change sides. Whetstone was at a loose end, suspended from his command in the previous autumn and sent back to England after falling out with Stokes, his senior officer. Leaving Gravesend on 17 June with Henshaw, carring Morland's evidence against Willys and a covering letter written two days earlier, Whetstone was allegedly anxious to serve the king and hoping for a knighthood. In due course he managed to meet Montagu clandestinely in Copenhagen and to hand over a letter from Charles offering him an earldom. However, the admiral was unwilling to show his hand until there was a successful rising in England.

Hyde had previously written to Montagu's cousin stressing the admiral's unique opportunity to contribute to a restoration. Montagu later acknowledged to the king that he had received his first letter whilst in the Sound;[64] he was certainly of questionable allegiance at this time, and was probably privy to plans for the royalist rising then in train. Hyde confirmed that Charles asked him to move the fleet to the coast of Flanders so that he and the Duke of York might embark. Instead Montagu hedged his bets and brought the fleet back to England, claiming that he had run short of provisions. His return to home waters without orders led to his dismissal from the command, and he retired to his estate at Hinchinbrooke to wait upon events.[65]

The royalist rising of summer 1659, like all its predecessors, was a complete fiasco. The royalists in England were divided over the venture, and harvest time was the worst possible moment for raising men. Unwisely, Charles had been led by Mordaunt to believe that organizations were in readiness in several counties. Mordaunt's trust met on 9 July and agreed that the rising should take place on 1 August, though the date was later put back. The Knot was not represented at the meeting and Willys, as usual, was opposed to the proposal, speaking strongly against it at a meeting on 24 July. Hauled before the Council of State five days later, he may have disclosed the details. Mordaunt's arrest had been ordered on 28 July, but he hid in London after his rising in Surrey had failed and reached Calais safely on 7 September. Only in Cheshire under Sir George Booth did the rising make any headway. Lambert led a force to put down the rebellion and easily defeated Booth's motley band on 16 August. Parliament treated with leniency those captured or arrested, releasing them over the next few months without preferring charges.

It is not clear how closely Thurloe was in touch with political affairs through the autumn of 1659 and the early weeks of 1660. Although most of his former friends and colleagues were away from the capital, some who remained probably kept him up to date with developments. St John had returned to the Council of State on 21 May, soon after Thurloe's dismissal. Whitelock was appointed Lord President in August and later reluctantly joined the Committee of Safety. Marvell was still employed by the government and in July was given lodgings in Whitehall. Morland too was back as a clerk to the Council under Scobell, and in August was charged with the care of all papers relating to foreign affairs. John Clarke, Thurloe's relative by marriage, though absent for a few weeks relieving Lockhart at Dunkirk, was a member of the Committee of Safety appointed at the end of October.[66] Thus Thurloe could continue to glean information from these and other influential contacts in parliament and government. The vast quantity of Dutch intelligence in Thurloe's papers, probably dating from 1659–60, suggests that some of his sources were still reporting to him.

When Lambert turned out the Rump Parliament on 13 October Thurloe must have felt that events were repeating themselves. He of all people knew that it was impossible to govern the country without more money and that only parliament could provide it. After Richard's fall the Rump had agreed to pay the former Protector's debts of almost £30,000 and had raised cash by selling furniture and pictures from the royal collections, though the deer from the parks seem to have been reserved for the Councillors and their friends, Robina Lockhart getting a fat buck from Hampton Court, St John and his son two each from Rockingham forest. Somerset House was sold, though the chapel was saved, and a plan to sell Hampton Court Palace came to nothing. A timely loan from the East India Company brought in some cash to pay the army at home and the troops at Dunkirk.[67] Even so the government's debts stood at almost £2 millions by the end of the year.

Lambert's dismissal of the Rump Parliament was accomplished by military force, but had been relatively peaceful. Morland later alleged that he had stirred such jealousies between Scot and Lambert that Scot was about to obtain an order to send the general to the Tower.[68] Parliament had stationed two regiments of foot and four troops of horse in Palace Yard, but Lambert and his men stopped the Speaker's coach on its way to the House and escorted it back to his home. The House was then closed. The Committee of Safety appointed by the army in the wake of the Rump's ejection quickly cancelled the recent Acts of Parliament which hindered the raising of revenue to pay the army, and sent officers to Scotland and Ireland to obtain approval for its actions. Ludlow, who had taken Henry Cromwell's place, was already on his way from Ireland and was met with the news at Chester. In Edinburgh Monck strongly censured the dissolution of parliament, causing the Committee to despatch Lambert to command the northern army, whilst sending further representatives to Edinburgh in the hope of persuading Monck to give his support.

Thurloe remained a mere spectator of these events and, deprived of all his offices, lacked both power and an earned income, though his holdings of land still made him comparatively wealthy. It is small wonder that his first concern, while settling in at Lincoln's Inn in November, was to attempt to obtain some of the money owed him by the government. His detailed accounts for the period 26 January to 30 June 1659 contain several matters of interest. The Council were quick to note that there was no receipt for £300 which Thurloe said he was engaged to pay, nor was there a receipt for £60 paid to Mr Barret – that is, Willys – by Mr Secretary's own hand on 15 June, over a month after he had been dismissed. The amount expended, almost £2,000 over five months, was much larger than the sums laid out in earlier years. Over £1,139 was still owing, in addition to £525 for his salary. His contract for farming the Post Office had been nullified by Act of Parliament on 11 October, but he claimed an abatement of rent because of the disruption caused by Booth's rising in August and further sums for postage by members of parliament – claims strictly in accordance with his letters patent.[69]

While Thurloe was thus occupied Lambert was posting north to Newcastle, and Monck, having secured Scottish revenues to pay his troops, was marching for the border. In London the apprentices rioted on 5 December, demonstrating for a free parliament, and there was some bloodshed. The Anabaptist Vice-Admiral Lawson brought the fleet into the river and declared for parliament, rejecting the Committee's overtures. Encouraged, Mr Speaker Lenthall recalled parliament to meet on 26 December, when members promptly secured the revenues and ordered the troops to their quarters. As Monck crossed the Tweed on 2 January 1660 he met no resistance, for Lambert's army had melted away, its dispersal hastened by Fairfax, who emerged from ten years in retirement to take control of York at the end of December. At York Monck was asked either to arrange for the restoration to parliament of the members excluded in 1648 or for a new parliament to be elected. Many petitions to the same purpose were received as he marched south, a huge batch reaching him at St Albans on 30 January 1660.[70] After he had arranged for the regiments quartered at Westminster to be moved away, Monck entered London with his troops on 4 February.

Samuel Pepys, working as a clerk to George Downing (himself back at Westminster as one of four tellers of receipt at the Exchequer), opened his diary on 1 January by noting that twenty-two of the old excluded members had been at the door of the parliament House for the last week, but had been denied entrance. On 19 January, when he heard that all the clerks of the Council of State had been turned out, Downing, about to leave for the Low Countries to resume his appointment as resident with the United Provinces, suggested that Pepys might apply as a replacement. But the diarist was content to bide his time until his kinsmen Montagu reappeared on the national scene.

On 2 February, while Pepys was noting that the Strand was full of mutinous soldiers clamouring for a free parliament and their wages before marching out to make way for Monck's army, Thurloe's paper about Post Office revenue was being read to the committee for inspecting treasuries. Claiming about £3,000 'for disbursements in the business of intelligence and other public services to the Commonwealth', he described how, when his Post Office monopoly was removed and others took over the business, he carried on to the end of the quarter for which he had already paid rent. He had no desire to apply the profits to his own use, but had retained them to set off against a debt due to him from the state. He had therefore given the Exchequer a receipt for the whole sum he had claimed in the previous November. He reminded the Council that he had voluntarily increased the rent by £4,000 a year. The committee resolved that the warrant for such a payment was null and void, and ordered that the paper be referred to the Council for a report to parliament forthwith. Political life is always uncertain and Thurloe's fortunes seemed at a nadir when the Council reallocated his former coach house and stables in Whitehall.[71]

Monck was well received by the Commons, but was persuaded by the Council to humiliate the City of London by breaking down its gates and apprehending a number of its common council. This task completed,

Monck found that parliament had accepted a petition that any person proposing or mentioning restoration should be guilty of high treason. The news sent him straight back to the City to reopen communications with the Lord Mayor. From there he wrote to parliament demanding that it dissolve and call a new election. It was a Saturday night, 11 February. The City streets had been crowded all day, and after dark the mob was still calling for a free parliament. About seven or eight o'clock Monck appeared among them on horseback. 'Pray be quiet', he called. 'Ye shall have a free parliament.' Immediately there was a loud cheer, and soon the bells were ringing and bonfires in the streets were signifying the end of the Rump Parliament by roasting rumps of mutton and beef, while healths were drunk to the king. Evelyn, the other great diarist of the period, called the occasion the 'first good omen'. The reactions of Thurloe, as he sat in his chamber at Lincoln's Inn, are not recorded.

Monck was now in absolute control of events, but outwardly at least he was not yet convinced that restoration of the monarchy was inevitable. He addressed a further letter to parliament calling on it to provide maintenance for the army and fleet, to appoint a Council of State which would call a new parliament of the three nations to meet in April and establish a Commonwealth with no king, single person or House of Lords, and to arrange for its own legal dissolution. The excluded members took their seats and a new Council of State began to sit daily. Scot, who had been made Secretary of State on 17 January, was dismissed on 23 February, and Thurloe was recalled four days later as one of two new Secretaries. His reappointment was not without opposition in the House, but the majority in favour was decisive: 65 votes to 38 in a formal division. His colleague was Colonel John Thompson, one of Monck's personal staff. The change of attitude to Thurloe was extraordinary. In the previous July he had been omitted from the list of commissioners for Cambridgeshire in the Militia Act, and in January had not been appointed a commissioner for raising the assessed revenue from the county. But he did not regain control of the Post Office, which was vested in Isaac Dorislaus on 1 March 'without prejudice to any persons who may have claims on the same'.[72]

The moving force behind Thurloe's recall was Monck himself. Sufficient correspondence between the two has survived to demonstrate their mutual trust and understanding. Disputing early in 1658 a royalist allegation that Monck had refused to obey Cromwell's orders, Thurloe had written that there was no man more loyal and dutiful in the three nations. Monck must have quickly realized that Scot was quite unsuited to the temper of the times and equally have desired the solid backing of Thurloe in the post that he had made his own throughout the Protectorate. St John's advocacy for his old friend and one-time steward may also have been influential in both Council and parliament. Jessop, who had been dismissed with Thurloe in the previous May, was already back as clerk of the Council, 'the kind of man', a modern historian as written, 'by whose patient work in the background empires are built, great fortunes sustained, fleets and armies kept at sea or in the field'.[73]

As might have been expected, Thurloe's recall to the centre of power was viewed with suspicion by many, though welcomed by his friends. The historian Bischoffshausen prefaces his study of Thurloe's work by quoting several contrasting reactions to the reappointment. Thus Hyde was 'extreme sorry to hear that Thurloe is again like to get into employment, who knows so well the way of doing mischief, and who is . . . without any remorse for what he has already done', an opinion which soon reached Thurloe, reported by one of his agents at Brussels who examined a letter written to a gentleman of quality in the west of England. On the other hand Downing, welcoming the news of his re-employment, wrote: 'Yourself and none in England as yourself doth know the schemes of our affairs abroad.' Broghill, writing from Dublin and denying reports that he and his friends were working to secure Ireland for the king, was as enthusiastic: 'I am heartily glad we are now restored to a government, which invites you to that employment you so long and meritoriously discharged.' Longland wrote from Leghorn: 'I have that assurance of your honour's wisdom and integrity that the whole nation will receive much benefit from it.'[74]

Another contemporary letter presents a more positive royalist attitude than Hyde's:

You may perhaps see many things that may shock you, as particularly Thurloe's being made Secretary of the Council of State, but I am told from many good hands that it is to our master's advantage, and already some false brethren discovered and a list of those villains is in his hands.

This writer seems to have heard of Morland's revelations and attributed them to Thurloe. It is certainly untrue that Thurloe had sent the court a list of traitors to the king's cause. Broderick, though he had earlier accused Thurloe of malice towards the royalist party, was not surprised at his return. He welcomed Scot's dismissal and thought Darell had proved himself inadequate as clerk through inexperience and that Jessop was necessary for the sake of continuity. Another royalist informant reported to Nicholas that the greater part of the Council of State was moderate, 'St John the very worst, Thurloe as bad and Thompson not much better, both secretaries of state but not of the council'.[75]

Though recalled to duty, Thurloe lacked the amenities he had earlier enjoyed. Gone were his chamber and adjoining closet in Whitehall, his comfortable family home at Kensington for use at weekends. For a few days he had to travel from Lincoln's Inn, but on 2 March the Council ordered that he be provided forthwith with lodgings at Whitehall.[76]

The course of future events are still far from certain, but shortly after resuming office Thurloe took the precaution of opening a line of communication with Hyde. By 20 March he had received what seemed a reliable report that Monck had vowed to bring in the king, and by 13 April Hyde was telling Sir John Grenville that he had received very frank overtures from Thurloe, with many great professions of resolving to serve the king. Thurloe had been too wise to make his submission in writing. The king tended to be suspicious of Thurloe's approach, which was accompanied by inquisitive questions and unwelcome offers to advise His Majesty on what was needful.

This seems to be the principal motivation for Thurloe's apparent defection to the winning side. He had already suffered the mortification of nine months' exclusion from his oversight of foreign affairs and his control of intelligence. Just before his recall in February Longland had comforted him with the thought that 'sometimes 'tis better to be a spectator than an actor', but it was in his nature to want to be at the centre of affairs and to meet head-on the manifold challenges of the times. He could not bear the thought of another abrupt break, and showed no sign of releasing his grip on events.

Moreover, he was hedging his bets by telling Downing that he would pay up to £200 for a source of constant intelligence on the Stuart court and arrivals and departures there. Further afield, Longland asked whether he would pay £500 a year (with occasional sweeteners of £100) for weekly letters from 'the place you desire' and Lockhart had recruited a new source at Bayonne to report on the French court, which was still in south-west France while preparations for the king's marriage to the infanta went forward. Lawson wrote from the Downs enquiring whether Thurloe wanted to continue receiving reports on French naval movements in the Channel from a source acquired on Scot's instructions.[77]

The changed atmosphere in London had caused Montagu to return to the capital. He had been reinstated as general-at-sea jointly with Monck on 23 February, and Pepys recorded that Thurloe called on him on 2 March. On the same day Pepys was writing of great talk of a single person, three names being mentioned as possibilities – Charles, George (Monck), or Richard again. Although he later denied it, St John was said to 'speak high for the last names'. Morland, better placed then Pepys, reported to Hyde on 3 March that Montagu, St John and Thurloe 'want to let in Dick Cromwell again'. Parliament confirmed Thurloe's appointment as joint Secretary of State, and on the same day decided that the national religion was to be the Confession of Faith put forward in 1646 but never enacted.

After securing the revenues and borrowing some ready cash, parliament obligingly issued writs for a new House to assemble on 25 April and dissolved itself on 16 March, as Monck had requested and as St John had proposed in a motion carried five days earlier. Thurloe was recommended by Monck as a candidate for Bridgnorth in Shropshire, but the general's letter was returned on 11 April with the news that Bridgnorth would elect two 'very high royalists'.[78]

A small though significant event had occurred in the City on 15 March, when a painter calmly effaced a republican inscription outside the Old or Royal Exchange, providing another excuse for bonfires in the streets. Bordeaux witnessed this incident, but Pepys had noted over a week earlier that 'everybody now drinks the King's health without fear'. According to Morland, writing on 9 March, Willys had told Thurloe that the king's arms were open to embrace him. 'I resolve to go the nation's pace, no faster', he had replied. A fortnight later Morland was still reporting efforts by St John and Thurloe to set up Monck or to restore Richard, though St John withdrew from the Council on 30 March, condemning Monck as a rigid cavalier.

Others were hastening to make their peace with the king. Ann Thurloe's cousin Nicholas Lechmere hit upon the ingenious idea of drawing up a pardon for himself and paying £200 for it – a good example, Mordaunt told Charles on 24 March, to induce others to return betimes to their duty. But Thurloe's reputation for accurate intelligence was deterring others. Asked why he did not go to obtain pardon from Charles, the Speaker replied that any approach to him was known in London within ten days. Unaware of the Speaker's reservations, Whitelock, in great extremity on account of the stone, wrote asking him to include his name and that of his son James in any list praying for His Majesty's gracious pardon.[79]

Lambert, in the Tower since 5 March, caused some alarm when he escaped on 11 April, though he was soon recaptured in Northamptonshire. Mordaunt's trust had at last put together a complete organization, county by county, to support the royalist cause. A couple of days after the dissolution Monck received at St James's Sir John Grenville, who had brought a letter from Charles. Terms for a restoration were discussed and Monck at last declared himself ready to serve the king. Shortly afterwards Mordaunt and Grenville went to Brussels with proposals for Charles to move to Breda, near Flushing at the mouth of the Scheldt, whence he was to send Monck a declaration which he could present to parliament.

When Thurloe went to see Bordeaux on 31 March to thank him for the politeness shown him since his return to office, he was assured of French amity and readiness to mediate if it would contribute to the welfare of the nation. The French made advances through Thurloe and Monck in an attempt to persuade Charles to enter France and to be restored from there to his kingdoms, but the notion was coldly received in Council. Charles did consider making use of the port of Dunkirk, but Lockhart, who was back there as governor, would not hear of it. Needless to say, Lockhart was quickly dismissed from all employment after the Restoration.[80]

Soon after arriving at Breda Charles despatched letters to Monck, to the Lords and Commons, and to the Lord Mayor of London. They were received in London before the new parliament assembled and while Lambert was still at large. When the House met on 25 April, with Jessop as its clerk, the members elected Sir Harbottle Grimstone as Speaker. His was a name well known to Thurloe, for Grimstone and Sir Thomas Barrington had been elected as members for the county of Essex in 1640, and his father of the same name had been member for Colchester in the parliament of 1626. Old peers entitled by rank to sit in the House of Lords, summoned by the Earl of Manchester as their Speaker, also assembled for the first time since their House had been abolished. Whitelock recorded that the City forces made a gallant show in Hyde Park, where there was much good cheer. There were about twenty thousand of them, and some were close enough to the Oxford road at Tyburn to see Lambert being brought back by coach as a prisoner.[81]

On 1 May, as seamen helped to erect a huge maypole in the Strand at the foot of Drury Lane, Monck went to the House and announced that Grenville had brought a letter from the king. Sir John was called in and handed the letter to the sergeant for the Speaker. The king's letter and declaration were read and well received. A return to a constitution of king, Lords and Commons was accepted without dissent, and a committee was appointed to draft a reply to His Majesty's gracious proposals, after which all the documents were to be printed and published. Grenville was called to the bar of the House and handed the reply, with £500 to buy a jewel. He can scarcely have believed his ears after eleven years in the political wilderness. As recently as August 1659 he had undergone two trying examinations by the Council. On 8 May the Lords and Commons stood bareheaded in Palace Yard while the heralds proclaimed the king, a ceremony repeated at Whitehall, at Temple Bar and in the City. 'Shouts and acclamations filled the town', Mordaunt told Charles, adding that the Lords had inserted in his title the words 'Defender of the Faith', at first omitted by the Commons.[82]

Montagu was then ordered to take the fleet to Flushing and bring back the king. Pressure had been brought to bear on Vice-Admiral Lawson, and there was no trouble on board the ships. Montagu, with Pepys in attendance and giving passage to six representatives of the Lords, twelve of the Commons and fourteen from the City of London, boarded the *Naseby* in the Downs and sailed immediately.

Thurloe was still viewed adversely by the royalist representative. On 13 May Mordaunt reported to Hyde that St John, Pierrepont and Thurloe were still plotting opposition to Monck. 'Without a doubt,' he wrote, 'there are not in nature three such beasts, from whose villainy and treachery I beseech Almighty God defend His Majesty, your Lordship and those that depend on both, for their malice extends to all under that notion.' But St John and Thurloe were not at liberty to witness the Restoration. On 14 May a Bill of Attainder was introduced against St John and six more of the old guard. Parliament also resolved that Mr Secretary Thurloe, 'being accused of high treason, be secured' and that the sergeant-at-arms should forthwith put the order into execution. A parliamentary committee was appointed to examine him, to meet the next afternoon at the inner court of wards.[83]

Extracts from private letters written on 15 May convey a little of the excitement caused by the arrest. 'Today Thurloe is impeached of high treason for something he did lately,' wrote one correspondent, 'and they sent to apprehend him, but I cannot tell whether they met with him or not.' 'They have secured Thurloe,' wrote another; 'some think rather to squeeze some discovery out of him, than for anything capital.' This writer added that Oliver Cromwell's widow and his daughter Frances Rich had disappeared from their lodgings at the Charterhouse. A third letter of the same date, after reporting Thurloe's impeachment and apprehension, went on to say that he had 'yesterday said that if he were hanged he had a black book which should hang half of them that went for cavaliers'.[84]

Reporting on 18 May, the Venetian resident gave vent to a vituperative condemnation of Thurloe. 'He has no equal in rascality and crime', he wrote.

Oliver raised him from nothing to be Secretary of State solely because of his knavish disposition and his thorough opposition to the king. During the time of the two Protectors, when with absolute authority he exercised that honourable office, he never gave satisfaction either to the people or to foreigners, and his only profession was to deceive and betray the innocent. . . . If he falls into their hands the great wealth indirectly acquired during his secretaryship will not avail to save his life. His offences have been too glaring and call for the vengeance of

Heaven, especially for the death of so many innocents in the time of Cromwell.[85]

Guavarina had long been dissatisfied with Thurloe's apparent dilatoriness in forwarding negotiation with Venice, but in truth it had proved impossible to interest councillors in policies that might jeopardize the Smyrna trade. This outburst merely confirms the underlying royalist sympathies of the writer, who had long before complained that everything was upside down at this court.[86] To classify convicted plotters and practitioners of insurrection and political assassination as innocents was stretching verbal expression too far.

Thus it was that Thurloe, deprived three days before his arrest of an official appointment connected with the tax assessment for the Isle of Ely but also paid £250 for intelligence expenses during his tenure of office,[87] was forced to remain in the Tower while the final acts of the Restoration were carried through at Flushing, Dover, Canterbury and London. The Duke of York, who had held the post of Lord High Admiral since he was four years old took over the fleet on its arrival in the Scheldt, and the *Naseby* became the *Royal Charles*.

The king, met by Monck when he landed at Dover on Saturday 26 May, travelled by coach to Canterbury, where he attended a service at the cathedral the next day. Afterwards he sat alone with Monck, who handed him a list of some forty persons recommended as best able to serve him on his Privy Council. Only two had worked for the royalist cause, the rest being described as ex-rebels or Presbyterians, or both. The list does not appear to have survived, but it would be surprising if Monck had omitted Thurloe's name from it. Charles wisely left it to Hyde to deal with this unexpected intervention.[88]

On Monday the king reached Rochester and on Tuesday, his birthday, entered London. From his place of confinement Thurloe must have heard the noise of the celebrations. There is no record of his thoughts as all that he had worked for during eight long years at the centre of government came crashing down amid the tumult of cheering and healths, trumpets and bell-ringing. From what is known of his Puritan character it is probable that he accepted everything as the will of God, even when circumstances turned against him and the 'good old cause' as he knew it.

Only a few days elapsed before the gossips had more to write about Thurloe. One reported on 5 June that he had been with the king and was said to have turned over a leaf in a black book, making some tremble – two of the Duke of Buckingham's servants, 'and it may be higher'. Andrew Newport, a member of the royal household, wrote a week later: 'Thurloe has been with the king privately, and with the chancellor since.

'Tis said that he will be (as he used to call it himself) Ingenious.' It is difficult to guess the exact meaning of this last intriguing remark. Possibly the writer meant to convey the impression that Thurloe would be able to talk his way out of the corner in which he found himself. Alternatively the word intended may have been ingenuous – one that he was fond of employing, and one appropriate to his character. What is certain is that his meetings with Hyde must have given rise to those reports on foreign affairs during the Protectorate already discussed.

The idea that Thurloe's 'black book' would have caused more than minor embarrassment has been discounted by historians. Hyde, who apparently retained no memory of Thurloe as secretary to the opposing commissioners at Uxbridge fifteen years earlier, had never concealed his dislike of the man who had become Secretary of State. He had greeted his return to office with dismay and supported the widely held view that Thurloe welcomed conspiracies, for they enabled him to 'lay about him and commit all whom he suspects'. Many politicians become victims to their own propaganda and Hyde may well have been pleasantly surprised by mild-mannered reality when the two men came face to face.[89]

Thurloe had to wait until 27 June before he was given his liberty, but he then seems to have been released without conditions. Indeed, the Commons passed a resolution on the 29th that he might have free liberty to attend the Secretaries of State at such times as they should appoint and for so long as they should own his attendance to be for the service of the state without trouble or molestation, notwithstanding any former order of the House. Charles had appointed two Secretaries of State, Sir Edward Nicholas and William Morrice, who had played a significant part in the Restoration. Morrice and Sir John Grenville had in 1659 been elected members for Newport in Cornwall. Monck, allied to Morrice by marriage, invited him to London, where he thereafter reported to Monck on the temper of parliament. It was in Morrice's room at St James's that Grenville first saw Monck, with Morrice guarding the door. He accepted his appointment as Secretary of State as early as 5 May, but it could not be made public until after the Restoration. Morrice was active behind the scenes throughout the month.[90]

It is often said that nobody is indispensable. Had Thurloe been ill again, or dead, the king's government would have managed without him. But he was available, and his knowledge and experience, freely put at the disposal of the new administration, must have been invaluable. Nevertheless he was not one of them; his function now was to disengage himself and to seek a new life away from the hurly-burly of politics, the complexities of foreign affairs and the intrigues of intelligencers.

7
FOREIGN AFFAIRS, 1657–1668

The Protector in all these cases governs himself by the Protestant cause (John Thurloe)

England's interests abroad at the beginning of 1657 centred on the prosecution of the war against Spain in two separate areas. Blake's fleet, which had remained on station throughout the winter after Montagu had brought the bigger ships and prizes home in the autumn, now stood ready to repeat the successes of the previous year. Nearer home the hope was to formalize the understanding with Mazarin, to provide as agreed the six thousand troops to fight under Turenne, and thus to gain Dunkirk or another Channel port. Across the Atlantic, Jamaica seemed secure. A decision had been taken in April 1656, Thurloe told Montagu, to send twelve hundred reinforcements to the Caribbean, with provisions for six thousand more for four months.

When Blake reported his plans to intercept the Spanish fleet from Mexico, Cromwell sent as reinforcements two large ships and four frigates. There was a degree of urgency because it was thought de Ruyter might use the Dutch Mediterranean fleet to carry or escort the Spanish silver from the Canaries to the Netherlands. Arriving at the Canaries on 20 April, Blake found the Spaniards in harbour at Santa Cruz, Tenerife. He attacked immediately and sank or otherwise destroyed five or six galleons and ten other vessels without loss.

The news was brought home by Captain Story, who had taken part in the action. On 28 May, immediately after the bill for settling the post had been read, Thurloe reported the success to the Commons. Although the English fleet had obtained no benefit in plunder, he told them, the enemy had never suffered a greater loss. Characteristically he added: 'It is the Lord's doing, and the glory is his'. Members at once moved for a day of thanksgiving and settled on Wednesday 3 June at St Margaret's, and appointed ministers to preach.

Members also agreed that the narrative of the action should be printed, that Story, Blake and all his captains should be rewarded, and that Thurloe and Downing should prepare a letter of thanks to Blake, to be signed by the Speaker. Blake was to have a jewel worth £500 and

Story one of £100, the Council to pay. The Protector, too, sent his personal congratulations with the jewel on 10 June, together with instructions to leave fourteen ships before Cadiz, send five to the Mediterranean and bring the rest home.[1] But Blake was not to see his native country again. He died on board the *George* a few hours short of Plymouth on 7 August, and ten days later Thurloe and most other members of the Council attended his funeral in Westminster Abbey.

The treaty with Mazarin had been signed on 13 March 1657. Cromwell had a larger vision of a confederation comprising France and all the northern Protestant states – England, Sweden, Denmark and the United Provinces – to fight Spain and the emperor. He is said to have told Stoupe, his Swiss confidant, at a time when he was apparently disposed to accept the offer of the crown, of a grand design to be announced at the opening of his reign. He supposedly envisaged a council of seven for the maintenance of the Protestant religion to sit at Chelsea, with four secretaries for four territorial divisions. Mazarin, more practical, held out for a bilateral treaty when Thurloe raised the question of a wider grouping. The agreement was to last a year. A week before signing the treaty, Lockhart entered Paris in the French king's coach, attended by the representatives of the queen and the cardinal, the ambassadors of Portugal, the United Provinces, Venice, Savoy and Genoa, Marshal de Turenne and 'others of high quality'.[2]

Occasionally the other demands upon the Secretary's time seem to have distracted him and the complexities of domestic policy to have led to a temporary neglect of foreign. Thus in spring 1657 Thurloe found it difficult to maintain his tight grip on foreign affairs because he was absorbed by the long debates about Cromwell's title and the written constitution. The Venetian resident complained on 10 April that he must wait days and sometimes weeks to speak to the Secretary of State, who was overwhelmed, he wrote, with parliament, Council and other meetings, 'so that he never has a moment to breathe'.[3]

It was in April, too, that Sir John Reynolds, Commissary-General of the Horse in Ireland, was selected to command the troops being sent to Flanders. Some nine years younger than Thurloe, he had fought for parliament in the civil war and in Ireland, where he had been rewarded with land. Knighted by Cromwell in 1655, he was now an Irish member at Westminster. On 5 May, in the midst of deliberations over the kingly title for Cromwell, the Commons gave him leave of absence to assume his command. He crossed from Dover to Boulogne on 17 May, and in June his troops, marching over countryside that was to become depressingly familiar to another generation of Englishmen, joined Turenne's army at St Quentin.

To the consternation of the English government that army, instead of

heading north for the coast of Flanders, was directed east towards the
Ardennes to besiege Montmédy. By July Thurloe was addressing frantic
letters to Reynolds asking for a report on the condition of his forces. The
country was threatened by the Spanish troops and royalist regiments in
Flanders, where it was given out that they would be across the Channel
before the end of the year and were already receiving deserters from
Reynolds's ranks. 'I hope 'tis false', wrote Thurloe. To make matters
worse, a large quantity of provisions and stores had been shipped and
held in the Downs awaiting orders, with the costs to the French under
the treaty rising daily, a situation that had 'some calamity in it', Thurloe
wrote on 16 July. The ships eventually sailed to Calais and the French
sent commissioners to pay the bills. There was, of course, disagreement
over the prices and costs of demurrage.[4]

Thurloe's papers are generally confined strictly to business and there
is seldom a glimpse of the private lives of the Secretary or his friends, but
his correspondence with Lockhart in Paris sometimes struck a more
personal note. Thus in February Lockhart thanked him for seeing his
wife and undertook to obtain for Mrs Thurloe 'any of the knacks' she
might desire from the Saint-Germain fair. Later in the year Thurloe
acknowledged his debt to Lockhart for looking after Peyton, a nephew of
his first wife, and asked him to give the young man a pass and protection
to go to study at Saumur, one of the two Protestant universities permitted in France. Lockhart undertook to write to a professor at the university asking for reports on Peyton's behaviour and progress in his studies.
In return he felt able to ask for favours for his own brothers. A couple of
months earlier he had put forward the names of two brothers of Swift,
his secretary, and of the husband of his wife's nurse for places as lieuten-
ants in the levies being raised for Jamaica.

In another letter Thurloe remarked that if Lord Falconbridge was in
Paris he should be encouraged to come over and 'prosecute his former
intentions', hinting that His Highness would approve, a reference to
Viscount Falconbridge's suit of Cromwell's daughter Mary. Falconbridge
had enlisted Lockhart's aid when passing through Paris in the spring,
and Lockhart had pleaded his cause with Thurloe as a means of reaching
the Protector's ear, denying charges of Romish sympathies levelled
against the viscount and enlarging upon his personal qualities. The
Secretary also sought more material favours on Cromwell's behalf. When
Thurloe asked Lockhart to acquire for the Protector 'another quantity of
French wine', the ambassador responded by sending three lots, one each
for Cromwell, Thurloe and Desborough, of the best that could be found.
Early in September Lockhart reminded Thurloe that His Highness
should send over a man to choose wine, for now was the time to buy
Burgundy.[5]

Neither Cromwell nor Thurloe was disposed to blame Lockhart for the French action in deploying the English forces so far inland. It could not have been expected that the court of France 'should have dealt so uncertainly with a prince who they profess so great a value for'. When Thurloe wrote on 23 July, however, he stressed that His Highness hoped to hear soon of the surrender of Montmédy and to receive some account of a resolution of the French court more certain and agreeable to the treaty than anything yet undertaken. So far six thousand men, the fleet and provisions had been put to the service of France with no advantage to England. As it happened, Lockhart had seen the French king and cardinal on 18 July and had spoken of His Highness's resentment at the conduct of the campaign. The cardinal excused this as unavoidable but, surprisingly, offered England any other place until Dunkirk could be handed over. Lockhart appreciated the uselessness of anything other than a seaport, but nevertheless sought instructions.[6]

Montmédy fell at the end of the month. Reynolds reported that Turenne seemed well disposed towards English interests but Lockhart, with the court and the cardinal at Sedan, feared that French eyes were now turned towards Germany instead of the Channel port. Reynolds was ordered to march towards Guise, east of St Quentin, which was at least in the right direction. His men must have presented a far from pretty sight, 'many marching without breeches and stockings which is a shame to our nation'. Lockhart, 'animated by the just resentment expressed' in one of Thurloe's letters, remonstrated sharply with His Eminence during an audience and was heard with patience. Besides making his complaints about the conduct of the campaign, Lockhart was more than once urged to enquire about the safety and welfare of Protestants in Piedmont and in France, for rumours were reaching England of an impending massacre, of ministers banished and of churches pulled down. Instructing him to press Louis to intervene powerfully with the Duke of Savoy, Thurloe wrote that what was required was not an edict but action.[7]

On 19 September Turenne appeared before Mardyke, a fortress east of Dunkirk, and took it four days later. Reynolds's force, much reduced by disease and desertion, was saddled with the task of providing a garrison for Mardyke through the winter months, while Thurloe found himself ordering twenty thousand oak palisades for its defence. Later he saw two interesting letters from Turenne to Bordeaux remarking on English surprise at the labour required to make the place defensible through the winter and complaining about the tardy arrival of the carpenters and palisades.

The garrison repelled a night assault by royalist forces, but for a time Cromwell refused to reinforce it. Two regiments held in readiness at Dover and Yarmouth, and the French army around Calais and

Boulogne, were considered sufficient reassurance for the winter months. Even so, Thurloe complained, it would cost up to £8,000 to victual Mardyke till January. By mid-November he was telling Lockhart that men were dying at the rate of ten or twelve a day; several companies of troops had to be sent over soon afterwards. It did not help when Mazarin admitted to Lockhart that Turenne had let slip an opportunity to take Dunkirk, which was poorly defended.[8]

Lockhart had his own troubles: his wife was seriously ill with puerperal fever after a long and cruel labour in giving birth to a boy in Paris at the end of September. Although she eventually pulled through, she had not receovered when Thurloe wrote early in December forbearing to trouble Lockhart with business at such a time. Reynolds, who had been indiscreet enough to have a meeting with the Duke of York, who was serving with the opposing Spanish army, obtained leave to visit England in December, but the pink in which he sailed was wrecked on the Goodwin sands and he was drowned. After informing Lockhart of this loss, Thurloe wrote only once more before he was struck down himself with the serious illness which forced him to retire to his house at Kensington.[9]

France and Flanders had not been the only areas to occupy his attention during the summer of 1657. The death of the Emperor Ferdinand III late in March alerted the whole of Europe to the political options available in the election of a successor. Cromwell's government, like others, wished to use diplomatic pressure to influence the result. Thurloe heard from Lockhart that the cardinal was going to court the Germans in a shower of gold. According to Lockhart, the king of Hungary, not yet of age, was 'more a Spaniard than his father was'.[10]

Then in May the international balance in northern Europe was violently upset when Denmark, encouraged by the Dutch, declared war on Sweden. The Danish invasion of the Swedish duchy of Bremen 'set the war wholly on a new foot', Thurloe wrote afterwards, and 'most of the states in Europe found themselves concerned to intermeddle in it'. Cromwell was naturally horrified to see two Protestant powers at war. He promptly sent emissaries to both sides to make peace, and an envoy to Muscovy as mediator between the Grand Duke and Swedish king.[11]

When on 14 March Richard Bradshaw first heard in Hamburg of his impending mission to Muscovy, he wrote at once to Thurloe enquiring if it were true and, if so, for a couple of trusty servants to accompany him. He soon received official notification of his appointment and by mid-April was ready to depart, even though funds had not reached him and a local quarrel with English merchants in Hamburg had not been resolved. This disagreement, in which Bradshaw felt himself aggrieved by royalist sympathizers, was to run on like a festering sore in his correspondence for the rest of Thurloe's Secretaryship. Bradshaw was also concerned about procuring an interpreter, a present for the Grand Duke and his money. On 2 May he acknowledged receipt of his instructions, according to which he was to press the Grand Duke to make peace, whilst representing to him the advantages of opening the Baltic ports to trade and of having Swedish rather than Polish territory on his western boundary.

From Lübeck, Bradshaw reached Riga on 25 May and was well received by the Swedish provincial governor. Alarmed by the prevalence of plague there, he took refuge in the neighbouring territory of the Duke of Courland. He despatched letters to the Grand Duke and to the Swedish king, but appreciated the weakness of his position in being merely an 'orator' not an ambassador for his Highness, an error of protocol difficult to explain (unless it was a parsimonious effort to save additional salary and allowances). The Grand Duke's chancellor responded to his letter with an offensive communication calling for amended credentials.

Bradshaw, realizing that even if he were to be admitted to Russia he would be held in quarantine for six weeks at the frontier, asked Thurloe for instructions and repeated his request for a Russian interpreter. His wife joined in by demanding a physician, chaplain and a cook for her husband while Thurloe tried to keep up the envoy's spirits by assuring him that he had the confidence of those at home. On 4 September Bradshaw's agent in London informed Mrs Bradshaw that Thurloe was taking care of the envoy's requirements; at the same time Bradshaw was instructed to continue his journey to the Grand Duke, 'if he will receive you'. After waiting ten weeks from the despatch of his amended credentials, Bradshaw wrote on 27 November that he would return if no reply were received after three months.[12]

He needed the King of Sweden's permission to make his return journey overland, but travelled to Memel to await it. A pass was obtained in early January 1658, Carl X commenting that others besides Bradshaw had been held three or four months at the Russian frontier. Only on 20 March, when he was in Stettin on his way back, did Bradshaw receive a letter inviting him to Moscow to be received by the czar. But it was written in Russian instead of the customary Latin, and Bradshaw could not get it translated till he reached Hamburg again.[13]

To the King of Sweden Cromwell sent Major-General William Jephson, MP for Stockbridge in the Long Parliament, to travel through Hamburg to the king's headquarters in the field, as Rolt had done before him. His instructions, dated 22 August 1657, authorized him to offer English horse and foot to take over the Duchy of Bremen and defend it, provided Sweden would pay all the charges. He was not, however, to make the offer unless the matter was first raised by the Swedish king. Cromwell had for some time eyed the Duchy of Bremen, strategically placed between Sweden and the United Provinces, first asking for it at the end of 1656 as security for a loan of £100,000. But he was not tempted by extravagant Swedish offers of territory in the summer of 1657, and in any event was forced by October to reduce the amount of money England could offer.[14]

Philip Meadow was taken once more from Thurloe's office to serve as envoy to Denmark. It had at first been intended that he should follow Jephson through Hamburg, but late in August it was decided instead to send him direct to the Sound, and Montagu was asked to provide a suitable ship. He embarked at Dover on 3 September and was at Elsinore by the 10th.[15]

His instructions were admirably clear. He was to wait on the King of Denmark, express the Protector's affection and good will, assure him that nothing would be done to break or infringe peace and affirm that England was ready and willing to do all in her power to foster the alliance. At a private audience he was to say that nothing had been more unwelcome than the news of war with Sweden. Two crowns in amity with England and of the same religion, if allied, could be a terror to the common enemy and of great advantage to the Protestant interest. His Majesty must be sensible of the great disturbance of freedom of trade and navigation, especially in the Baltic, the needs of the Commonwealth for commodities from those parts being well known. Meadow was authorized to offer to settle differences with the crown of Sweden and was to argue that a Protestant alliance would be much more secure than an alliance with Spain, Hungary, or any of that 'Austrian family who have and always will prove a broken reed to such princes or states as lean upon them'.[16]

Meadow faced a daunting task. The Danes were allied with Poland and Brandenburg; the latter had changed sides once more. Thurloe was concerned about the attitude of Hungary, since its young king was almost certain to be elected emperor. He feared the old imperial design to control the Baltic. He instructed Meadow on 2 October to find out 'by money or otherwise' whether Denmark was obliged not to make peace without her allies. In a further letter of 27 November setting out his thoughts and instructions, he mentioned that the Dutch were better disposed than formerly and that Downing would be sent to The Hague to mediate between Portugal and the United Provinces, themselves at war after the Dutch had taken several of the Portuguese fleet from Brazil.[17]

Taking up his post in January 1658, Downing wrote at once to Thurloe and Lockhart promising a regular exchange of correspondence. Worried about the security of letters passing through Flanders, he gave Thurloe a cover address at The Hague and asked for one in London. He did his best, with French support, to mediate between the Dutch and Portuguese, but he soon became drawn into the negotiations about the northern war. By the end of February he was able to report that the Dutch were ready to join France and England in promoting peace in the north, but by that time peace had in any case already been signed and on 12 March Thurloe wrote for information on Dutch reactions.[18]

Jephson had reached Wismar, on the Baltic coast about halfway between Lübeck and Rostock, and reported on 8 February the feat of the Swedish king in taking advantage of exceptionally hard frost to march across the ice of the Little Belt and so take the island of Fünen from the Danes. Carl X pressed on and in a few weeks had crossed the Great Belt and Zealand to reach the gates of Copenhagen. It was Meadow's opportunity. He went forward to meet the king, who jocularly told him that God had shown him the way and built him a bridge. He could hardly do less than go over, though he had scarcely expected to meet the English mediator on the way. By sheer hard work and diplomatic skill Meadow managed to achieve peace by the Treaty of Roskild at the end of February 1658. Sweden was enlarged to its 'natural' frontier on the Sound by taking the Danish provinces on its eastern borders. It was a triumph for one who, writing of some troublesome subsidiary business a couple of months later, used the words: 'yet I hope at last so to bend both ends as to make them meet together'. He had bent the inclinations of two headstrong monarchs and made them meet in peace, though it cost him a sword and a horse admired by the Swedish king and duly presented to him.[19]

Cromwell had promised Sweden £30,000, paid in three monthly instalments, but Thurloe had to write to Jephson in December (in one of his last letters before his serious illness) explaining that the treasury was as usual empty after paying off the fleet. He promised payment when it became possible, though undated secret instructions to Jephson revealed that in the wake of exhaustion from the civil war, the Dutch war and now the war with Spain, no contribution to Sweden was possible. Back at work in spring 1658, Thurloe fired off a broadside of questions to Jephson trying to discover the Swedish king's intentions now that peace had been made. His minister in London had, it seems, suggested impossible things. If Swedish intentions were known and acceptable, Cromwell would be ready to join a Protestant league. Should the Dutch be brought in? What about terms for a treaty with Poland? Perhaps Sweden could make English mediation a condition of peace? Jephson was given leave to return as soon as he had reported the king's intentions and would probably be relieved by Meadow.[20]

Thurloe soon had another job for Jephson. The imperial election was due in the summer when the Habsburg candidate, the king of Hungary, would be eighteen years old. In April Jephson was sent to Berlin in an effort to influence Brandenburg against 'that Austrian family' always distrusted by Cromwell. He had an interview with the Elector at the end of the month, but made little impression. Since the end of the Thirty Years War, politics had begun to succeed religion as the prime motivating force of European states. Calvinist Brandenburg, in alliance with Catholic Hungary and Poland, had stabbed Lutheran Sweden in the back in Pomerania; later in the year, when Leopold had been duly elected emperor, a League of the Rhine was formed consisting of both Catholic and Protestant states. Although Cromwell and Thurloe had both for a time tolerated a war against their fellow-Protestants in the United Provinces, neither had ever been happy about it and they considered it an impediment to their principal objective, Protestant unity.[21]

There was renewed talk of sending Bradshaw to Russia. In April his agent in London was desperately trying to find out whether a decision had been reached, going four times in a week to Whitehall in a vain attempt to see Thurloe, who was 'sometimes at his house at Kensington, sometimes in physic, and sometimes with His Highness'. Reporting this to Bradshaw on the 16th, he added a postscript that Cromwell had not yet made up his mind. In truth, the idea seems to have been quietly dropped.[22]

Meadow stayed at Copenhagen until a treaty had been finalized between Denmark and Holstein. He signed and sealed it as mediator, as he had done previously at Roskild. He was rewarded with the Order of the Elephant, 'a burdensome knighthood' as he described it, but he refused an annual pension from the Danish crown. Then he set out for Hamburg, a tedious march of 240 miles with his retinue and baggage, crossing the two Belts and passing through devastated country. Arriving on 20 May he found his new instructions accrediting him to the Swedish instead of the Danish king. That he was still described as an envoy, not an ambassador, continued to rankle because of the disadvantage in matters of precedence.[23]

Meadow related to Thurloe his efforts to recruit a source of intelligence at Copenhagen who would report freely to Isaac Ewer, Meadow's secretary, but to no one else. This young man, son of Thurloe's half-brother William, is mentioned in the records from March 1655 onwards as handling intelligence payments in Thurloe's office. He had recently helped Meadow materially in his negotiations. Subsequent correspondence suggests that Ewer was posted to Frankfurt and that Meadow took on Lawerin, formerly with Bradshaw and initially an informant of Scot.

It seems unlikely, therefore, that Meadow's attempts to recruit a new agent in Copenhagen had borne fruit.[24]

Thurloe, however, did not lack foreign intelligence. Besides his reports from overseas he was at this time seeing a great many letters intercepted in London from the correspondence of the Swedish, Danish, Dutch and French representatives there. Morland was proving an expert at this business, taking care not only with the speedy and accurate forgery of copies to be sent on to the addressees, but also in the use of paper and ink of the same quality and wax of the same colour for the counterfeit seals, which received impressions as sharp as the originals.

Thurloe's own foreign and diplomatic staff in London had slowly expanded. Someone called Merry had been engaged at 200 marks (£133) a year on the departure of Meadow,[25] but from about October 1657 the post of assistant Latin secretary was in the hands of the poet Andrew Marvell, whose complex Horatian ode on Cromwell's return from Ireland had, *inter alia,* prophesied his indefatigable rise to power. Marvell, described by John Aubrey as of middling stature with a roundish cherry-cheeked face, hazel eyes and brown hair, had first been recommended for the job by Milton in February 1653. On that occasion Meadow had been appointed instead, and Marvell had spent the intervening years as tutor to Cromwell's ward, living at Eton. His devotion to the Commonwealth and Protectorate had found expression in several pieces, including a Latin verse on Oliver St John's embassy to the United Provinces, a long poem in English on the first anniversary of Cromwell's government, and in rhyming couplets a celebration of Blake's victory at Tenerife.

Meadow stayed at Hamburg throughout the early summer of 1658, emphasizing how much good would be done by payment to Sweden of the promised subsidy and reporting that the French had contributed 550,000 crowns. The Electors from Germany as well as the Dutch were attempting to mediate between Sweden on the one hand and Hungary and Poland on the other, but Carl X was being uncooperative. He refused to see the Germans.[26]

In July Meadow started for Kiel to meet the Swedish king, but because of smallpox Carl X changed the rendezvous to Neumünster, thus shortening Meadow's journey. He met Jephson, back from Berlin, and was well received by the king, but had to report that 'all things tended to a general war and combustion'. Leopold William, Archduke of Hungary, was now Emperor. Brandenburg had allied with Poland, then suffering under an old, infirm and childless king and occupied by Muscovites, Cossacks and Austrians. Moreover, the Dutch were again sending a fleet to the Baltic. Then in August came the bombshell, when the Swedish king's plans, of so much interest to Thurloe a few months previously, were at last revealed. In open violation of the Treaty of Roskild, he crossed from Kiel to the coast of Zealand and again marched on Copenhagen. If Denmark were defeated, Meadow considered, Norway would follow, and then the king could abbreviate his title and simply call himself King of the North. Frederick III of Denmark described him accurately enough as 'a prince who aspires at nothing save war'. Thurloe's efforts to secure peace had apparently come to nothing.[27]

The Protector's chief fear had been that Sweden would be defeated, leaving the emperor victorious on the shores of the Baltic. Now it was obvious that the Danes could not hold out unaided and that Sweden would control both sides of the Sound, closing it at will or imposing whatever tolls she liked. Downing doggedly pressed on with negotiations at The Hague, but the Dutch had moved too fast, despatching a fleet under Opdam with six thousand troops to defend Copenhagen. In England things were almost at a standstill. The Protector was sick – in fact dying – and the succession remained uncertain. Even so, Cromwell achieved one more ambition across the Channel before he died.

The agreement with the French had nearly run its course when the year 1658 opened, but the Secretary of State was completely out of action. Lockhart wrote on 9 January to say that he was very upset to hear of Thurloe's illness. In a letter of 11 January Marvell excused the Secretary's inability to write himself but said that he was getting better. On 4 February Firbank reported him still 'not yet abroad, but I hope God will enable him to put his hand to the plough again'. Four days later Thurloe was back at work, writing to Lockhart complaining that His Highness had done more than required by the treaty, the French far less. On 10 February a royalist source in England reported that Thurloe 'has had raving fits, but is somewhat recovered'. On the same day Lockhart, very worried about the renewal of the treaty, asked Falconbridge to obtain the Protector's directions in the continued absence of the Secretary of State – because of the slow and at times unreliable postal service between London and Paris he was unaware that Thurloe was, in fact, back at work. After another twelve days, though weary with writing and 'being but crazy in my health', Thurloe found time to show himself a true Puritan and no bigot. 'It is very pleasant and truly profitable too', he wrote,

> to read what you have writ about the cardinal's discourse of death and the vanity of the world which . . . doth shame those who have nothing of his share in the power and pleasures of the world and yet find a great sweetness in it and are loath to leave it. I shall not fail to read this part of your letter also to His Highness, [he added] that those expressions of kindness may not be lost.[28]

The blockade of Ostend and Dunkirk was resumed at the end of February with thirteen sail under Goodson. They had an immediate success when in capturing three Dutch-hired transports and driving two ashore. The transports, making for Ostend, were intended to carry Spanish troops for a landing at Yarmouth. Such an invasion had no hope of success in the face of English sea power and it seems doubtful whether it would have taken place even had the transports arrived safely. Thurloe had forwarded the Protector's orders for the withdrawal of the bigger ships for the winter, but Montagu arrived off the coast of Flanders on 4 May to take command in the *Naseby,* the only eighty-gun ship in commission.[29]

The vexed question of the right to search neutral vessels soon came to the fore. Spain and the Dutch had made a treaty in 1650 providing that the goods of a belligerent should be free from molestation if carried in neutral ships. This confirmed long-standing Dutch ambitions to protect their carrying trade by establishing the free passage of enemy goods in neutral ships. England, however, had always maintained the right to search for and seize enemy goods in neutral bottoms, a practice expressly reaffirmed in treaties with Sweden and Denmark in 1654. Montagu had been told in August 1657 that there was no doubt that both in international law and under all existing treaties he could search Dutch ships for Spanish bullion and other goods. Now off the coast of Flanders he found that Spanish supplies in Dutch bottoms were being escorted by Dutch warships and were thus beyond his reach.[30]

A new treaty with the French had been signed in March, specifying that the siege of Dunkirk should start between 30 April and 20 May. Lockhart sent Swift to report to Thurloe with a copy of the treaty. The English were required to bring their force at Mardyke up to its original strength of six thousand men. Though the numbers always fell short, Thurloe was kept very busy arranging shipments of money, biscuit, wheatmeal and hay to Dunkirk.[31]

The French army received a setback at Ostend. Forwarding an account of it to Monck in Scotland, Thurloe, quite the armchair strategist, commented that the French made a strange mistake in accepting plans which had been offered to His Highness nine months earlier but then rejected as ridiculous.[32] Regrouping, Turenne advanced from Amiens and on 15 May was joined before Dunkirk by the English foot from Mardyke. When a Spanish relief force camped among the dunes along the coast north-east of the fortress, Turenne decided to attack. The action took place on the very day that Cromwell and his Council were keeping as one of fasting and prayer for God's help.

The English did well in the battle, in which they and the French were victorious, though they returned to discover that their camp before

Dunkirk had been pillaged by a sortie in their absence. However, block-aded by Montagu's fleet, Dunkirk did not long resist Turenne. The garrison capitulated on 24 June and marched out next day. Louis XIV entered and handed the town's keys to Lockhart, who now became military governor of England's new foothold on the Continent of Europe. Precisely a century had passed since the loss of Calais. 'Your servant is now master of Dunkirk', Lockhart reported, but he did not disguise the difficulties of garrisoning the fortress without money or provisions. He had been forced to borrow 2,000 livres from the cardinal, a loan that was apparently still outstanding almost a year later when Bordeaux tactfully mentioned it to Thurloe.[33]

News of the victory of the Dunes reached London on 16 June, and of the surrender of Dunkirk ten days later. A day of public thanksgiving was to be held on 21 July. In his memoirs, James Welwood alleges that Mazarin had attempted to double-cross Cromwell over the cession of Dunkirk. Cromwell, he claims, sent for the French ambassador and upbraided him for his breach of faith. Brandishing a copy of the cardinal's order, he is supposed to have threatened to come over himself and demand the keys if Lockhart were refused them. Apart from Mazarin, only Turenne, the queen mother (Anne of Austria) and a secretary were privy to the order. Suspicion fell on the queen mother as Cromwell's source, but according to Welwood it was the secretary – perhaps the Italian recruited by Lockhart – who kept up a secret correspondence for several years.[34]

Welwood offers another somewhat unlikely tale revealing Cromwell's love of intrigue and clandestine operations. Thurloe used to tell, Welwood claimed, how he was once commanded by Cromwell to go at a certain hour to Gray's Inn and there deliver a bill of £20,000, payable to the bearer at Genoa, to a man he would find walking in a particular place, habit and posture. Thurloe complied without exchanging a word with the stranger, and never knew to his dying day the reason for this transaction or the recipient. If the allegation has any substance, it seems improbable that so large a sum was intended for mere intelligence purposes. It could only have been military aid for some Protestant community, perhaps in Switzerland. Certainly the royalists heard of or related several stories of Cromwell sending large sums abroad, one of them specifically mentioning £20,000 to raise Swiss troops to help the Huguenots.[35] Neither of Welwood's stories is otherwise confirmed by contemporary sources though both may contain an element of truth, albeit greatly exaggerated.

The possession of Dunkirk and Mardyke pleased Thurloe mightily. There is a much-quoted passage in his review of foreign affairs written in 1660: 'By having these places of strength in his hand [Cromwell] carried at his girdle the keys of a door into the continent.' The advantages that Thurloe could see were, first, that France would in future be obliged to honour its treaties and to agree every action with England because its own back door was open; secondly, that the English presence would encourage the Protestants in Flanders to throw off the Spanish yoke, whilst England stood ready to assist any Protestant interest on the Continent; and finally, that Dutch shipping would be under threat from both sides of the strait, whilst English shipping would no longer be subject to interference from privateers at Dunkirk and Ostend. Henry Cromwell took a more realistic view. 'I make a question (if you stay here)', he wrote to Thurloe on 30 June, 'whether that security will not prove a dear purchase.'[36]

Lockhart certainly had a big job on his hands, particularly as William Swift, his secretary and trusted assistant, had died almost at the same time as Dunkirk fell; Lockhart took care to see that his widow was provided for. The fortifications stood in urgent need of repair, there was a civilian population of 5,100 to oversee, while military occupation was bound to lead to tension. The French, too, were still demanding the use of Lockhart's troops in the field, when he was desperately short of stores, victuals and money. All these preoccupations were reflected in his correspondence with Thurloe, who was also disposing ships of the fleet to support the siege of Gravelines while Montague remained in the Downs.[37]

English shipping was also active in one more theatre. Although the lucrative trade with Spain had been interrupted by the war, the Mediterranean was attracting many seaborne traders, mainly to Leghorn and Smyrna. Thurloe was well served by his correspondents John Aldworth at Marseilles and Charles Longland at Leghorn, who had recruited sources of his own in Rome and another who had been sent first to Toulon and then to Spain. Representations from Longland in the previous November about the depredations of pirates from Majorca and Tripoli against English trade had led to the despatch of a small force of warships to those waters. Though Thurloe kept up a desultory correspondence with Captain Stokes, who commanded it, he was better supplied with commercial and naval intelligence by the two shore-based officials, and by despatches from Constantinople.

In February 1658 Stokes redeemed seventy-two captives at Tunis. At Thurloe's bidding the Council in May authorized the payment by the customs of almost £2,900 to Stokes for this service, which cost him 10,000 dollars in payment to the dey. (At this date the customs retained one half of one per cent of its total revenue specifically for the redemption of captives). In July the Council decided to maintain the Mediterranean fleet for a further six months from 1 October. Thurloe was one of a committee of seven directed to speak to merchants trading in the Mediterranean, to arrange for victuals to be sent and to see that the Admiralty commissioners be requested to maintain the force at its present strength.[38]

On 20 July Thurloe was at Hampton Court, where Cromwell's favourite daughter Bettie Claypole was seriously ill and the Protector himself ailing. Three days later Nieuport, returning as an ordinary instead of extraordinary ambassador after a visit to Holland, reached Gravesend and sent his son on ahead to Westminster with a letter for the Secretary of State. Failing to find him, the young man went on towards Kensington; Thurloe met him on the road and took him into his coach. On arrival at Whitehall he quickly made arrangements for the Protector's barge to be prepared and for Marvell to go in it to welcome Nieuport. The ambassador, aware of the unfortunate timing of his return, tactfully went up river by night without ceremony. Accompanied by the Protector's master of ceremonies in a coach-and-six, Nieuport later drove to Hampton Court and was met by Thurloe at the inner gate of the first court. At an audience attended by Lawrence as Lord President, Strickland as the Council's expert on Dutch affairs and Thurloe as Secretary of State, Nieuport spoke briefly of his country's quarrel with Portugal, of Holland's desire for a maritime treaty with England and of her anxiety about the Baltic situation. He was then conducted back to his coach.[39]

Thurloe had lost his watchful eye in central Europe when in May 1658 the Protector recalled Pell from Zürich. After travelling down the Rhine, Pell reached England on 13 August. Although he was never able to see the Protector again, he waited on Thurloe four days later. It was on this day that Cromwell was reported somewhat better and managed to go out of doors for an hour. This news encouraged Nieuport to remind Thurloe that in the previous October he had sent him a draft of nineteen articles for a maritime treaty, which had formed the subject of a conference in November. He offered to wait on the Protector at Hampton Court again at his convenience to conclude the business,[40] but Cromwell's recovery was brief and he died before any progress had been made.

Towards the end of October Richard Cromwell's Council debated sending a fleet to the Sound on learning that the Dutch fleet had passed through the narrows at Elsinore and been saluted by the castles on either side, both now in Swedish hands. Though Sweden was reluctant to acquire a new enemy, the rival fleets engaged and a few ships were lost on each side. The Dutch pressed on and joined forces with the Danish fleet off Copenhagen, while the Swedes sought refuge in the harbour at Landskrona located in territory they had recently acquired on the eastern side of the Sound. In this way they avoided a renewal of action with the Dutch and Danes.[41]

As soon as he returned to duty on 9 November Thurloe was very fully occupied in negotiations with the Swedish and Dutch representatives in London and in sending new instructions to Downing. The first task was to draft with Fiennes a reply to a paper presented by the Swedes. Nieuport was quick to press him about the proposed maritime treaty, and three days later Dorislaus obliged with a translation of the Dutch ambassador's report of their conversation. On 19 November Nieuport visited Thurloe at Kensington, where he had gone to rest before the state funeral of Oliver Cromwell. Early in the following month he was at Nieuport's house with Wolseley and Strickland, with Jessop in attendance as clerk, to haggle over seemingly interminable complaints of captured shipping.[42]

The Secretary was also being pestered by Guavarina, the Venetian resident, who in the previous August had been attached for the debt of a trifling sum. His complaint that his coach had been stopped in the streets by the bailiffs had been considered by the Council on the day before Cromwell died. Thurloe was appointed a member of the committee formed to deal with the issue. Now in January 1659 the Venetian was complaining again of assaults, robberies and false accusations.[43]

Thurloe had earlier told Downing at The Hague that the Dutch ambassador was alarmed at the prospect of an English fleet entering the Sound and suggested that it would be useful to spread rumours of a naval expedition to that area. A fleet under Goodson did sail late in 1658. Thurloe ensured that it was not delayed by lack of pilots, but it encountered so much ice at the Skaw that it could not enter the Sound and returned to England without incident. Nonetheless, as Thurloe pointed out to Monck, the mere movement of the fleet had deterred the Dutch from despatching as planned reinforcements of four thousand foot and twelve warships. Yet since these, too, are likely to have been turned back by the ice, the English deterrence was perhaps more theoretical than real.[44]

Not until 21 February 1659 could Thurloe give the Commons a full and, in the opinion of the Venetian resident, clear account of the affairs of northern Europe from 1655 to date. The French historian Guizot saw Thurloe as the only speaker who raised the level of debate to the natural dignity of the subject, revealing a man of strong convictions and mature experience. But he detected in Thurloe, too, a lack of confidence in the strength and durability of the power he served. The Dutch, Thurloe pointed out, already had thirty ships in the Sound and were sending more – twenty frigates, ten fireships and ten despatch vessels. His Highness Richard Cromwell had made preparations, but thought that the

House should be informed and offer advice. But there was total silence when Mr Secretary sat down. Then Sir Henry Vane asked which side had broken the peace and started the second war. Thurloe, knowing that Sweden had denounced the Treaty of Roskild and invaded Denmark while alleging that the Danes had failed to comply with its terms, replied cautiously that although both sides had been heard, the English government was still in the dark. His Highness, however, wished to espouse neither side. It was in England's interest to stop the war.[45]

Downing had informed Thurloe on 28 January that the English parliament was a laughing stock abroad. The betting was twenty to one on nothing coming from it. But when the debate was resumed on 23 February Vane and Heselrige insisted on parliament's right to provide a powerful navy if required, to appoint or approve the sea commanders and to raise the necessary revenue. None of these duties should be surrendered to a single person and his Council. Several judicious contributions to the debate were made by an Admiralty commissioner, John Clarke, who had fought in Ireland and under Blake at the capture of the Scillies. Clarke had sat in all the Protectorate parliaments and had become close to the Secretary through marriage to Thurloe's 'sister', Joan, widow of his half-brother Isaac Ewer. Writing to Downing, Clarke condemned parliamentary sloth in authorizing the fleet's despatch. 'The House stands stiffly upon their own rights and powers', he added. It was left to Sir Richard Onslow, a leader of the 'Country party', to move that 'a very considerable navy be forthwith provided and put to sea for the safety of this Commonwealth and the preservation of the trade and commerce thereof'. The motion was carried without a single voice against.[46]

Thurloe had to intervene in the debate again the next day to deny an allegation about an underhand engagement with Sweden. The Dutch, he said, had not quibbled about the objective of their fleet – it was prepared in order to help the king of Denmark. He went on to speak of the peace made with the Dutch in 1654. With hindsight, he wished that the war had been prosecuted to its utmost so that the Dutch would either have to accept England's offer of a coalition as one people or be ruined, but they had offered peace and agreed to parliament's demands against the House of Stuart. He had heard that the Dutch thought themselves so hard put upon that they would never be content until they had extricated themselves from the terms of the treaty. Turning to Spain, he appeared to support a perpetual state of war. Queen Elizabeth, he declared, would never be persuaded to make peace. Despite the opposition of James I, parliament had forced a war in the 1620s and in 1641 had denounced peace with Spain without their consent. 'Those things have weight with me', he said, but added that the decay of trade had not been due to Spain but to the Dutch: 'Dunkirk is more considerable than men are aware of.' He ended by urging the Commons to stop talking and to authorize action.[47]

Vane spoke again complimenting Mr Secretary for his speech, but going on to suggest that there might be some secret treaty with Sweden of which Thurloe himself was unaware. The fleet sent to Jamaica should have gone to the Sound instead and fallen on the Dutch. The affair had all along been managed to support the interests of a single person and not the public good. The Solicitor-General and others criticized Vane's insinuations, but he was not pressed to withdraw. Candles had long been brought in and it was almost 11 p.m. before the question was put. The House then resolved to ask the Protector to put into execution its vote concerning the fleet, but added a proviso 'saving the interest of this House in the militia and in making peace and war'.[48]

On 5 March there was news that Copenhagen had been taken by the Swedes, in spite of the Dutch presence. A week later Montagu dropped down the river from Whitehall to join the *Naseby* and put to sea with a powerful fleet of almost forty ships with five fireships. He later told Pepys that he had tried to encourage Richard Cromwell at their farewell interview, avowing that he would rather see him dead than giving way to 'such things as were then hatching and afterwards did ruin him'. The Protector had replied that he would follow the advice, whatever it might be, of Broghill, Jones, Thurloe and Montagu himself. This contradicts reports reaching royalist sources that Richard had withdrawn his confidence from Thurloe.[49]

Meanwhile, at The Hague, Downing had been working with the French ambassador to prepare a joint treaty with the United Provinces about their relations with Sweden and Denmark. He reported regularly to Thurloe on his progress, but on 15 March the Protector himself wrote suggesting that negotiations would be better left to 'our men with the Kings of Sweden and Denmark'. It would also be wiser for neither England nor the United Provinces to send their fleets. The Protector wrote again at length on 30 March and 1 April about the treaty, but these letters must have been lost or were still in transit when on 9 April, after sitting all day until midnight, Downing and his French and Dutch colleagues completed their work and sent off the resultant treaty to Thurloe in London for it to be rendered in Latin.[50]

The receipt of this document three days later caused consternation in Whitehall. The Protector wrote at once to Downing instructing him not to sign, and on the following day to Montagu to say that he was to pay no attention to Downing's treaty: 'We do in no sort approve of those articles, being (I know not upon what mistake) framed contrary to our instructions.' Thurloe wrote to Downing in detail, though apparently in great haste, on the 14th. Whitehall's main objection was that the English fleet was obliged by the treaty to give no assistance to either side for three weeks, while Opdam's fleet was left in the Sound at liberty to act against Sweden. 'He may fight and beat the Swedish fleet, bring over all Brandenburg's army and His Highness' fleet might stand still and look on.'

Downing was left in no doubt about the enormity of his indiscretion. Thurloe referred to articles 'we dislike throughout', hoping that Downing would not have signed them. He would receive further instructions shortly. In the meantime, if he had despatched a copy to Montagu, he must immediately recall what he had sent, 'or all is lost there'. Downing later received a considered reply signed by the Protector, criticizing each article in turn, and also an express with amendments agreed by Nieuport, Fiennes and Thurloe.[51]

The resulting tripartite treaty between England, France and the United Provinces, calling on Sweden and Denmark to return to the terms of the Treaty of Roskild, was signed at The Hague on 11 May. Montagu had arrived in the Sound but his fleet had little effect, for de Ruyter had reinforced the Dutch and Danish fleet to nearly eighty ships. Moreover, by 9 May the Protectorate was at an end and Thurloe was out of office.

Another matter that had engaged the Secretary's attention throughout Richard's short Protectorate was the effort made by both France and Spain to bring their conflict to an end. Because of this and of the Anglo–French approach to northern affairs, he was in constant touch with Bordeaux. For his part, Bordeaux assured Thurloe of the high esteem in which he was held by Cardinal Mazarin. Bordeaux wisely refrained from asking for an audience with the new Protector until fresh letters of credence arrived, but he saw Thurloe, who offered to call on him with an assurance of the regime's continued friendship. The new government had requested the French court to wear mourning for Oliver Cromwell, and the French government to lend no less than £50,000.[52]

Thurloe's prolonged illness hindered negotiations throughout October 1658. In the meantime Bordeaux recruited Falconbridge, the Protector's son-in-law, for the French service, at first offering only to pay his expenses. But Falconbridge let it be known that he would prefer jewels for his wife to money and had expected a pair of Barbary horses for himself. When Bordeaux reported that Thurloe had avoided seeing him, Falconbridge attributed this to offence at the delay in advancing the loan. They met on 11 November and again two days later at Thurloe's Kensington home. Bordeaux gave no encouragement to Thurloe's hints about money and made it clear that France would not pay towards the English fleet if the outcome was war with the United Provinces. Nevertheless, he claimed that France had been pressing for action to prevent Sweden's defeat.[53]

Meetings between the ambassador and the Secretary of State continued at intervals. In addition to northern affairs and the Spanish treaty, they discussed the freeing of three Roman Catholic priests and the possibility of five or six hundred men from Lockhart's garrison assisting Turenne in the siege of Oudenarde. Lockhart had in fact arrived back in England on 20 November and was about to resume his role as ambassador to the French court. But when, in February 1659, Thurloe sent his chief clerk to Bordeaux one evening to apologize for his unavoidable absence, the clerk was forced to admit that although Lockhart would be sent with full instructions, their contents remained in doubt until settled by parliament.[54]

Thurloe saw Bordeaux on 9 April and discussed the Spanish treaty. His Highness, he said, regarded the timing as most inopportune. It would mean that Spain would conquer Portugal, the emperor would defeat Sweden, the Dutch would be in danger, and France and England would be riven by internal strife. Nevertheless Lockhart had been instructed to treat.[55] Reading between the lines it is possible to discern the Protectorate's genuine fear that an easing of pressure would free Spain to honour her comitment to Charles Stuart. Restoration of the monarchy was the principal fear, and all other policies must be subordinated to its prevention.

In spite of the worsening political climate at home Thurloe strove to give continuity to the nation's business and maintained frequent contact with Nieuport as well as Bordeaux. The latter found nothing controversial in the draft proposals for a tripartite treaty on northern affairs, which Thurloe brought him on the evening of 20 April following the disowning of Downing's effort. They also discussed the urgency of peace with Spain. A few days later Bordeaux sent his secretary to Kensington, where Thurloe received him civilly but would not discuss northern affairs with him. Montagu's fleet had reached the Sound on 6 April. He had offered his services as mediator to the kings of Denmark and Sweden but neither seemed inclined to accept, so Thurloe informed Monck on the 26th. In an undated letter of about this time, the Secretary expressed the opinion that neither the King of Sweden nor the King of Denmark would make peace while one expected aid from England and the other help from the States General. It was therefore important to let them know that the two countries were united on policy.[56]

Nieuport was consulted about the terms of the tripartite treaty. On 23 February he reported considerable difficulty in persuading Sweden to give up any of the advantages secured by the Treaty of Roskild. However, his main business with Thurloe was to lodge yet more complaints about maritime affairs. In December 1658 Thurloe had reported to the Council two memorials from the ambassador about the seizure of Dutch vessels by English warships in the Mediterranean. The Council sent a sharply worded reprimand to Stokes letting him know that it ran contrary to the mind and intention of His Highness to do anything to the prejudice of those in amity with England. At the same time Stokes was to continue to prevent enemy goods passing in the bottoms of friends and allies, a conflict of interests that would bedevil relations between belligerent warships and neutral merchantmen for centuries to come. Complaints were not, however, all on one side. In the previous August Thurloe had been ordered to prepare for the Council a list of injuries received by the English from the Dutch.[57]

In February 1659 Nieuport claimed that although an assurance had been given that the Protector and Council would not allow any English warships to go to sea with commissions from a foreign power, he could name three with commissions from the kings of Sweden and Portugal. In March he asked for the immediate release of two Dutch vessels brought into the Downs by Swedish privateers. The Commissioners of customs later reported that since the privateers had not been fitted out in England they were not under English jurisdiction.[58]

Bordeaux saw Thurloe yet again on 29 April, when they debated the relative merits of a short or long truce or peace with Spain. England, said Thurloe, would prefer a long truce or real peace, but Bordeaux argued that a longer period would give Spain opportunities to overthrow Portugal and relieve Flanders. According to Bordeaux, Thurloe seemed convinced by his adovocacy and promised an answer the same evening, but not until 2 May was he able to send word that His Highness had agreed to a truce and that Lockhart had been instructed accordingly. The Secretary and ambassador also agreed to send parallel instructions to the resident ministers at the Swedish court to promote by mediation an accommodation with the United Provinces and to use similar good offices on behalf of Poland and Brandenburg.[59]

Thurloe was unable to do anything to exploit the tripartite treaty, for he had lost office two days before it was signed at The Hague. He wrote a farewell letter to Downing on 27 May saying that he had tried to find out whether Downing would be kept on at The Hague. In fact, the new Council did consider a replacement but decided to keep Downing at his post.[60]

When he wrote to Monck on 26 April Thurloe had believed peace between France and Spain to be imminent, and in fact a truce was signed the next day. Here again his firm control of the country's overseas interests was to be sorely missed. He later wrote that a great opportunity to get the best out of France and Spain had been lost because of the change of government in England.[61]

In May Montagu asked the new government for orders to make the fleet useful. There was no response and after lying at anchor all summer, he became restive. On 10 August he wrote at length about the state of negotiations since the arrival of three English commissioners in July. Nothing had been left out, he wrote, again requesting certain and positive orders. He waited only another fortnight. On the 24th the commissioners at Copenhagen reported that he had sailed with the fleet, leaving two frigates and a ketch and taking Meadow with him. Meadow, in fact, stayed at Elsinore pestering the Council for his recall. He had earlier refused a Danish pension, but now accepted 10,000 rixdollars (about £1,800) from the Swedish king, not least because his servants had not been paid and his own salary was a year and a half in arrears.[62]

While Thurloe was out of office six members of the Council, with Henry Lawrence as President, put their signatures and seals to a document of remarkable constitutional interest – an agreement with the Dutch made on 30 July 1659 concerning the Hanseatic towns of Lübeck, Bremen and Hamburg. Its interest lies in the fact that it refers to the treaty being

> between the Most Serene and High the Lord Protector of the Commonwealth of England, Scotland and Ireland, of the one part, and the High and Mighty Lords the Estates General of the United Provinces of the other part

and goes on to state that the agreement is made by 'the Commissioners of His Highness the Protector'; such a single person had not existed for three months, and this paper suggests that in turning Richard out the army had achieved nothing more than placing the office of Protector in commission. It may be that since the Council had issued no amending ordinance and parliament had passed no new constitutional legislation, the Commonwealth was still governed in law by the Protectorate set up by the Petition and Advice. One may still wonder what Thurloe would have made of this piece of equivocation had he remained responsible for foreign affairs.[63]

When Thurloe was recalled to office in February 1660 it was specifically for the control of foreign affairs that his expertise was needed. Affairs in the north appeared likely to settle themselves without much diplomatic assistance, for Carl X of Sweden had returned to Stockholm in December 1659 and news of his death there reached London on 5 March, brought by a vessel docked at Hull. The Swedish ambassador had an audience with the Council on 14 March to inform members officially that the king had been succeeded by a minor son with a queen regent, whose government was content to make peace all round. There was nevertheless a tangled web of alliances to be unravelled. On 9 March the Council received a memorial from the Danish representative in London, another from the commissioners at Copenhagen and a letter from Downing at The Hague. All were referred to Thurloe to consider and report. It is a measure of his domination of the field of foreign affairs that the Council thought it unnecessary to appoint a committee. From Danzig Thurloe heard of the conclusion of peace between Sweden and Poland, signed at Oliva, then a small town in its own right but today lost in the urban sprawl connecting Gdynia, Sopot and Gdansk.[64]

Over the previous months protracted negotiations between France and Spain had taken place at Bayonne. Lockhart had set out from Fontainebleau in the previous July, still keeping up the appearance of ambassador of an important European state, travelling in a coach-and-six with a retinue of three pages and nine footmen. He reported regularly to the President of the Council, but as the representative of a distracted country ignored by both sides, he was unable to make any significant contribution. Mazarin remained cool and the Spanish negotiators were more inclined to pay attention to Charles Stuart, who put in an appearance on the frontier as soon as he knew that the royalist risings in England in August 1659 had failed. The Treaty of the Pyrenees had finally been signed on 28 October 1659, and Lockhart was recalled in the same month.[65]

The Restoration, coming three months after Thurloe's return to office, ended his active career. According to Thomas Birch, he was often solicited by Charles II in the early years of his reign to return to public office, particularly in the field of foreign affairs. Thurloe, however, doubted his ability to serve with other members of the administration. Cromwell, he told the king, had sought men for places and not places for men. Nevertheless he still retained a sense of duty to his country. Reviewing his papers in August 1660, he came across a copy of a projected alliance between the French king and the States General, which had reached him a few days before his retirement. He took the trouble to make a summary, condensing its articles so as to show the scope of the alliance and its reference to the honour and integrity of His Majesty and the kingdom. Although he recognized that Chancellor Hyde might have received the information from other hands, he thought it his duty to send him the summary.[66]

It must have been a blow to Thurloe to hear of the sale of Dunkirk to the French. As Henry Cromwell had predicted, this key to the Continent had proved an expensive acquisition, costing about £100,000 a year to garrison and provision. Charles II got four million livres from the

French for it. Peace with Spain had been quickly negotiated, but in August 1664 the second Dutch war broke out. As before it was fought entirely at sea, but this time, after a promising start, it ended disastrously for England. Thurloe was no longer able to exert any influence on affairs, and was forced to remain silent in retirement.

8

PERSONAL AND FAMILY AFFAIRS FROM 1645

It is a fair ornament of a man, and a great convenience both to
himself and to others with whom he converseth or dealeth, to
act regularly, uniformly, and consistently *(Isaac Barrow)*

Throughout his career, John Thurloe had tended to remain in the
background and the details of his public life and official work are often
lost amidst its shadows. Of his personal and private life over the same
period, even less is known. It is clear that he had two wives, but no
formal records of either marriage have been traced. His first, to a
Peyton, lasted no more than four years, ending with her death around
1641, when Thurloe was in his mid-twenties. He seems to have remained
a widower for some time. The only clue to the date of his second
marriage is an undocumented statement by Birch that the couple's third
son was born in 1651, which would place the marriage around 1647,
perhaps a year or two earlier.

Thurloe's second wife, Ann Lytcott, was the third daughter in a family
of fifteen children, nine of whom survived infancy (see Genealogical
Table 2). Their father, Sir John Lytcott, knighted by James I, was a
gentleman of the privy chamber. His wife Mary was a sister of Sir
Thomas Overbury, who had been poisoned in the Tower through a
notorious court conspiracy in 1613. Sir John had inherited the lease of
the manor of Molesey in Surrey, on the south bank of the Thames
opposite Hampton Court, and in 1638 purchased the freehold for
between £800 and £900. On his death at the age of sixty-five in September 1641, the manor and all his other freehold lands in England were
conveyed to his sister-in-law Muriel Oldisworth and three nephews,
including Nicolas Lechmere, to hold in trust for his widow and children.
The widow and trustees sold the estate in April 1647 with the rectory
and parsonage of East Molesey for £4,000. It must be presumed that a
share of this inheritance reached Ann Thurloe. Under her father's will
she had been left 1,000 marks (£333) and all the furniture of one
bedroom after her mother's death or remarriage.[1]

It may have been soon after his second marriage, or perhaps on
admission to Lincoln's Inn in 1647, that Thurloe sat for his portrait. Its

present owners, the Chequers Estate, catalogue it as the work of William Dobson. Dobson, appointed sergeant-painter to Charles I on the death of Van Dyck in 1641, had accompanied the king to Oxford in 1642–3 and there painted many of the royalist leaders. He returned to London in the summer of 1646 and may have spent the last months of his life (he died in the October) painting some of the parliamentarians. However, he worked only very briefly in London after the first civil war and the attribution of the Thurloe portrait appears doubtful.

There is an eager, uncertain look in the face of the thirty-year-old staring out from the head-and-shoulders picture. A thin moustache covers his upper lip and he gives the appearance of what indeed he was at this stage: someone still awaiting the opportunity to show his real worth. The Cromwell Museum at Huntingdon has another portrait of Thurloe, also attributed somewhat questionably to Dobson. This three-quarter-length study shows a man of rather more mature looks with brown shoulder-length hair, a moustache and faint goatee beard. He wears a black doublet with lace cuffs and a restrained white collar with a bunch of lace at the throat. In an age when fame could come at an early age to those with influence or rank he had had to struggle upwards by his own exertions, though assisted by St John's patronage. But he had done well in his first official employment at Uxbridge, and now looked for further chances to demonstrate his abilities.

Shortly after Thurloe's departure for The Hague early in 1651, he proved the will of his half-brother Isaac Ewer of Hatfield Broad Oak in Essex, a colonel of foot in the parliamentary army, who had died of plague in Ireland shortly after the surrender of Waterford in August 1650. Ewer, distinguished by a large, black, bushy beard, had fought as second in command of Robert Hammond's regiment in the New Model Army at Naseby, and in the second civil war took part in both the capture of Chepstow by storm and the surrender of Colchester. He became Governor of the Isle of Wight just two days before receiving orders to move Charles I to Hurst Castle on his final journey, and had later served as one of the king's judges and was a signatory of the death warrant. He made Thurloe sole executor of his extensive Essex property, charging him also with the care and tuition of his two children, Thomas and Joanna, 'entreating him to have a tender care of them'. Thomas was then sixteen years old, his sister probably somewhat younger. Thurloe's own eldest son John was also a beneficiary under the will.[2]

Thurloe presumably continued to occupy his chamber at Lincoln's Inn during his first year or so with the Council. By the time he took up his duties his second family consisted of three sons, the youngest a year old. That his second son had been named Oliver was probably more in compliment to St John than to Cromwell. It is not known where the family were living. Thurloe's name has been linked with a number of properties in East Anglia and the Home Counties, including a farmhouse in the main street of Stevenage, parts of which survive incorporated in a later building on the site. But no documents support this or most other alleged associations.

Thurloe's appointment as Secretary of State at the end of 1653 was marked by the casting of a gold medal chased by Thomas Simon, the foremost engraver of the time, from a model in wax by his brother Abraham. Thurloe's head appears on the obverse, a right profile with long wavy hair crowned by a skullcap. His doublet is buttoned and he wears the usual plain collar. The engraver's initials, 'TS', appear on the truncation. On the reverse is a double cypher of Thurloe's Latinized initials, 'IT', and the words 'Secr. Thurloe' beneath it.

Simon, appointed chief engraver and medal-maker to the Protector, was also responsible for engraving the seals and the gold silver coinage of the Protectorate.[3] The artistic skill of the Simon brothers is well attested and it is probable that in the Thurloe medal we have the best surviving likeness of the Secretary. Nearly a century later it was reproduced as an engraved frontispiece to the first volume of Thomas Birch's edition of the State Papers. The medal hangs on a stone obelisk at the foot of which are a Holy Bible, coins of the Protectorate, scrolls bearing the legends 'God with us' and *'Pax queritur Bello'*, the arms of England, Scotland and Ireland, the Covenant, books, quills and an inkpot. To the right is a gatehouse and to the left can be seen the masts of the parliamentary fleet. Everything has a significance for Thurloe's career.

Alongside his official employment at Whitehall, Thurloe was constantly dealing with matters arising from the drainage of the Isle of Ely. The work continued to make fitful and rather slow progress. St John, on circuit in March 1655 despite a warning about the troubled state of the country, told Thurloe that he would inspect the works in the south level as soon as he had finished. Since the adventurers had only the summers of 1655 and 1656 in which to complete the digging, St John arranged to meet them at Downham. By summer 1656 work had to be suspended in the middle level because money had run out through non-payment of taxes, and Thurloe was urged to intervene. All the same an additional twenty-three manors of five hundred and ten acres apiece had been created, nine in the south level, eleven in the middle, and three in the north. A further five had been formed near the villages of Doddington and Whittlesey.[4]

Thurloe had by then become an adventurer himself and was allotted five hundred acres beside the river Nene near Doddington. Another adventurer with five hundred acres in the south level was Vice-Admiral

Goodson, who wrote to Thurloe from Jamaica early in 1656 asking him to pay £400 or £500 out of his salary to his wife. Thurloe was not present at a meeting at Ely on 29 September 1656, when it was ordered that the laws of Romney Marsh in Kent should be used in the Great Level and that Bedford and the rest – including Thurloe, made a lord commissioner on that day – should have the same powers as its lords. A steward, clerk, bailiffs and jurats were appointed. St John, at Longthorpe in September and October, kept Thurloe informed of progress. In turn, the Secretary found time to keep him abreast of London news, including the capture of part of the Spanish American treasure fleet. In due course St John told him that Bedford was to be Governor and Thurloe himself Deputy Governor of the company. Further meetings of the company were held at St John's chambers at Lincoln's Inn in January and May 1657, after which the business seems to have lapsed until after the Restoration.[5]

In August 1656 St John visited Wisbech to see what progress had been made in building Thurloe's fine new mansion there on the site of the castle. The Norman fortress had been replaced by a medieval episcopal palace for the diocese of Ely. However, the bishops rarely used the place and in the latter half of the sixteenth century it served as a prison for religious dissenters, at first Protestants, later mainly Jesuits. It was cleared of prisoners in 1600 and between 1609 and 1619 Bishop Lancelot Andrews, editor of the Authorized Version of the Bible, spent £2,000 on repair work. The buildings then covered two acres surrounded by four acres of grounds with access by drawbridge over a forty-foot moat. During the 1630s the bishop, Matthew Wren, was a zealous Laudian whose property was to be sequestered by the Long Parliament. Wren himself was taken into custody in 1641 after the Commons had voted him unfit and unworthy to hold or exercise any office or dignity in church or Commonwealth.[6]

One of the new elite of the Interregnum, Thurloe – by his tenure of the manor of Wisbech Barton, with those of neighbouring Elm and Tydd St Giles – was profiting from rents formerly paid to the diocese. When the properties of the dean and chapter of Ely Cathedral were alienated in 1652 the manor of Wisbech, with all its rents and tithes, was acquired by two London merchants. There was a block of land between the churchyard and the street, four acres of pasture north of the river, a large barn and seven acres of arable and pasture ground. Thurloe did not acquire the manor until 1658, but he had evidently held property in and around Wisbech since at least the mid-1650s. His papers contain a letter from James Edwards, his bailiff or rent collector at Wisbech, dated 14 January 1656. Holdings of fields totalling a hundred and sixty-one acres are mentioned. In the same month he was asked to recommend an officer and soldiers from Wisbech for a troop of militia, suggesting that his connection with the town was already far closer than that of a mere parliamentary representative.[7]

Even earlier he had interested himself in the town's well-being. There is a curious order to the commissioners for customs in May 1655, directing them to instruct their collector at Wells to take £50 from the money received from the new impost on coals between October 1654 and March 1655 and to pay it to the 'town-men' of Wisbech (or as the mayor might direct) for the poor of the town. A proviso enjoins that no disposal should be made without the consent of the Secretary of State. The only reasonable interpretation of this document is that Thurloe was nursing a parliamentary constituency by diverting public money to private charity, an uncharacteristic lapse from his normal standard of rectitude.[8]

Cromwell had held Wisbech Castle while Governor of the Isle of Ely, but had caused it to be slighted on his withdrawal. Thus when Thurloe decided to make it his home it was 'one of the ruins that Cromwell knocked about a bit' and had to be almost entirely rebuilt to a new, more modern design. The front elevation of the new mansion was to be an almost exact copy of St John's seat of Thorpe or Longthorpe Hall. Seven steps led up to the front door, with half windows of rooms in the basement showing on either side. Pillars supported a balustraded balcony over the porch, and there were three windows on either side of the entrance and balcony doors. A second floor had three dormer windows on the front. Above it was a flat roof with four clusters of chimneys and a central access shaft. The architect may have been John Webb, a nephew and pupil of Inigo Jones, though Sir Peter Mills has also been credited with both Thorpe Hall and Wisbech.[9] The house was demolished in 1816 and replaced by a Regency villa which still stands facing the church across Museum Square, its grounds neatly enclosed by two crescents of houses. The garden walls and gate piers probably date from the seventeenth century and may have belonged to Thurloe's mansion.

Thurloe had little time to visit Wisbech, but he evidently had some affection for the place. In 1654 some burgesses had deposited a few books for common use in a room over the church porch, traditionally the original location of Wisbech Grammar School. Before he left the town at the Restoration Thurloe contributed thirty-two works to this embryo library, and donated £50 for the purchase of more. In 1656 he had given £150, the interest to be used for apprenticing three poor children yearly, and also made gifts of £50 to construct a causeway and £46 10s. for a sluice.[10]

In the seventeenth century the parish church contained a number of galleries or boxes and in 1657 a special one was added for Thurloe's use, at the charge of the town bailiff. After two centuries or more of use all the box pews and galleries were removed in 1856. In the absence of the bishop, Thurloe, as lord of the manor, confirmed William Coldwell in his living, and early in 1657 presented an Independent minister as vicar of Ely.[11]

Elected a capital burgess of Wisbech in November 1657, Thurloe arranged for the grant of letters patent to his colleagues by the Lord Protector on 29 July 1658, only five weeks before Cromwell's death. He was re-elected in the following November. In January 1659 the corporation paid £2 costs to the under-sheriff of Cambridgeshire at the election of Thurloe as a burgess to sit in parliament. This indicates not that the under-sheriff elected him, but that he had allowed him to represent the borough of Wisbech rather than the Isle of Ely.[12] Thus Thurloe sat for the Isle of Ely in the parliaments of 1654 and 1656, but in 1659 for Wisbech. He was also successful on that occasion at Huntingdon and Cambridge University, where he received a record vote in his favour.

One other matter concerning Wisbech may be mentioned. Determined to impose its authority on the people in religious matters, the Council issued a reminder on 22 December 1657 to the Lord Mayor and Justices of London and Westminster to see that the ordinance taking away the festivals of Easter, Christmas and other holy days was observed and to prevent the traditional solemnities. A correspondent at Wisbech, seeing a report of this order in the printed news, wrote to Thurloe that he wished it had reached Wisbech, 'where this paltry people at the schoolhouse have again had solemn preaching all that day' and the next. It showed their spirit of contrariness: when formerly the vicar preached they used to open their shops, and now they did the opposite. Nevertheless he was fully persuaded that truth would flourish in this place in the Lord's time. This was only one of many Protectoral directives which may have disturbed the way of life in Thurloe's adopted town. For example, in the previous June a proclamation prohibited travel on Sundays (except to and from a place of worship), the opening of shops or inns, and the holding of fairs or markets, and declared that all were to attend church or chapel. Any who disobeyed were liable to heavy fines.[13]

Family affairs sometimes obtruded on Thurloe's official duties. In the midst of all the controversy about the institution of the Protectorate under the Instrument of Government, and his continuing care of foreign affairs, intelligence and security, Thurloe found time in December 1654 to write a letter on behalf of his mother-in-law Lady Lytcott, who had been striving in vain to recover a loan made by her husband. Later his friend Philip Jones was able to follow up the business for him in South Wales.[14]

Thurloe learned in November 1655 from Scotland that Leonard Lytcott, a member of his wife's family, was in serious financial trouble. It appears that he had invested money with a merchant who had gone bankrupt. Thurloe pressed Lord Broghill to come to Lytcott's aid. Although he made plain his distaste, Broghill undertook to try to obtain for him a post in the Scottish customs and excise. At the same time he tried to persuade Lytcott, who until then had done well in the army, not to go to London; money for the journey was in any case lacking. Lytcott evidently recovered, for in 1660 he marched south with Monck at the head of his regiment. Another instance of Thurloe's involvement was that of William Ewer, nephew of Isaac Ewer, the parliamentary colonel and regicide, and thus of the Secretary himself. He had gone to Ireland with Ewer and in May 1656 was unemployed, a victim of the reduction of forces there. With some diffidence Thurloe recommended him to Henry Cromwell as 'a very sober man, and valiant, and otherwise capable of trust'.[15]

Like all men of influence at this time, Thurloe received many requests for patronage. These began as early as March 1654 when Whitelock wrote to him from Sweden requesting him to put in a good word with His Highness on behalf of his son James. A month later one of the heralds begged a place as a trustee or commissioner for the improvement of forests. From Scotland Monck was a constant suitor and in July 1657 admitted to Broghill that he was ashamed to ask any more favours of Thurloe. Nevertheless, a month later he pleaded for his Clarges brother-in-law to obtain a vacant post as an Admiralty commissioner and went on to excuse some derogatory remarks about the Post Office made by Clarges in parliament. Thurloe must have found them irritating, but Monck assured him that no malice towards him had been intended. Clarges did not, in fact, get the post in spite of writing personally to Thurloe and to Cromwell. Again, in the following April Monck asked Thurloe to receive Clarges to discuss 'a little thing in Ireland'. Clarges, a tireless busybody, later induced Monck to appoint him at £150 a year as agent and solicitor in London for the forces in Scotland, and sought to perform a similar service for Henry Cromwell in Ireland. This proposal was turned down, for Clarges, as agent for the Irish Council, was already providing a regular flow of informative letters to Dublin.

Oliver St John was another to make use of his somewhat privileged relationship with the Secretary of State. In February 1655 he sought an appointment for a barrister connection of the Mashams and Barringtons, and at the end of that year Thurloe had to seek out one of St John's sons in London and ship him off to Jamaica. In December 1658 St John begged a favour for another son. 'My wife is much troubled that her son should lose his hopes and returns you early thanks for your fond trouble', he added.[16]

The enrolment book of the Hanaper in Chancery contains records of two patents granted to Thurloe in 1657. The first, of 11 July, gave him and his heirs in perpetuity a patent to hold a fortnightly market at Wisbech. The second, of 20 September, was a warrant for the office of Postmaster-General of England, comptroller of the Post Office, for five years from 29 September at a rent of £10,000 a year payable at the Exchequer quarterly.[17]

In addition to his property and offices, Thurloe may also have acquired or adopted a coat of arms during the Interregnum. The 1787 volume *Respublica* includes an illustration of the arms of John Thurloe of the county of Suffolk, Secretary of State and Privy Councillor. They are blazoned as 'sable a chevron ermine between three cinque-foils or'.[18] This entry is immediately suspect, for Thurloe had no connection with Suffolk apart from the presumed derivation of his surname from one of the villages of Great or Little Thurlow in that county. The College of Arms has no record of a grant, though these particular arms have been used by a family named Thorley. Nevertheless the evidence that Thurloe used the arms for his seal is to be found in the Whitelock papers, which contain at least two examples on letters to the ambassador in Sweden, the earliest in January 1654, only a month after Thurloe had become Secretary of State.[19] The lack of registration at the College of Arms is not surprising, for all honours conferred during the Interregnum were nullified at the Restoration.

Sometime in the mid-1650s, when Thurloe was at the peak of his powers, he posed again for what was the grandest and most imposing of his portraits, painted by an unknown hand. The canvas, now in the National Portrait Gallery, bears a three-quarter-length view of him standing beside a table with a coloured cloth on which lie a pen and inkpot. The fingers of his left hand rest delicately on the table while his other hand holds a letter, clearly addressed to John Thurloe Esq., Secretary of State. Thurloe has shoulder-length hair, is clean-shaven and has a somewhat severe expression, though he looks healthy and prosperous enough. Although Sir Francis Russell and others described him as 'the little secretary' the portrait shows a man of average, even quite impressive stature. He wears the usual white square collar over a dark doublet and cloak. Since the two serious illnesses that were soon to assail him probably left him looking older than his forty-one years, it seems likely that he commissioned the portrait in summer 1657 to celebrate his elevation to the rank of Privy Councillor. Thurloe may also have been painted around this time by Samuel Cooper, the celebrated miniaturist who portrayed so many of the national figures of the Protectorate, as of the royal court.

As a Privy Councillor Thurloe not only gained a vote in the Council but was also entitled to use the title 'Right Honourable'. In fact correspondence had usually been addressed to him in this style ever since he became Secretary of State three and a half years before. Privy Councillors were often – and correctly – referred to as the Lords of the Privy Council, but had no individual right to adopt the superior title. Nevertheless, at this time many of them were addressed as 'My Lord' and letters reaching the Secretary often began with this salutation and referred to him as 'your lordship'. The rector's son had indeed come a long way.

In November 1657 Thurloe received a further appointment carrying huge prestige: a governorship of the Charterhouse, a charitable foundation housed in the buildings formerly occupied by the Carthusian order near Aldersgate Street. Cruelly suppressed by Henry VIII in 1535, the Charterhouse and its property had come into the hands of the powerful Howard family. In 1594 one Thomas Sutton, who had amassed a huge fortune from Durham coal and marriage to a rich widow, made provision for a hospital and almshouse in Essex. He did not, however, obtain possession of the property he had in mind before 1610, and in May 1611 he bought the Charterhouse (an English corruption of the French word *Chartreuse*) from the Howards for £13,000.

In the following month he obtained royal letters patent to transform his charitable foundation there as the hospital of King James. It was to provide board and lodging for folk who had fallen on hard times, and schooling for boys whose parents had no estates to leave them. The foundation was to be staffed by a master, a preacher and a registrar, but overall supervision was in the hands of a body of governors. A list of the first governors gives us an immediate indication of the standing of the Charterhouse as a charity: the Archbishop of Canterbury, the Lord Chancellor, the Lord High Treasurer, the bishops of London and Ely, and a judge afterwards Chief Justice of the Common Pleas.[20]

The governorships were held in 1657 by the new men of the Commonwealth and Protectorate. When the governors and master met on 2 November to elect a replacement for Dr Lawrence Wright, the governors present were Nathaniel Fiennes and John Lisle, Lords Commissioners of the Great Seal, Bulstrode Whitelock, one of the Lords Commissioners of the Treasury, John Glynne and Oliver St John, both chief justices, William Lenthall, Master of the Rolls, Philip Skippon, a major-general and Privy Councillor, and Sir Arthur Heselrige, a baronet and veteran parliamentarian. Wright, sometime physician in ordinary to Cromwell, had died on 3 October after over five years as a governor. The record of the assembly relates that

> we . . . do elect choose nominate and appoint the right honourable
> John Thurloe principal Secretary of State and one of His Highness'

most honourable privy council to be one of the governors of the lands, possessions, revenues and goods of the Hospital of King James founded in Charterhouse within the county of Middlesex . . . and do order that a patent or grant of the said place be forthwith sealed and sent to Mr Secretary accordingly.

Each governor had the right to nominate a poor man to be entered as one of the brethren and also a poor scholar for the school. The names went on waiting lists until vacancies occurred. Thurloe made his two nominations in May 1658 during an assembly at which Richard Cromwell was elected a governor.[21] In August of the following year, while Thurloe was out of office, a request reached him from a man called Daniel Johnson in the Dunkirk garrison, reminding him that Lockhart had already appealed to him to make his only son a scholar of Westminster or the Charterhouse. 'If beggars may be choosers,' he went on, 'the Charterhouse would be better', being near to friends who could keep an eye on the lad in the absence of both parents.[22] It seems that Thurloe was never able to honour this request.

In February 1658 the Secretary was offered another and somewhat surprising appointment as Chancellor of Glasgow University. The chancellorship had been vacant since the execution in 1649 of James, Duke of Hamilton, an active royalist who had led an army south into England in 1648, only to suffer defeat and capture at Preston. It appears that the post was now offered to Thurloe in recognition of his zeal in promoting the spread of the Gospel in the Highlands. He was sent the oath for signature and return to the university. It seems unlikely that Thurloe, who never went north of East Anglia, was able to do very much for the university, but he held the post until the Restoration, when it was returned to the Scottish nobility in the person of the ninth Earl of Glencairn.[23]

The university archives contain a document, signed by James Nutley, one of the clerks of the signet, dating from the Protectorate of Richard Cromwell and certified to be His Highness's command by Mr Secretary Thurloe. It is a warrant to pay the principal of the college £40 yearly from university funds as augmentation and the university £100 a year from the revenues of the former dean and chapter of Glasgow, over and above the £200 a year already allowed by Oliver Cromwell from this source. The warrant refers to an earlier charter of March 1656, itself confirming the university's ancient revenue and privileges and bestowing new income.[24]

With the birth of his daughter Ann on 16 May 1658 at the Countess of Mulgrave's house in Kensington, Thurloe had four sons and two daughters living. According to Morland he had lost two infant children at the beginning of 1657, so the new baby was probably a good deal younger than her brothers and sister. One of the boys had been sent to lodge with a Dr Carteret in Jersey, presumably to further his education. In October 1657 the captain of a small warship reported from Cowes roads that he had been prevented by bad weather from calling at Jersey as ordered to pick up Thurloe's son after convoying several vessels to St Malo.[25]

The dowager Countess of Mulgrave had been the first earl's second wife, married as long ago as 1619 and a widow since 1646. She was tenant of about fifteen acres of glebe land belonging to the vicarage of Kensington. Her house must have been large, for it was assessed at £35, besides £10 paid to the poor, in a survey of 1649, and at £60 under the Act of 24 November 1653 for contributions from the parish of Kensington towards maintenance of the army and navy.[26] These financial burdens, or perhaps mere loneliness, caused the dowager countess to take in paying guests. The Thurloes had taken only part of the house, for two separate reports confirm that the countess continued to live there. They had been preceded by Sir Orlando Bridgeman, a royalist forbidden to live in London, whose wife Dorothy had also borne an infant daughter at the house two years before Ann's confinement. The second Earl of Mulgrave, stepgrandson of the dowager, had been a member of the Protectorate Council and summoned to the new upper House, though never taking his seat. He died suddenly on 23 August 1658.

The records for December 1658 contain one of the rare reminders that Thurloe the statesman and parliamentarian, the Secretary and chief executive officer of government, was also a family man. George Downing wrote from The Hague asking whether Mrs. Thurloe liked any of the patterns of table linen which his wife had sent.[27]

After Thurloe's dismissal by the restored Rump in May 1659 he lost his official accommodation, and not until 20 September was he reallocated his chamber and adjoining closet at Whitehall. In the interim it had been assigned to one of his former assistants. Thurloe had probably left his family in Cambridgeshire and during summer 1659 lodged in John Upton's house at Hammersmith. In November he paid £10 for readmission to a chamber and garret at Lincoln's Inn. This was number 13 in Dial Court near the chapel. Twelve days after his admission to Dial Court, John Dodington was admitted to Mr. John Thurloe's chamber on the ground floor in Gatehouse Court, Chancery Lane Row. A modern tablet recording Thurloe's residence, placed by the Cromwell Association, has been affixed to the outside wall of these chambers overlooking Chancery Lane.[28]

Dodington, who had become Thurloe's secretary, was a member of a Somerset family with many connections with Lincoln's Inn. His grandfather had been admitted in 1595 and his father Francis in 1622, while his uncle Christopher, by then Recorder of Wells, had been called in 1631 and made a bencher in 1654 with seniority of 1648. Thurloe's selection of John Dodington as his secretary is at first sight surprising, for his father had fought for the king in the civil war and in March 1644 behaved with unusual severity towards prisoners at the capture of War- dour Castle in Wiltshire. Subsequently fleeing to France, he had been on the list of those excepted from pardon presented by the parliamentary side at Uxbridge, and he had similarly been among those whom Louis XVI had been asked to expel from France with the royal princes.

John probably did not share his father's views. Admitted on 23 January 1655 to Lincoln's Inn,[29] in 1658 he bought the office of first Re- membrancer in the Exchequer, responsible for the collection of reve- nues with potential profit from fees. His position was confirmed by letters patent issued under the Privy Seal on 29 July, in the closing weeks of Oliver's Protectorship – 'well approving of the ability of the said John Dodington', the document went on, he was to enjoy the office for so long as he should well demean himself. In spite of this promising introduc- tion, the court queried his experience and postponed his confirmation of appointment for two days. It was then approved with a show of reluc- tance, the court noting that there were many precedents for denying admission for want of skill. In the event Dodington was disappointed in the income received from this source.[30]

Dodington was married to Hester, daughter of a baronet, Sir Peter Temple. Learned and ingenious, he translated several books from French into English, including a history of Cardinal Richelieu's admin- istration, dedicated to Thurloe, and 'for pure spite' a translation of a satirical Spanish work, *The Visions of Dom Francisco de Quevedo Villegas.*

One of the first things Thurloe must have had to arrange after his release from detention in 1660 was a new home for his family. Matthew Wren, Bishop of Ely, had emerged from nineteen years' captivity on 15 March 1660 and at the Restoration all his lands and property were returned to him. Thurloe had to hand over his mansion on the site of Wisbech Castle and most of his other properties in the bishopric.

His choice fell on a house at Great Milton, a village about nine miles from Oxford in a valley south of what was then the main road to London. Rows of thatched cottages face a triangular green where three roads meet, one descending steeply past Thurloe's house, now known as The Priory. At the bottom of the hill the road curves round to the left and begins to rise again past the church on the way to Little Milton. In Thurloe's time there were three more large houses in the neigh- bourhood: the vicarage, the manor house where Thomas, son of Lord Keeper Coventry, was in 1662 succeeded as lord of the manor by his son George, and the seat of the royalist Smith family. All three houses stand today, as does The Priory. Richard Atwood had been vicar for fifty-one years when he died in 1658. His successor Samuel Nicolls, having no legitimate title to the living, disappeared at the Restoration, to be replaced by John Cave who, as farmer of the prebend, was able to present himself. There is no record of any Thurloe connection with this representative of the restored Anglican priesthood.[31]

The Priory, a name acquired only in the nineteenth century, is a substantial stone building with three gables fronting the road and gardens descending in terraces. In the oak-beamed entrance hall and main reception room are wide low-arched Tudor fireplaces, and there is oak panelling in the principal rooms. It had belonged to Dr John Wilkinson, who in the opening years of the seventeenth century was a fellow of Magdalen College, principal of Magdalen Hall and tutor to Henry, Prince of Wales, elder brother of Charles I. Wilkinson was forced to leave Oxford whilst it was the royalist headquarters, but he was restored in 1646 and in the following year became president of Magdalen College. At his death in January 1650 the house passed to his nephew, Henry.

Henry Wilkinson was an exact contemporary of Thurloe. Oddly, there was another Henry Wilkinson, also a friend of Thurloe, connected with the university at this time. Taller and older, he was known as 'long Harry', while the Great Milton Harry was called Henry Wilkinson junior or 'Dean Harry'. He succeeded his uncle as principal of Magdalen Hall in 1648 and became lecturer in moral philosophy in the following year. His wife Elizabeth died at the end of 1654 and, like his father, was buried at Great Milton. Called Rabbi Wilkinson and denounced as a madman by Anthony Wood, the peevish Oxford historian who 'never spake well of any man', Henry junior seems to have been an able, though somewhat bigoted, Puritan. He was unable to subscribe to the Restoration Act of Uniformity, left Oxford in 1662 and continued to serve as a Nonconformist minister in Leicestershire, Essex and Suffolk for the next thirty years. It appears that Thurloe first stayed at his house as a guest and then rented it.[32] Hitherto he had enjoyed little enough family life, and must have looked forward to a more peaceful and restful existence after his immense labours.

He still, however, lingered in London. At assemblies of the governors of the Charterhouse held while Thurloe was detained, a start had been made on clearing out the men of the Commonwealth and admitting or readmitting royalists. Even so, Thurloe was able to nominate Robert Lytcott, presumably a nephew, as a poor scholar at the assembly of 18 May 1660 when he was actually in custody, though he was unable to oblige Monck, who had written to him on 11 April pressing for the admission of Enoch, son of Matthew Line, a deserving person who had served the Commonwealth as a chirurgeon-at-sea. At this meeting two former governors were restored, and the continued governorships of Fiennes, Jones and Fleetwood appeared to be in question.

On 6 June at another assembly missed by Thurloe, still in detention, it was decided that 'Lord' Lisle, who had quitted the kingdom and was unlikely to return, should be removed and replaced by Algernon Percy, Earl of Northumberland. This was John Lisle, a bencher of the Middle Temple who had drawn up the sentence on Charles I. Made a Commissioner of the Great Seal in 1649, he had sat as member for Southampton in the parliaments of 1654 and 1656 and had been called to the 'other House' in 1657. Now he had fled to Switzerland. Northumberland, who replaced him, had been dismissed by Charles I from command of the fleet in June 1642. Although he was a member of the Committee of Safety a month later and of the Committee of Both Kingdoms in 1644, he was always a peacemaker and had been a parliamentary commissioner at Uxbridge. He had held aloof from public affairs under the Protectorate, refusing to sit in the 'other House' in 1658, thereby working his passage back to acceptability to the restored monarchy.

The bishop of Ely made his reappearance at an assembly on 17 July. Again Thurloe was not present, but they came face to face at another on 10 December. It is fascinating to conjecture how they treated each other. Thurloe at least has the reputation for amiability, courtesy and mildness to persons of all parties. At this assembly it was agreed to write to Lenthall and St John, asking them whether or not they would attend, and to Heselrige and Vane requesting their resignation.

Thurloe attended one more assembly, on 22 January 1661. By then Heselrige had died in the Tower and St John had resigned. Lord Chancellor Hyde was elected in lieu. It was on this occasion that Whitelock and Thurloe were taken aside by the earls of Manchester and Northumberland and told when the list of governors had come before the Council for review, the king had remarked that they were not fit to be there.[33] Whitelock did not resign, though he gave up attending, but Thurloe took the hint before the next assembly. He wrote his letter of resignation on 22 May, but it was not in the hands of the governors when they met the next day. He was thus able to make a final nomination at this meeting. The governors decided that all their pensioners and officers ought at the time of their admission to take the general oath of allegiance. Since most of them had been admitted 'in the time of the late troubles', the bishop of Ely and the Master were asked to meet and swear all those who had not hitherto taken the oath.

The governors did not meet again until 2 November, when they took note of Thurloe's letter, received via the Lord Chancellor, in which he made a free and voluntary surrender of his place as governor. Sir Orlando Bridgeman, Chief Justice of the Common Pleas, was elected in his stead. Sadly, Thurloe's nomination of Robert Lytcott was disallowed in 1662, when almost the entire list of May 1660 was declared null and void because so many had been nominated 'by governors attainted or fled the country for treason'.[34]

In October 1660 Thurloe had also been replaced as Chancellor of Glasgow University by William Cunningham, Earl of Glencairn. Glencairn, a Scottish royalist imprisoned at Edinburgh in 1655, had followed Monck to London as a Scottish commissioner and had been warmly received at court after the Restoration. The next year he was made Lord Chancellor of Scotland.

At a council of Lincoln's Inn Society on 2 July 1661, Isaac Ewer, sometime a clerk to the Council and later one of Meadow's secretaries in Denmark, was admitted to Thurloe's chamber and garret in Dial Court on payment of £10, though he also had to pay Thurloe's arrears before admission. By then Thurloe's collection of documents must have been safely hidden away in the false ceiling of the garret. They were discovered there about thirty years later by a clergyman who had borrowed the chamber from a friend during the long vacation.[35]

The country was settling down again in its old traditional ways. The restoration of the episcopate had saved the Church of England from extinction. In the previous year Hyde had expressed fears that all the bishops would soon be dead and the church doomed. The seventy-seven-year-old Bishop Juxon, who had attended Charles I on the scaffold, was made Archbishop of Canterbury and Gilbert Sheldon Bishop of London. Four Presbyterian divines were offered bishoprics and one of them accepted. Juxon, a man of exemplary character but limited ability, demanded the restoration of Lambeth Palace library, which had been bequeathed to Cambridge University by Bishop Bancroft and sent there by a parliamentary order of 1647 after the collection had been perused to see whether any books concerned the state. The committee appointed to examine Thurloe in May 1660 was given the additional task of securing from the Puritan preacher Hugh Peter all books and papers from Lambeth library still in his possession. The library was restored to Sheldon in 1663, when he succeeded to the archbishopric on Juxon's death.[36]

Early in June 1660 Thurloe was cited in Whitelock's defence of his conduct during the Interregnum, and some weeks later was more seriously implicated in the effort of his old friend St John to rebut charges of complicity in the execution of Charles I. St John – who had been sent to the Tower on 10 July, soon after Thurloe's release – denied that Cromwell had shared his bed or his lodgings before and after the king's death. He and his wife were then living at Lincoln's Inn, and there was but one bed. He denied having a hand in a book justifying the king's execution, the contents of which he had not seen before publication. He also dealt with an allegation that Thurloe had told some of the army that St John and Cromwell had advised the king's death. At that time, nearly twelve years before, he said, Thurloe was not acquainted with the army, was his own private servant, and did not serve Cromwell, 'not being recommended by me to him' until five years later, after two years in the employment of the Council of State. He referred his accusers to Thurloe's testimony, contained in a letter to the Speaker, Sir Harbottle Grimstone.

On this point Thurloe avowed that he was himself quite ignorant of the whole business. He believed that the trial and execution of the king were very far from St John's judgement. Indeed, he had heard him express his dislike of regicide and of army proceedings for some time beforehand. Setting out his case at length, St John went on to affirm that he never knew of any intention to try Charles for his life until the public announcement, that he then made clear his dislike and dissatisfaction, as many witnesses could confirm, and that since he was not then in the House of Commons, he had had nothing to do with the business.

St John likewise denied any hand in altering the form of government to a Commonwealth. Many witnesses could confirm his consistently declared preference for a system comprising king, Lords and Commons. He had refused the command to judges to assist in constitutional revision and had always manifested his dislike of the removal of the House of Lords and of the seclusion by Colonel Pride of members of the Commons in 1648. As for acting the part of *éminence grise* – or, in his own words, 'a dark lantern' – in setting up and managing the Protectorate, there were many witnesses to the contrary. He had been ill at the time and at his worst in December 1653 when Cromwell became Protector. True, Cromwell had summoned him to the 'other House' and made him a Commissioner of the Treasury, but he had 'never intermeddled' nor received a salary besides that due to him as a judge. As soon as the legal term ended he would go to the country and seldom saw Cromwell except to pay his respects at the beginning and end of terms.

He had earned the army's displeasure for his well-known if rather subdued opposition to the Protectorate and he wholly denied having given private advice to Thurloe. Mr Secretary, out of respect to one who had bred him from a youth in his service, used to visit him once or twice a quarter. The final charge, that he had assisted in setting up Richard Cromwell and had endeavored to the last to restore him, was equally false. He had been quite unaware of Oliver's intention to nominate his son to succeed. Oliver's death and Richard's proclamation took place when he was sixty miles from London, and he knew nothing before they were public knowledge. He thought it strange that anybody should think him guilty of so great a folly as to work for Richard's restoration.

Thurloe's evidence supported his former master throughout. It told of their first meeting after the Protectorate had come into existence and of St John's disgust with the Instrument of Government, adding that there was nothing to connect him with the Petition and Advice. Thurloe knew of no communication between St John and Cromwell, for the Chief Justice had refused to meddle in anything except his judicial duties. He had, in fact, been the subject of a complaint to the Council for refusing to proceed on laws made by the Protectorate government. The truth was, Thurloe wrote, that 'some who loved and valued him had something to do to preserve him under that government.' He denied that St John had advised Cromwell about the succession or had known anything about the nomination of Richard. He did not believe that St John had worked for Richard's restoration, for he had often heard him oppose it.[37]

In spite of this spirited defence, the House of Lords voted St John's perpetual incapacity to perform any official function. Now in his sixties, he lingered for a time at Peterborough but in November 1662 decided to live abroad, travelling by way of Le Havre and Basel to Augsburg, where he remained for the rest of his life. Though never a sympathetic character, nor much liked by his contemporaries, St John was a man of strong political and religious views. His utter opposition to the royal powers as exercised by Charles I did not mean that he was opposed to monarchy as an element of the constitution or to its legal framework, a distinction not appreciated by his political opponents. Thurloe owed him much, for he could never have reached the position he acquired in the 1650s without the start in public affairs St John had given him.

It must have come as a relief to Thurloe when on 8 August 1660 the committee of the whole House of Lords considering the Bill of Indemnity resolved to strike out the clause referring to himself.[38] Three weeks later, after a difficult passage through both Houses, the Act of Indemnity and Oblivion received the royal assent. Thirty surviving regicides were excluded and ten of them, including Scot, were executed – hanged, drawn and quartered – in the autumn. Others fled to the Continent or to America. Of these three more were captured in Holland in the following year. Downing, who was officiously responsible for this, came in for a good deal of adverse criticism. All three were put to death, and finally Sir Henry Vane junior – not, in fact, a regicide but a parliamentarian for whom Charles II nurtured a strong dislike – was executed in 1662, meeting his fate, like the others, with dignity and courage.

Thurloe's half-brother Isaac Ewer had, of course, been classed as a regicide because his signature was on the death warrant. Not surprisingly the Commons resolved on 9 June 1660 to except him, and some twenty others who had already died, from the general pardon and oblivion, and to subject them to such pains, penalties and forfeitures as should be thought fit to be inflicted by another Act which they intended to pass. Just over a year later, having heard the evidence against them all, the House resolved that a bill should be introduced for the confiscation of all their estates, real and personal. Thurloe, as sole executor, would have to handle the state's claim on his half-brother's estate.

It cannot have been extensive. Two years earlier Thurloe had told Henry Cromwell that Isaac had been no gainer by the wars and had left 'a much less estate behind him than the world may possibly think'. Neither he nor his family had received any reward for his services and even the arrears due to him were still outstanding.[39] Revenge against the leading regicides took a loathsome form when on 30 January 1661, twelfth anniversary of the king's execution, the bodies of Cromwell, Ireton and John Bradshaw were disinterred at Westminster, hung up to be reviled at Tyburn (near the present Marble Arch) and then flung in a common pit there. It must have been a dreadful day for Thurloe, as for others who had served and respected the dead men.

Thurloe and his friends still excited the suspicions of the new government. At the end of August 1660 Sir Edward Nicholas, former secretary to both Charles I and II and now one of the Secretaries of State, received a report of meetings between Wharton, Thurloe and seven others (including Colonel Clarke and Philip Nye) at the house of Gervase Bennet. In the following January John Upton's house was searched and some armour discovered and confiscated, but Thurloe's goods found there were restored to him.[40] Upton was a merchant who had supplied provisions for the Protectoral navy. In 1650 he had married Jane Lytcott, one of Ann Thurloe's sisters, at St Mary Abchurch in the City. As a kinsman of Thurloe he had provided accommodation addresses and had acted as paymaster for some of Mr Secretary's agents during the Interregnum. For a time he had also been a commissioner of customs.

In 1663 the authorities received a report containing information about several former servants of the Protectorate. Lamenting that St John should have been allowed to depart, the author went on to suggest that Thurloe's house should be searched and his people examined: 'Could he be gained he might yet discover much both old and new.' There is, however, no record of any action being taken. This document, endorsed 'concerning public affairs', seems to have been filed and then forgotten.[41]

By now Thurloe's secretary John Dodington, who had been called to the bar in November 1661, was in trouble at Lincoln's Inn, where he was alleged to have affronted a bencher in his chamber 'with opprobrious and misbecoming language', causing his suspension. It is impossible to say whether this was a political quarrel or had anything to do with Dodington's arrest a fortnight later. On 15 July 1663 he found himself in the Tower, and in the following month he petitioned the king for his examination and liberty. Being innocent of treasonable speeches or practices, he asked for his release and pardon. He had, he wrote, promoted His Majesty's interest and was heartily sorry for any indiscretion he might have committed. It sounds like an apology, prompted by a guilty conscience, about something he preferred to leave unspecified. Evidence in his later career of a quick temper and outbursts of vituperation may be relevant here.[42]

When this petition brought no response, Dodington wrote again on 5 October to Joseph Williamson, a clerk in the office of Sir Henry Bennet, successor to Nicholas as Secretary of State, begging the king's directions either for his release or his maintenance. His family were ill and could not bear the expense. Again, nothing happened. His wife and children were refused access to him without a special order. But early in February 1661 his father, Sir Francis, who had returned from abroad immediately after the Restoration, managed to obtain a warrant to see him. So did his wife Hester.

Early in 1664 the Privy council decided to disperse several prisoners hitherto held in the Tower, and in April Dodington was suddenly taken a close prisoner to Hull. Late one night he was ordered to be ready to go to sea within a few hours. He owed his warder £54 for board and lodging, but met with insults when he raised the matter. The Lieutenant of the Tower, he protested afterwards, was fitter to keep lions and bears than prisoners. At Hull he immediately asked the Governor, Lord Bellasis, formerly of the Sealed Knot, for parole within the town, since the warrant for his detention mentioned no specific crime.[43] Cases of detention without trial had certainly occurred under the Protectorate, but this was a particularly strange affair. Even if it had originated from Dodington's connection with Thurloe, or was prolonged because of it, Thurloe was in no position to help his friend.

Dodington survived and was eventually even able to gain the confidence of the king and the administration. Bennet, by then Lord Arlington, recommended him as secretary to Falconbridge upon his appointment as ambassador to Venice in 1670, belatedly confirming Thurloe's confidence in his abilities. 'He is very capable of serving you,' wrote the Secretary of State, 'being a very good linguist, and besides a very ingenious gentleman of fine parts.' His adventures on the journey across Europe and during his subsequent appointment as resident after the recall of Falconbridge unfortunately lie beyond the scope of this work. Dodington retuned to London at the end of 1672 and died a year later.[44]

Few echoes of Thurloe's former responsibilities can have disturbed his quiet country life with his family at Great Milton, where they were assessed for nine chimneys under the hearth tax of 1666. The family was fortunate to be well away from London, where bubonic plague broke out in April 1665. It was a far more severe epidemic than that of 1646, the last in Thurloe's memory. The worst month was September, when in one week seven thousand out of a total of eight thousand deaths in London were put down to plague. One of its victims was Thomas Simon the engraver, who had made Thurloe's gold medal twelve years before.

Fleeing the plague, the court left Whitehall in July for Hampton Court, moving to Salisbury in August and to Oxford in September, when the long summer drought was broken by rain. Parliament, too, met briefly at Oxford, and Charles remained there until the end of the following January (1666). Doubtless Thurloe, having been left in peace now for several years, felt no alarm at the proximity of his former opponents. Nor is there evidence that he feared a revenge killing by relatives of men he might have helped to bring to the gallows. None of his letters of these years seems to have survived. It may be that, all too aware of the danger of interception and use by the authorities, he took care to confine his writing to family and business matters of a sort unlikely to have been preserved by recipients.

A pleasant family gathering took place at Great Milton on 3 September 1665 when Ann Thurloe's sister Ursula, widow of George Clarke, a London merchant, married into the Upton family. The bridegroom was a second John Upton, nephew of the John who was married to Jane, another Lytcott sister. Upton, a bachelor of twenty-six, must have been a good deal younger than his bride. In the same year the manor of Astwood, near Newport Pagnell in Buckinghamshire, was settled on John Trevor and John Upton in trust for John Thurloe junior, Thurloe's eldest son. It is not clear whose influence lay behind this transaction, though it may have been that of Upton himself.[45]

The war with the Dutch at sea dragged on throughout 1666, and in September came the disastrous Great Fire of London, when almost four hundred acres of the City were devastated. St Paul's, the Royal Exchange and the Customs House were destroyed, together with some fifty other public buildings and eighty-seven churches. Although the lead from the roof of St Paul's ran in molten streams down Ludgate Hill and fire raged up Fleet Street, it did not reach the Temple and all the Inns of Court escaped Damage. In four days over thirteen thousand houses were destroyed, leaving two hundred thousand people homeless, a catastrophe comparable with some of the worst earthquakes in urban areas in modern times.

It is not known whether Thurloe was at Lincoln's Inn to witness the conflagration or the resultant misery. Certainly he was there at about the same time in the following year. The war had come to an end in July 1667 after the final humiliation inflicted by the Dutch fleet in entering the Medway, burning four English warships and towing away the *Royal Charles* as a prize. That led on 26 August to the fall of Hyde, who had been ennobled as Earl of Clarendon at Charles II's coronation in 1661. Forced first to resign and then to leave the country, he ended his life in exile, a fate Thurloe was fortunate to have been spared.

Four days before Clarendon's dismissal Thurloe had put his signature to a document directing the disposal of his real estate. It has not survived, and it is difficult to determine what he still owned. Probably the land he had acquired from fen drainage near Doddington was still in his possession. The manors of Whittlesey St Mary and Whittlesey St Andrew and some of the Wisbech property may have been his by right or had escaped return to the church. Possibly he still held the property settled on him by St John almost thirty years previously. He may well have laid out some of his fortune, too, to purchase land during the good years. Even so, in the mid-1660s his estate must have been much smaller than it had been ten years before at the height of his power, when he owned extensive property within the diocese of Ely and elsewhere in East Anglia.

Thurloe had only just passed his fifty-first birthday. He may have undergone a recurrence of the illness which had laid him so low ten years earlier, or suffered a mild heart attack that had reminded him of his mortality. At all events he must have decided that the time had come to put all his affairs in order. He confirmed the settlement of his real estate when on 28 November he put his hand and seal to his last will and testament.

In days when wills were considered as much religious as legal documents and were dealt with exclusively in ecclesiastical courts, it was customary to insert an introductory passage expressing the testator's confidence in God and in his power of resurrection. Whereas with some it would consist merely of a conventional piece of piety inserted by the clerk who drew up the will, it is clear that in Thurloe's case it was an accurate reflection of his personal religious convictions. He opened by expressing

> entire submission to his will who is the Sovereign Lord of all things and hath the absolute disposition of me, mine and all creation, be-

seeching him to approve and confirm what I do and be gracious to and bless the wife and children which he hath given me, . . . I do in all humble confidence walk and cast upon him to be their God and the God of theirs for ever.

He went on to make provision for payment out of his real estate of any remaining dues once his funeral expenses and other debts had been met from his personal estate. He hoped that the funeral expenses would be very little, 'being content to stay for the honour of my body until the resurrection when I believe it shall be raised incorruptible and made glorious. . . .' He left his wife Ann her wearing jewels, which she had indeed purchased by her good housewifery, and such parts of his household stuff during her widowhood as she should please to make use of. His eldest son John was to have all his books except those which Ann might reserve for her own use and bestow on the rest of their children. He left £100 to his youngest son Nicholas, who received less than his brothers in the distribution of property.

Widowhoods were often short in the seventeenth century. Thurloe therefore made provision for the disposal of his household stuff after Ann's death or remarriage. It was to be used to raise money for apprenticing those of his three younger sons who were not placed in his lifetime. That being done, the remainder was to be divided between his two daughters Mary and Ann towards their portions payable on the twenty-first birthday of each or on the day of marriage if earlier. They, too, had been left shares of the property. If one of them were to die before inheriting, the surviving daughter was to have both portions; if both died, their shares were to be divided between their younger brothers still alive. Thurloe's eldest son, who already owned Astwood on trust, would receive the largest share of the property, but there was enough to allow each of the other five surviving children a small portion. His 'dear wife' was made sole executrix, and he appointed two overseers – his wife's brother-in-law, John Upton, and another kinsman. They were earnestly entreated to assist and counsel his wife and were each left forty shillings with which to buy mourning rings, a common practice in wills of this period.[46]

Some time earlier Whitelock had tried to interest Thurloe in the purchase of one of three adjoining properties in his possession on the north bank of the Thames between Henley and Marlow. Thurloe, however, had rejected the approach, asserting that the place was 'too great for him'. Undaunted, in December 1667 Whitelock started negotiations to sell him a farm near Hungerford, but little or no progress can have been made, for Thurloe was shortly afterwards taken ill once more.[47]

Back at Lincoln's Inn in January 1668, Thurloe suffered what in contemporary phraseology was called 'a great fit of the stone'. He endured retention of his urine for fifty hours, feeling the sentence of death on himself, his life being despaired of by his friends and physicians. But then, in excruciating pain, he passed the stone and recovered.

In the middle of February he gave his friend Wharton and a doctor of physic an account of his terrible experience. When the doctor had left them the two friends sat chatting, 'most about the things of God and his people'. As they were about to part Wharton told him where he meant to be on the following Sunday, and asked if he would be there, too. Thurloe mentioned the name of a clergyman, and said that if he were preaching and breaking bread, then 'I intend to be with him, for he presseth hard after nearer communion with God and helps others much therein.' No doubt for good reason at this time of religious intolerance Wharton does not identify the man in his account of the conversation, referring to him only as 'such an one'. As he said goodbye to his friend, Thurloe told him that he would not for anything have been without this late providence. 'I know the worst of death,' he said, 'and it is nothing for me to die.'

A week later he was dead. On 21 February he had appeared to be in his normal moderate state of health, but took a laxative in the morning. At three o'clock he dined with his ordinary appetite, sitting with another old friend, Colonel Philip Jones. When the meal was over he asked Jones to withdraw for a while because the medicine was having its desired effect. 'The occasion being over,' Wharton recorded

> he asked the colonel to come in again and walking with him towards the window, the colonel observed him to reel as if he were ready to fall and he caught hold of him to support him, but he never spake word and immediately died.[48]

It must have been a massive heart attack, attributable perhaps to the immense stresses of his years in office between 1652 and 1660. He was still only fifty-one years of age.

Thurloe was buried under the chapel of the Inn of Court in which he had spent so much of his adulthood. An inscription on the stone slab over his grave records that there lies the Secretary of State to the Protector Oliver Cromwell and a member of the honourable Society of Lincoln's Inn.

Thurloe's name today evokes little if any memory of the Secretary of State of the Protectorate. To those who know London it suggests a connection with the Square, Place and Street so called in South Kensington. As it happens there is a connection, though more remote than the seemingly obvious one, for John Thurloe himself never lived in Kensington.

Thurloe's younger daughter Ann, not ten years old when her father died, married in August 1683 Francis Brace, a widower of Bedford. The ceremony took place at St Benet's, Paul's Wharf, a church often chosen by couples who had obtained their license at the neighbouring faculty office. Although the bride was fully of age, the licence records that her mother had given her consent to the match. The younger of the two sons of this marriage, named John Thurloe Brace, married in 1713 as his second wife Anna Maria Browne, who owned over forty-two acres in sixteen holdings of tenements and fields in Kensington. It was from this valuable property that the Thurloe estate in South Kensington subsequently developed. Brace's great-grandson, John Alexander, began building there in 1826. It is appropriate that it should adjoin Cromwell Road and Cromwell Place, which may have taken their names from Cromwell House, Henry's former home at Hale House on the site now occupied by the Victoria and Albert Museum. Cromwell Road was driven through its garden in 1852.[49]

John Thurloe junior was admitted to Isaac Ewer's chamber – formerly his father's – at Lincoln's Inn in 1670 and was called to the bar on 9 May 1672 'on receiving sacrament'. Eleven days later he was ordered to pay his dues and receive the sacrament at the first opportunity in the ensuing term on pain of losing his call. This hints at a residual opposition on his part to the prayer book. It seems that Ewer and his cousin remained in ignorance of the hoard of documents stowed away in the roof of the garret. After their discovery in the reign of William and Mary and the subsequent decision to publish a selection, the Lincoln's Inn Society subscribed five guineas 'for the large paper [edition] of Mr Thurloe's collection of state papers'.[50]

Before that, in 1674, John took possession of the manor of Astwood in Buckinghamshire and gave a home there to his widowed mother. He died a bachelor at Amesbury in Wiltshire on 29 March 1682 and in the following year his mother, then sixty-three, caused a memorial inscription to be put up on the wall of the church there. He had given up his chamber at Lincoln's Inn in November 1678 and the little garret chamber above it some nine months before he died. The manor of Astwood passed to his sister Ann Brace, who settled it on her children in 1713. It was eventually sold by her son John Thurloe Brace in 1735.[51]

It appears that none of Thurloe's sons had male issue to carry on the name. His earliest biographer, Thomas Birch, writing in the early 1740s, confirms the death of John, the eldest, at Amesbury. He goes on to state that Oliver, the second son, married but died childless. Thomas, the third, died as Governor of James Island in the Gambia; Nicholas, the youngest, went to sea and was known to be still alive in 1678. Thurloe's elder daughter Mary married Thomas Ligoe of Burcott, Buckinghamshire. They produced a son and a daughter who respectively married a sister and brother named Hamilton.

Thurloe's executor John Upton lived until 1689. His second wife Jane, Thurloe's sister-in-law, died in August 1672 and Upton took a third wife a year later. In his will he left £10 each for mourning to Giles Lytcott, Ann Thurloe and Ursula Upton, brother and sisters of his second wife. When Ursula died in 1710 she remembered in her will her two Thurloe nieces, Mary Ligoe and Ann Brace.[52]

The name of Thurloe lived on for a time in his charity in the town of Wisbech. Only one of the original trustees survived the 1660s but the fund was still operating in 1822, when accumulated interest of £37 10s. was added to increase the fees for apprentices. His mansion, admired by Pepys in 1663, was offered to Wisbech Grammar School in 1811. The burgesses, hoping to acquire it later at a lower price, rejected the offer, only to see the place completely demolished five years later.[53]

Thus Thurloe passed out of the public memory along with so many other prominent men of the Interregnum. Only Oliver Cromwell himself, who had influenced the affairs of his country for many years and dominated them during the closing period of his life, has continued to attract popular attention, to be praised and reviled but never ignored by succeeding generations. John Thurloe deserves to be remembered as one who served him well and made a vital contribution to his government quite unsurpassed by any of his contemporaries.

9

CONCLUSION

My body and soul glorified shall be for ever with the Lord, in the hope and expectation whereof I am waiting until my change comes (John Thurloe)

In the relatively short period between 29 March 1652 and 15 May 1660 Thurloe, as Secretary to the Council of State and later as Secretary of State and a Councillor in his own right, had risen to be one of the most powerful men in the country, only to fall abruptly, to be restored briefly and, like many another man of prominence in the sixteenth and seventeenth centuries, to end with a spell in the Tower and an obscure enforced retirement. For over five years he had borne single-handed, and in spite of recurring illness, the burden of the multiple duties of Secretary of State, which in that era were usually shared between two office-holders. This arrangement was criticized because his absences inevitably slowed or even halted the machinery of government. Yet it does not appear to have occurred to Cromwell to appoint a second Secretary to share the workload and to cover absences caused by leave and sickness. He preferred to await the return to duty of the man he liked and trusted, the dependable and indispensable John Thurloe.

It is, perhaps, understandable that Thurloe has been largely forgotten in the centuries since his death, for his strength lay in his ability to act behind the scenes, ready with a prompt proposal but content to let others take the centre of the stage. It was not that he was unknown; his name was at least as familiar during his years in office as were those of Francis Walsingham and Robert Cecil, two of his eminent predecessors, in theirs. It was his concern for the constitution, his reluctance to formulate policy without the backing of parliament or Council, and his energy in forwarding the business devolved upon him by others that made him so invaluable. After examining and evaluating the evidence it may now be possible to give Thurloe greater credit for his political and parliamentary performance than that usually accorded by historians and to ascribe to him some responsibility for much of the initiation as well as the execution of foreign policy. He was certainly not timid in his conduct of intelligence operations and showed considerable initiative in seeking and developing new techniques and sources.

Thurloe played his part in the lasting achievement of the Common-wealth and Protectorate: the capture and plantation of Jamaica, the sustenance of the West Indian and New England colonies, the vast increase of overseas trade under the protection of the Navigation Act, the building, equipping and manning of a powerful fleet and its penetra-tion of the Mediterranean theatre.

As Secretary of State Thurloe gave unreserved loyalty to Oliver Crom-well, steadfastly supporting his decisions and backing his policies, even if on occasion he deplored both the Protector's failure to act as he himself saw fit and his deference to the advice of others. This view, expressed in a letter of 13 July 1658,[1] suggests that Thurloe was not so much an echo of his master's voice as someone who genuinely shared the ideas of the Protector on most questions of policy at home and abroad. Thus he, too, supported the appointment of the major-generals and sought to con-tinue their rule in the face of sharp and vociferous opposition. Equally, he based his approach to foreign policy in Europe on the advancement of the Protestant cause at the expense of Spain and the Austrian em-peror, and further afield on the growth of trade and commerce. Under-lining his regard for Oliver Cromwell, Thurloe bestowed support and friendship on his sons Richard and Henry and worked hard for the continuation of Cromwellian policies during Richard's short and largely ineffective Protectorship. The Restoration drove them apart – Richard into exile, as much to avoid his creditors (for his debts were never completely paid by 'the state') as in fear of reprisals, while Henry and Thurloe both enjoyed a peaceable retirement.

Like other men of his time, Thurloe witnessed the reversal of the revolutionary policies in church and state pursued between 1640 and 1660 and their replacement by measures more like those that had pre-vailed in earlier generations. More personally, it was his misfortune to see the triumph of the royalist cause that he had sought for so long to penetrate and undermine. Hyde's letter to Grenville stating that he had received 'very frank overtures' from Thurloe is the only evidence of his submission, and it suggests that love of his work and a reluctance to hand over half-completed and complex negotiations to others less experienced were the motives that induced him to offer his services to the king. It is also possible that – like Monck, Montagu and other leading men who had served the Protectorate – he had by then concluded that restoration of the monarchy was the only means of avoiding anarchy and securing stable government for the whole British Isles. The administration of Charles II was manifestly established by the will of a freely elected parliament. This alone was perhaps sufficient to induce him to give it his allegiance, even if he retained reservations about according it his respect.

Nevertheless an untrammelled House of Commons seemingly did not rank high in Thurloe's estimation. He rejoiced that the institution of the Protectorate would bring arbitrary government to an end, preferring the judgement of a single person to that of a House which later showed itself capable of treating James Nayler in so arrogant and inhuman a fashion. Again, he welcomed the return of an upper chamber of nominated members as a check on the uncertain excesses to be feared from the elected representatives of 'the people'. Both views suggest that Thurloe, like his mentors St John and Cromwell, had not become a convinced republican. All three were implacably opposed to the theory of divine right as advanced by Charles I, and this antipathy led them by extension to feelings of revulsion for the whole House of Stuart. It was all very well for republicans to speak of power being derived from the people and expressed by their elected representatives in the House of Commons, but both Cromwell and Thurloe had seen the anarchical tendencies of a single House. For this reason neither Cromwell nor Thurloe was against government by a strong leader, a single person, even if he lacked a kingly title.

Here lies the fundamental paradox in the ideas of government held by both men. Although both rejoiced at the fall of the Stuart monarchy, neither was in principle opposed to monarchical government or, indeed, authoritarian rule. When Thurloe called for a godly magistracy he was chiefly concerned for the godliness of the chief magistrate, and saw what he sought in the character of Cromwell. As Sir Charles Firth observed, Cromwell believed in government *for* the people and not *by* the people, giving them what was good for them, not what pleased them.[2] St John, on the other hand, deplored Cromwell's and the army's domination of the political scene and was much more inclined towards the maintenance of the ancient constitution than to the introduction of experimental substitutes.

Because in his active years Thurloe represented the executive arm of government, there has been a tendency among critics to blame him for the oppressive measures introduced by the Protector or Council. He certainly seems to have been personally untroubled by the savagery of sentences passed on those found guilty of breaking the law. The fact that most punishments were in line with precedent and with general European practice salved his conscience on that score. Again, he was content in the early days of the Protectorate to avoid the fallibility of juries by welcoming the use of a High Court of Justice, though by June 1658 he was prepared to stand up to Cromwell by arguing for the trial of conspirators by the common law in the Upper Bench.

At all times he was in favour of preventive detention when a near certainty of guilt was present but no crime could be proved. Cromwell's government was subject to the fear of counter-revolution innate in all revolutionary regimes, but Thurloe's part in suppression was confined to censorship of all contrary opinion: through a monopoly on the dissemination of news; the provision of warrants on the Protector's or Council's authority for detention, banishment or transportation of suspects; and forwarding to the executive the fruits of his highly successful intelligence operations.

Mention has been made of adverse criticism of the immense sums of money supposedly spent on Thurloe's intelligence activities. In February 1668, a week before Thurloe's death, Pepys recorded that intelligence had been discussed in the House in the course of an enquiry into the miscarriage of the second Dutch War. Mr Secretary Morrice said that he was allowed £700 a year, whereas in Cromwell's time the allowance had been £70,000. Another member had confirmed this and added that thereby Cromwell carried the key to all the secrets of the princes of Europe at his girdle. But the surviving receipts for Thurloe's expenditure show that the figure of £70,000 was a gross exaggeration; the real total paid from the Council's contingency fund seems to have been between £1,200 and £2,000 a year, though Thurloe may have received additional funds from other sources.

He was certainly prepared to pay handsomely for intelligence from a well-placed agent. In March and April 1658 he pressed Downing in three successive letters to recruit sources at the Spanish court in Flanders and amongst Charles Stuart's circle. He mentioned then that he was prepared to pay up to £1,000 for a good one.[3] It is interesting that the statement made in parliament in 1668 included the very same metaphor that Thurloe himself had employed to describe the value to England of the possession of Mardyke and Dunkirk: 'By having these places of strength in his hand,' he had written, '[Cromwell] carried at his girdle the keys of a door to the Continent.' Now Cromwell was being credited with having carried – thanks to Thurloe – the keys to the secret cabinets of European rulers as well.

The intelligence Thurloe gathered suffered the defects of all information derived from human sources: some agents embroidered their reports to provide news that they assumed would be welcome, whilst others, pretending to have access to sensitive information, resorted to invention to keep themselves in business and in funds. None the less, his use of the penetration agent made it almost impossible for any faction to bring off a successful *coup* against the government.

A paper prepared for William Bridgeman, clerk to the Privy Council in the reign of James II, recommended reviving Thurloe's intelligence methods, including 'gaining over' (the modern term is 'turning') two or three of the principal members of every subversive movement; each would disclose the group's private consultations, their secret reports acting as checks one on another. Thus it would be possible 'to crush all their designs in the egg' and hinder them from ever coming to maturity, unless it was desired to permit them to develop so as to obtain more certain evidence for conviction.

The paper cited the cases of Cokayne, who with Goodwin and Nye had kept Thurloe secretly informed of all the consultations of his independent brethren and had a salary of £500 a year for his pains, and of Willys, who betrayed the counsels and undertakings of the royalists. Thus, by ploughing with their own heifers – as the writer picturesquely put it – Cromwell was able to frustrate those who had designs against him. The writer confessed that such methods were difficult, complex and costly, but concluded that the expenditure would be justified if it preserved the king and his government.[4]

Thurloe only occasionally resorted to the more controversial practice of employing *agents provocateurs*. The most notorious case, that of Sir Henry Slingsby in June 1658, caused Attorney-Generl Prideaux to express his sorrow that people should be thus seduced by men who brought them to the gallows and then laughed at them. It is quite clear, however, that the perpetrator of this deception acted without any authority.[5]

Thurloe's best, most reliable and most prolific source of intelligence information was provided at negligible expense by the interception of correspondence. The clandestine examination of the post, developed by Morland under his direction, was a most significant advance. The post, says the descriptive account of Thurloe's management of intelligence quoted above, conveyed all the poisonous distempers of the City into the whole kingdom. Even when it was well known that mail was being intercepted, letters of consequence were seen every post night. The surviving records demonstrate that letters of ambassadors and public ministers of foreign powers were opened and copied on a regular basis.

The practice gave rise to 'great mutterings and many complaints made', but these were disregarded. Some correspondents resorted to the use of foot posts and ordinary carriers in an attempt to outwit the authorities. In times of stress two or three messengers of the Council were sent to seize what letters they could find. The writer admitted that innocent correspondence was not returned on such occasions, so that many financial and legal documents were lost 'to the undoing of divers poor people (as I well remember)'.[6] It is impossible to excuse such highhandedness.

Much information was also gained from the interrogation or 'examination' of suspects. This seems to have been conducted in a most civilized manner. Barkstead, a traditional military man in charge at the Tower, and justices of the peace in the provinces, may have been somewhat more frightening to prisoners than Thurloe and the clerks who assisted him in this unlikely combination of roles. Threats there may have been, inducements there certainly were, but apparently at no time was torture used. In this respect the Saints lived up to their name. Although some writers have expressed surprise at the readiness of conspirators under interrogation to betray their fellows, allowance must be made for the religious climate of the times. Suspects were examined on oath; although some were strong enough to remain silent, it was morally unthinkable for many of them to commit perjury.

Finally there was Thurloe's wide circle of informants, not only abroad, but (as Bridgeman was told) in every city and town of note. He also maintained correspondence with the sheriffs, justices and the major-generals when they were in office. He pressed them very much in Cromwell's name, the writer averred, and in response they were glad to gratify both Cromwell and Thurloe.[7] The information derived from these far-flung sources seldom needed to be kept secret and most could be passed to Marchamont Needham for use as news and propaganda in his weekly publications. The rest was privately disseminated as required in Thurloe's letters to his correspondents. Their relief at seeing his hand again, after one or other of his bouts of sickness, was freely expressed by the regular recipients. Although many agents and informants complained of his failure to acknowledge or reply to their letters, the wonder is that he found time to write as much as he did. Letters to and from his agents abroad were invariably routed through cover addresses. Morland had to keep Dorislaus informed of the addresses in current use so that letters containing intelligence reports or instructions were recognized for what they were.

Thurloe was not entirely successful in protecting government secrets. A proportion of his political and intelligence correspondence was intercepted on the Continent by agents both of Charles Stuart and of foreign powers. Pell was sceptical when informed that a courier's horse carrying the mail from England had fallen into the Rhône near Lyons, remarking that the French received their letters unharmed. The amount of Thurloe's correspondence in Hyde's and Ormonde's papers reveals the degree to which they, too, were aware of their opponents' affairs through intercepted letters.

For his part Thurloe seems to have shown a somewhat reckless disregard for the dangers of interception. He failed to give Whitelock a cypher before he left for Sweden, and subsequently surprised the ambassador by entrusting to Swedish hands the letter containing the key. While Whitelock was at the Swedish court Thurloe was procuring, from one of his paid sources overseas, copies of reports from the Dutch representative there to his superiors at The Hague. These he sent on to

Whitelock as enclosures to his weekly letters, thus endangering his source while saving the time it would have taken to produce a suitably edited and disguised version. Yet in spite of Morland's defection and other leaks from clerks in the Secretary's office, the government's reputation for security remained high during Thurloe's Secretaryship. 'There is no government on earth', the Venetian envoy declared in November 1655, 'which divulges its affairs less than England.'[8]

All in all, it is impossible to escape the conclusion that Thurloe was an admirable controller of intelligence activities, given seventeenth-century conditions. He broke new ground with his insistence on the acquisition of penetration agents, his development of the clandestine examination of correspondence and his successful use of interrogation without recourse to torture. He was also exemplary in his dissemination of information to those who needed it or were glad to have it in order to refute rumour. In these respects his reputation is well founded.

Thurloe's network of agents and informants on the continent of Europe enabled him to guide English foreign policy by taking advantage of his extensive knowledge of events and likely developments. The fact that he earned the admiration of an international statesman of the stature of Mazarin speaks for itself. His relations with foreign ambassadors and residents seem to have been friendly and based on mutual respect and a genial tolerance of differing points of view. These men were often exasperated by his delay in replying to their enquiries and protests, but even when complaining they were careful to emphasize their personal friendship.[9] During the Protectorate delay was inevitable. Its system required papers first to be shown to the Protector, then discussed by the Council and one or more committees before the agreed reply or decision was returned to the Protector for approval and signature. If Bordeaux is to be believed, Thurloe tended to underestimate the time required by this process and promised more than he was able to deliver.

In spite of all his meetings and negotiations with Nieuport, it was never possible to agree on terms for an Anglo–Dutch maritime treaty without prejudice to English trading interests. Trade, he had written, was the great interest of the United Provinces; all their treaties were designed to give liberty to commerce, navigation and fishery. Nieuport admitted as much to Evelyn when he entertained him to dinner in November 1659. Indeed, he went further: 'the Dutch mind only their profit', he declared.

Throughout the years of the Protectorate the Venetian representatives in London were critical of the overcentralization of foreign affairs in the hands of a single Secretary of State who was often inaccessible or overwhelmed by the mass of business and who, like most of the members of

the government, was sometimes rather negligent towards – and so ignorant of – aspects of European affairs. One can readily appreciate that
Thurloe, with so many pressing problems nearer home, gave a low
priority to business with Venice, yet both he and Cromwell were better
informed than most Englishmen on all that went on in Europe. Others
found Thurloe hard to interview on occasion, as when Nieuport pleaded
for but half of a quarter of an hour of his time in the first fortnight of
Richard's Protectorate.[10]

Thurloe shared Cromwell's enthusiasm for the Protestant cause in
Europe and may have been in sufficient health in January 1668, just
before his death, to have rejoiced at the conclusion of a triple alliance of
the three northern Protestant powers – England, Sweden and the
United Provinces – negotiated by Arlington, one of the cabal of five
ministers then overseeing the administration. Bulstrode Whitelock,
whose *Memorials of English Affairs* were published in 1682, wrote that
'even secretaries of state, we know, are not always of the cabal, nor their
intelligence the most infallible.' It was certainly true that Thurloe,
though frequently consulted, was sometimes excluded from important
discussions of policy by Oliver, though seldom if ever by Richard.

The Protestant cause was not the only mainspring of English foreign
policy during the 1650s. Just as important were determined moves
towards the advancement and protection of national trading interests.
At the same time duties imposed on imported goods were calculated as
much to give protection to home industry as for production of revenue.
This important development, which carried with it a recognition of the
value of the fleet, dates from this period and its formulation and execution may owe as much to Secretary Thurloe as to Protector Cromwell.
There is some evidence that Thurloe's strategic handling of the fleet was
both sound and of long-lasting importance.

In spite of Thurloe's resolute opposition to cavaliers, Anabaptists and
any others who threatened the security of the government he served, he
shared with Cromwell a desire for national unity and mutual toleration
between differing groups within the state. This was very clearly demonstrated in a letter he wrote to Henry Cromwell after the capture of
Dunkirk. Having ascribed the military success to the hand of God, he
went on:

> The honour of these victories certainly belongs to the English nation
> and not to any party therein; and God favours therein the whole land,
> and would have men do so too. . . . We must not narrow that interest
> and fix it either upon men only of my opinion, or of our particular
> way, but make it comprehensive of all the saints; yea, do good, justice
> and right to all; and when things come to be managed with this spirit, I
> shall look for settlement, and a blessing with it, and not before; least of

all, whilst wrath and discontent steer affairs, which I am sure never yet wrought the righteousness of God, nor never will.[11]

Here surely is the real John Thurloe, a spokesman for all who yearned for an end to party faction and strife, so that the nation could work as one so that each citizen could pursue his personal bent in an atmosphere of freedom and justice for all. This was the kind of society he had advocated when he put words into the mouth of Richard Cromwell: a society governed liberally with liberty of conscience, a godly magistracy and ministry, and the army in the hands of godly men. Thurloe seems to have forgotten that something like that had already been tried, with unpromising results. At the end of the long and detailed negotiations between Cromwell and parliament culminating in the refusal of the crown, when William Pierrepont and Edward Montagu declared that they would never trust politics again, Thurloe told Sir Francis Russell that he now saw that 'nothing is so considerable in any business as simplicity'.[12] But parliamentary faction and religious intolerance made his simple, ideal state unobtainable in practice.

Thurloe lived to witness parliament's eventual rejection of a written constitution and the restoration, after eleven years of experimentation with other forms, of the traditional unwritten constitution of king, Lords and Commons. Several years before, in 1656, the younger Sir Henry Vane had issued a pamphlet advocating a republican form of government with a president, senate and house of representatives, somewhat similar to the one adopted by the United States of America over a century later. Commenting on Vane's scheme at the time, Thurloe remarked that it had at first been applauded, but was later thought impracticable.[13] It was never tried in England, and the systems introduced under the Instrument of Government and the later Humble Petition and Advice both foundered on the jealousy of the House of Commons of its own powers and on the reluctance of the army to surrender the ascendancy it had acquired through victory in the civil wars.

Thurloe must have been shocked by the manifest licentiousness and occasional intolerance and cruelty of the court of Charles II, but he would probably have felt that the will of God was being carried forward in the 1660s just as surely as it had been in the 1650s. He shared Cromwell's advocacy of measures designed to improve religious toleration. Whilst he was in office passions were too strong to countenance any idea of a compromise with prelacy, yet he was to live to see the episcopate ascendant and the Book of Common Prayer accepted and in use in the parishes. Division and dissent remained, but a marked reluctance on the part of some justices to enforce the Act of Uniformity allowed Nonconformity to flourish in many places unchecked, itself a significant legacy of Cromwell's efforts to secure toleration for all shades of Protestant thought and practice.

At the same time – and despite Charles II's preferences – there was no diminution in the national fear and hatred of popery. When Thurloe wrote of Spain in 1656 as 'the most potent and cruellest enemy in the world against the church of Christ', and again in 1657 of the Spaniards as 'the greatest enemies Jesus Christ hath in this world', he was only giving expression to a view of Roman Catholicism and its adherents typical of his times.[14]

Thurloe's letters and his will reveal a personal faith rooted in the love and wisdom of an all-seeing God and in the certainty of a glorious resurrection. He saw the hand of Divine Providence in all the successes, political and military, of the governments he served. When there were setbacks they were ascribed, by others as well as Thurloe, to a temporary withdrawal of God's favour. For example, Reynolds's drowning and the outbreak of disease amongst the English army at Mardyke were described in a letter which came into Thurloe's hand as 'sufficient passages that God will not bless their actions'.

He must have been far from content with the High-Church reaction dominating the Restoration church settlement. He had seen his friend Dean Harry leave the Church of England rather than conform, and there is evidence that he himself remained an Independent. With Whitelock and Wolseley, he attended a conventicle in May 1667 to hear Dr John Owen preach at the house of Whitelock's brother-in-law. Owen, who had been with Cromwell in Ireland and Scotland and been vice-chancellor at Oxford during the Protectorate, was an exact contemporary of Thurloe and remained one of the most eminent Puritan divines, publishing anonymously a string of tracts during the 1660s. Wharton's account of their final discussion of religion strongly suggests that Thurloe did not attend services of the established church when it was possible to find something more in line with his own brand of Protestantism.[15]

Thurloe walked the earth in a society seething with philosophical and scientific as well as religious ideas. The reference to books in his will and his gift to Wisbech Library show that he was something of a collector, and presumably therefore a reader, of the literary output of the times. Much of the political thought of the era was disseminated in pamphlets which had come his way as a matter of course during his active career, but there is no eviddence about his general reading during his retirement. It has never been suggested that Thurloe aspired to great intellectual heights – not for him a fellowship of the newly formed Royal Society, which attracted men of academic distinction such as Dr John Wallis, Dr John Wilkins and others whom the Secretary may once have known. No doubt he had been proud to have been elected to parliament to represent one of the two great English universities, and to have been chancellor of a Scottish seat of learning, but he must always have been conscious of his lack of academic training outside the practice of the law.

Although Thurloe accepted presents from his colleagues and corres-pondents, the surviving evidence suggests that he resisted all temptations to corruption. Even a political opponent gave him credit for his rectitude. Writing in March 1659 as events moved towards the collapse of the Protectorate, Broderick drew attention to the misbehaviour of Philip Jones and Barkstead, both of whom had amassed personal fortunes, but rejoiced that Secretary Thurloe

> dares boldly defy them, having taken no man's money, invaded no man's privilege, nor abused his own authority, which is and merits to be great, the weight of all foreign and almost all domestic affairs lying on him. . . . And though intelligences have been infinitely chargeable, yet without it, into whose hands had this nation fallen?. [16]

This is a remarkable tribute, all the more telling because it comes from the pen of one so vigorously opposed to all that Thurloe stood for. Broderick gives him a clean bill for resistance to both the main temptations of his office – corruption by money and by the abuse of power itself. The passage was written soon after the attempt by some members of parliament to lay at Thurloe's door responsibility for Overton's imprisonment without trial and the exile of Rowland Thomas to slavery in Barbados. It shows that Broderick had been convinced by Thurloe's strenuous self-defence.

None the less the temptations of his office must have been great. At one point the state papers contain a request to Thurloe to indulge in a piece of international dishonesty by providing antedated letters of marque to an English ship which had taken a valuable French prize in Mediterranean waters without any kind of authority. Unfortunately his response to this approach is missing, but on the basis of his moral character and respect for the law he may perhaps be given the benefit of the doubt.[17]

From what little we know of it, Thurloe's family life seems to have been simple, loving and happy. There were many periods when he was working sixteen hours or more a day, but there were also quieter times when he would have been able to devote more attention to his wife and children. Far too little is known of Ann Thurloe. She must have been strong and healthy to have borne and reared a large family, though her domestic responsibilities were eased by the presence of servants to sweep, wash, scour, cook and serve. More important, perhaps, it was Ann who nursed her husband through his dangerous illnesses. The fact

that she was not with him at the end was due to his practice of periodically returning to Lincoln's Inn – not, as has been suggested, for the
duration of the legal terms, when Isaac Ewer would have been using the
chamber, but rather during the vacation intervals. On this final occasion
his illness must have prevented his return to the country at the start of
the Hilary term.

Thurloe lived in an age and in a society which, partly because of the
widespread opportunities for patronage and nepotism, attached much
importance to family connections. In a manner difficult for the modern
English man or woman to appreciate, people were well informed not
only about their own families but also about the cross-connections by
marriage between those of a wide circle of distant relatives, as well as
friends from particular neighbourhoods or of like political or religious
persuasions. As this account has shown, Thurloe was devotedly loyal to
his Ewer half-brothers and their families, as well as to many relatives by
his two marriages and to the kin of his benefactors St John and Cromwell.

Thurloe had been extremely fortunate to have attracted at an early age
the attention of so influential a patron as Oliver St John. His own origins
would have been insufficient to provide him with anything more than a
competent living had he not acquired this valuable patronage. What is
impressive is the manner in which Thurloe, having acquired this assistance, then made the most of the opportunities thus offered him: to
study law at Furnival's Inn and later to practise it at Lincoln's Inn; to
serve the parliamentary commissioners at Uxbridge as a painstaking and
reliable secretary; to work unstintingly for the ambassadors at The
Hague and to represent them convincingly when reporting to the Council of State. Thus by a fortunate turn of fate he became the Council's
Secretary at a time when his qualities of clear thought and energetic
action were much needed, and was quickly able to attract the eye of Lord
General Cromwell as he had earlier impressed St John.

When Cromwell became Protector and revived the office of Secretary
of State it was natural for him to offer it to the man occupying its nearest
equivalent post, and again Thurloe was not slow to show his appreciation
in the sort of loyal service that enhanced his own power and influence.
Finally his friendship with George Monck, nurtured largely through
correspondence during the general's long spell in command in Scotland,
secured for him not only a return to office in the closing months of the
Interregnum, but also a recommendation to the new royal ruler that
permitted him to preserve both his head and his liberty.

It was stated by a contemporary foreign observer, the Venetian resident, that Thurloe had no friends,[18] an allegation often repeated,

though his friendship with Henry Cromwell was too well known to be ignored. In fact, it is plainly nonsense to suggest that he had no others. All his correspondence reveals the amicable understanding that developed naturally between him and the overseas representatives of the state, both civil and military. His periodic visits to Lincoln's Inn during his retirement are unlikely to have been spent in private legal work or to have been arranged for that purpose. On the contrary, they provided opportunities for renewing contact with his friends, as Philip Wharton's sensitive account of his last few weeks makes clear. Moreover, it is important not to read the Venetian's observation out of context, for it was written in summer 1659, a few weeks after Thurloe's dismissal and the recall of the Rump. When considering a bill of indemnity, some Rumpers wished to extend its provisions to all who had supported the Cromwells, father and son, while others pressed to except Thurloe, Barkstead and a few more. It is not surprising that Thurloe, committed as he had been to wholehearted and prominent support of the Cromwells, found little backing then among members of the Rump, yet in the changed circumstances of February 1660 they voted by a sizeable majority in favour of his recall.

There is insufficient evidence to form a judgment on the nature of Thurloe's recurring illnesses. He became a person of note when he was already in his mid-thirties, and nothing is known of his health record up to that time. Perhaps he never enjoyed prolonged well-being. He had been brought up in a county where, to quote the contemporary poet Edmund Waller, 'hasty death and pining sickness reigns'. It is possible that it was this Essex sickness which dogged him throughout his life.

It has been suggested that his illness was mental or psychological rather than physical in origin and was provoked by the strain of too much work and too many seemingly insoluble problems.[19]

Admittedly the stress of office cannot have helped what seems to have been a delicate constitution, but contemporary references to fever, ague and raving fits do not accord with nervous breakdown or exhaustion. The details of his death, recorded by Wharton on the testimony of Philip Jones, the only person present, point to a coronary thrombosis or possibly an apoplectic stroke, neither a surprising fate for one who had been subject to the pressures of high office for such a long period.

In an age when the tenure of any office under the crown or the republic was looked upon by many as personal service to the monarch or Protector, by others as a licence to extract fees and by a few as a right to an income in return for minimal exertion, Thurloe saw his role quite plainly as service to the public and to the nation as a whole. His achievement lay in his devotion to his duty to God and Man as he saw it, in his single-minded pursuit of efficiency in administration and of godliness in living. There was nothing hypocritical about the expressed desire of the Puritan leaders to carry out the will of God. Thurloe could lay down his burden in the knowledge that he had done his very best for God, his nation and his family.

Abbreviations Used in Notes and Bibliography

Locations

BL	British Library
Bod	Bodleian Library
CCRO	Cambridgeshire County Record Office
ECRO	Essex County Record Office
GLRO	Greater London Record Office
LPL	Lambeth Palace Library
PRO	Public Record Office

Sources

Add	Additional manuscripts
Admissions	*Lincoln's Inn Admissions*
app	appendix
CCC	*Calendar of Committee for Compounding*
CCSP	*Calendar of Clarendon State Papers*
CJ	*Commons Journals*
CSP	Clarendon State Papers
CSPD	*Calendar of State Papers Domestic*
CSPV	*Calendar of State Papers Venetian*
EHR	*English Historical Review*
f.	folio
fn	footnote
HMC	*Historical Manuscripts Commission*
LJ	*Lords Journals*
MSS	Manuscripts
PCC	Prerogative Court of Canterbury
Rawl	Rawlinson
RSLI	Records of the Society of Lincoln's Inn
TSP	*Thurloe State Papers*
VCH	*Victoria County History*

Books fully described in the bibliography are referred to in abbreviated form in the Notes. Places of publication are given only for works published outside the United Kingdom.

NOTES

Introduction

1. Bod: Rawl MSS C989, f. 169.
2. P.M. Handover: *The Second Cecil 1563–1604* (1959) 138.
3. Evans 337.
4. Bischoffshausen: introductory quotation 6; Aylmer 167, 258; Trevor-Roper in Roots: *Cromwell: A Profile*, 132fn; Davies 29.
5. Woolrych: *Commonwealth to Protectorate*, 378.

1 A Long Apprenticeship, 1616–1652

1. VCH Essex ii:4, 120; iv, 188; *Repertorium: the History of the Diocese of London* (1710) 499.
2. William Watson: *Historical Account of Wisbech* (1827) 430.
3. GLRO: London Consistory Court 22 January 1633/4.
4. BL: Egerton MSS 2645, ff. 122, 154, 237.
5. ECRO: D/DU 472/14.
6. ECRO: D/DC 23/356.
7. Bland 9, 13, 14, 16; Admissions 2 July 1646.
8. Nickolls 24. The text is I Samuel 30:24.
9. On 17 February 1659. Rutt iii:309.
10. Longleat: Whitelock papers ix, f. 222.
11. Longleat: Whitelock papers ix, ff. 229, 243, 245, 255.
12. Clarendon: *Rebellion* ii, part 2, 568, 574.
13. The Uxbridge Treaty is described in Clarendon: *Rebellion* ii, part 2, 568–94 and in Whitelock: *Memorials*, 122–9. Further references in TSP, i:59–70; Coke 330; VCH Middlesex ii:44; iv:60–61; Thomas Tracks E 281 (12); Zachary Grey: *An Impartial Examination of the 4th vol. of Daniel Neal's History of the Puritans* (1739) app. 50. The opposing propositions are printed in S.R. Gardiner: *Constitutional Documents* 275–86. See also Daniel Lysons: *The County of Middlesex* (1800) 176, 178, 179.
14. Admissions 2 July 1646; RSLI ii:ii–iii.
15. H.C. Maxwell-Lyte: *Historical Notes on the Great Seal of England* (1926) 15, 347; Whitelock: *Diary*, 9 June and 13 July 1648.
16. Longleat: Devereux papers iv, f. 252; HMC *12th Report* app. ix, 175–6; Aylmer: *The State's Servants*, 234.
17. Darby 66–7.
18. Bod: Rawl MSS A2, ff. 134, 140.
19. Young 24.
20. Darby 74; Wells i:200.
21. Ibid., i:220.
22. CSPD 1651:29, 34, 72; CJ vi, 535; Bod: Rawl MSS C129.
23. TSP i:174, 177, 178.

24. CSPD 1651, 170; Bod: Rawl MSS C129.
25. TSP i:181, 182.
26. TSP i:183–5, 189.
27. TSP i:186, 187.
28. TSP i:190–5.
29. Bod: Rawl MSS C366, f. 270.
30. BL: Add 4200, f. 113, printed in EHR (1906) 319–22; Clarendon: *Rebellion* iii, part 2, 457.
31. VCH Bucks iv:155; Admissions 27 May 1647; CSPD 1650:219, 374:Abbott: i:452; ii:387, 406; CCC 393, 465, 603, 658.
32. HMC Portland MSS i:631.

2   The Council of State, 1652–1654

1. CSPD 1651–2:198, 203.
2. TSP i:205.
3. CSPD 1651–2:213, 223.
4. Wells i:230, 242.
5. Ibid., 251, 264, 265.
6. Ibid., 268, 277; CSPD 1652–3:216.
7. TSP i:358; Bod: Rawl MSS A9 f. 112.
8. CSPD 1651–2:224.
9. CSPD 1651–2:392.
10. Firth and Rait ii:658.
11. Wedgwood 70, 144; EHR (1897) 121; Davys 10.
12. CSPD 1649–50:533.
13. CSPD 1650:38, 56, 197, 223.
14. CSPD 1651:455; 1651–2:392; 1652–3:96; HMC Buccleuch and Queensberry MSS ii:part 1, 51.
15. EHR (1902) 104.
16. Shaw ii:1–4, 381.
17. CSPD 1652–3:87, 99.
18. The text is Daniel 7: 18.
19. Underdown: *Royalist Conspiracy* 25, 30, 36, 46, 67.
20. CSPD 1652–3:13, 94; 1653–4:14.
21. TSP i:303; CSPD 1653–4:133.
22. CSPD 1652–3:246, 453; Aylmer: *The State's Servants*, 254, 256.
23. CSPD 1653–4:201, 205, 229.
24. CSPD 1652–3:311; 1653–4:251; BL: Add 22546, ff. 109, 111, 113, 115, 118, 123.
25. TSP i:240, 249, 323, 338, 339.
26. Woolrych: *Commonwealth to Protectorate*, 195, 297, 298, 301, 308, 345–46; CSPD 1652–3:405; Rutt i:xi.
27. TSP 491, 635.
28. Rutt ii:78fn; TSP i:545, 546.
29. TSP i:576.
30. TSP i:591, 621; Fraser, A. 107fn; Longleat: Whitelock papers xv:f. 31.
31. Worden 333–4; Woolrych: *Commonwealth to Protectorate*, 156–57.
32. Gardiner: *Constitutional Documents* 405–17.
33. Woolrych: *Commonwealth to Protectorate*, 360, 362, 369; CSPD 1653–4:297, 301, 309, 314.
34. Bischoffshausen app, letters 6, 9; TSP ii:225.

35. CSPD 1653–4:382, 386; BL: Stowe MSS 142, ff. 60, 61.
36. Longleat: Whitelock papers xv:ff. 107–8, 117.
37. CSPD 1653–4:66, 350, 365, 372.
38. RSLI ii:398–401.
39. Bod: Rawl MSS A23, f. 307; TSP vii:914.

3　Foreign Affairs, 1652–1657

1. CSPD 1651–2:255, 279.
2. CSPD 1652–3:61, 82, 91, 125, 129, 343, 353; TSP i:227, 228.
3. Whitelock: *Swedish Embassy* ii:87; TSP i:583, 645; ii:22, 23; BL: Add 4156, f. 51.
4. TSP i:507.
5. BL: Add 32093, f. 320; Bischoffshausen app, letter 6; TSP ii:137.
6. TSP i:339, 359.
7. TSP ii:144, 154; Sherwood 60.
8. TSP ii:144, 154, 190, 195, 197, 211.
9. BL: Add 32093, f. 320; Add 4200, f. 113; printed in EHR (1906) 319–23; TSP i:499; ii:251; iii:21; PRO: SP 84/159, f. 186.
10. Sherwood 55; CSPD 1654:116; TSP ii:257.
11. TSP i:721; ii:259, 418.
12. BL: Add 32093, f. 326 (printed in TSP ii:113); Add 4156, f. 14. While a series of Thurloe's letters to Whitelock in Sweden are printed in Bischoffshausen app, quoting BL: Add 4991a for their provenance, and another series is to be found in BL: Add 373447, most of the originals are at Longleat: Whitelock papers xv; Whitelock: *Diary,* 12 June 1650.
13. TSP ii:255; Spalding 192–7; BL: Add 37347, ff. 198, 267.
14. Bischoffshausen app, letter 14; TSP ii:499; Spalding 198, 201.
15. Bischoffshausen app, letters 18 and 22; Vaughan i:22; TSP i:616.
16. TSP ii:38; PRO: SP 81/54, f. 76; Bod: Rawl MSS A328, ff. 75, 85.
17. Coke 397; TSP ii:652; EHR (1892) 41.
18. BL: Stowe MSS 185, f. 85.
19. Zachary Grey: *An Impartial Examination* . . . app 51; TSP ii:150.
20. CSPD 1655:23.
21. TSP iii:550, 634; iv:464; CSPD 1657–8:96, 453.
22. Whitelock: *Memorials* 647, *Diary,* 2 May and 18 October 1657.
23. CSPD 1655–6:79.
24. TSP ii:343, 404, 492; iii:558, 566.
25. Bischoffshausen app, letter 16; BL: Stowe MSS 185, ff. 187–200.
26. Bod: Rawl MSS A328, ff. 70, 74, 77.
27. BL: Stowe MSS 185, ff. 187–200; Longleat: Whitelock papers xv:f. 104.
28. BL: Stowe MSS 185, f. 83; TSP iii:16.
29. TSP iii:440, 549.
30. TSP ii:655, 668, 677, 680, 690, 725, 732; BL: Sloane MSS 4365, f. 3.
31. TSP ii:390, 527, 611; iv:79, 644.
32. Brown, H. F. 367, 370; CSPD 1652–3:219; CSPV 1647–52:250; PRO: SP 99/45, ff. 76, 84, 86, 94, 97.
33. Brown, H. F. 371–7; TSP iv:210; CSPV 1653–4:244; 1655–6:82, 177fn.
34. TSP ii:685, 696, 729, 744; CSPD 1655:165.
35. Morland 563, 566, 567, 579.
36. Vaughan i:20, 36, 67, 169, 185.
37. Vaughan i:214, 243.

38. Beresford 52, 55.
39. Vaughan i:259, 266; BL: Add 22919, f. 8; TSP iii:731, 734, 742, 745.
40. BL: Sloane MSS 4365, f. 70; TSP iv:304, 418; Vaughan i:354.
41. CCRO Huntingdon: Prescott MSS 98; TSP iv:724; v:616–44.
42. Vaughan ii:148; Morland 586, 587, 589.
43. Firth: *Clarke* iii:63; Vaughan i:336–37, 384; TSP iv:629.
44. TSP iv:107, 115, 293.
45. PRO: SP 78/113, ff. 76, 84; Vaughan ii:65, 66.
46. Carte ii 90
47. Carte ii:106; TSP iv:769; v:77, 79; CSPD 1655:241.
48. TSP v:208, 286; Vaughan i:452.
49. Carte ii:96, 102, 106.
50. TSP iv:745.
51. TSP vi:505.
52. Bod: Rawl MSS A54, f. 133; Vaughan ii:28; Carte ii:114; TSP v:400, 542, 557, 569.
53. TSP iv:30; William Foster: *The English Factories in India 1624–29* (1909) 74fn; *1630–33* (1910) xxxii, 186; *1655–60* (1921) 146, 154.
54. BL: Add 38100, ff. 231–2, 241, 262, 272–9, 324. The letters in this volume from four Swedish representatives are written in Swedish and German, but Sir Charles Firth's notes in English of the important points in Bonde's reports are at the front.
55. TSP iii:418, 708; iv:23, 141, 181, 246, 275, 279, 399, 407, 556, 645, 659.
56. TSP ii:561, 607; iii:173, 258, 386, 426, 575, 601, 698; iv:11.
57. TSP vi:158.
58. TSP iv:388–9, 656, 756; v:5.
59. R.W.K. Hinton: *The Eastland Trade and the Common Weal in the Seventeenth Century* (1959) 194; BL: Add 38100, f. 331; Whitelock: *Memorials* 620–3, *Diary,* 30 January 1656; TSP iv:486.
60. Whitelock: *Memorials* 627–30, *Diary,* 8 May and 12 July 1656; Spalding 207; 43rd Report of the Deputy Keeper of Public Records (1882) app ii:49–50.
61. Carte ii:102; TSP v:418, 470.
62. TSP iv:151, 158, 454, 505, 600, 604, 711, 748.
63. TSP iv:23, 40, 41, 55, 75, 87, 100, 104.
64. TSP iv:191, 198, 343.

4   *Political and Parliamentary Affairs, 1654–1657*

1. Firth and Rait ii:899, 969, 1007.
2. TSP i:594, 615; ii:67; Underdown 71.
3. CSPD 1654:327, 336; TSP ii:530, 538.
4. Rutt i:xvii, xix, xx, xxxii–v; TSP ii:614, 620.
5. Ashley: *Wildman,* 86.
6. Firth: *Clarke* ii:242–5; iii:24.
7. Rutt i:xli, xliii, xlvi, li, liii, cvii; TSP ii:681.
8. Rutt i:cxxxii, cxxxiii; Vaughan i:118.
9. CSPD 1654:297; 1655:128, 138, 139; CSPV 1655–6:107.
10. CSPD 1655:285, 298.
11. CSPD 1657–8:5.
12. CSPD 1655:240, 309, 319; 1655–6:54.
13. TSP iii:571, 593, 686.
14. TSP ii:640, 693.

15. CSPD 1655:261; Gardiner: *History*, iii, 318–21, 327, 340; EHR (1895) 473–77; TSP iii:486, 701; iv:117.
16. TSP iv:523; v:211.
17. TSP iv:436; Hardacre 126–30; CCC 734, 735.
18. CSPD 1655–7:15, 16, 237; TSP iv:321, 388.
19. TSP iii:266, 707, 727, 737.
20. TSP iv:685; CSPD 1652–3:332, 360; 1653–4:125, 136, 345; 1655:115, 116, 165, 322; 1656–6:136; Carte ii:95.
21. Shaw app, vii and viii.
22. CSPD 1655–6:294; BL: Stowe MSS 497, f. 78.
23. TSP v:45, 63, 176, 311, 328, 352; EHR (1895) 498–9; Firth: *Clarke* iii:71.
24. Rutt i:cxlvii, cl, clxiii–xxi.
25. TSP v:366, 419, 477; Rutt i:clxxix; EHR (1901) 737–9.
26. HMC Bath MSS ii:114; also in BL: Stowe MSS 185, f. 94.
27. TSP v:472; Rutt i:clxxxi.
28. TSP iv:373; v:120, 131, 177, 196–7.
29. RSLI ii:414, 415, 465.
30. Rutt i:cxc, cxci.
31. Rutt i:158, 228, 229, 237.
32. TSP v:786.
33. TSP v:788; vi:7; HMC *6th report* 441; EHR (1895) 503–6.
34. EHR (1902) 434; Firth:*Clarke* iii:87; Rutt i:360, 371, 377.
35. BL Lansdowne MSS 821, f. 294; Egerton MSS 2618, f. 51; EHR (1902) 429–42; Rutt i:378.
36. BL: Lansdowne MSS 821, f. 294; Rutt i:384.
37. Carte iii:89; TSP vi:107, 123; EHR (1903) 53–79; PRO: SP 78/113, ff. 113, 117.
38. Rutt i:388; PRO: SP 78/113, f. 118.
39. BL: Lansdowne MSS 755, f. 61.
40. Rutt i:396; BL: Lansdowne MSS 755, f. 62.
41. Rutt i:397–414.
42. TSP vi:219, 222, 243; BL: Lansdowne MSS 822, f. 57; Rutt i:418, 421; ii:3, 5.
43. Rutt ii:42, 43, 82, 90, 91, 93.
44. TSP vi:267; Rutt ii:116.
45. I am indebted to Dr John Morrill, in an address to the Cromwell Association printed in *Cromwelliana* 1981–2:20–25, for the thought underlying this conclusion.
46. Rutt ii:117–19, 122.
47. Rutt ii:164, 253; Firth and Rait ii:1058.
48. Rutt ii:176, 181.
49. Rutt ii:289, 301, 303, 309.
50. Prestwych 3–18; Rutt ii:511–15.
51. Rutt ii:313, 314.
52. BL: Lansdowne MSS 822, f. 75, printed in EHR (1903) 78.
53. BL: Lansdowne MSS 822, f. 132.
54. Bischoffshausen introductory quotation 2.

5   *Control of Intelligence, 1652–1660*

1. HMC Portland MSS i:323; Bod: Tanner MSS 60, f. 339.
2. Underdown: *Royalist Conspiracy*, 61.
3. TSP i:367, 408, 487, 495, 514, 630.

4. TSP i:409.
5. EHR (1954) 374–6; Underdown: *Royalist Conspiracy,* 83, 84, 87.
6. EHR (1988) 730; TSP ii:64, 70.
7. *Notes & Queries* 12th series, x, 101; CSPD 1654:274, 354; Bod: Rawl MSS A328, f. 120.
8. TSP ii:416; Bod: Rawl MSS A15, ff. 602–46; CPSD 1655:212.
9. TSP iii:95, 114, 151.
10. EHR (1888) 731, 734; TSP ii:330, 334, 336, 346, 353–5, 360, 384.
11. Vaughan i:4, 8.
12. TSP ii:385, 510.
13. TSP iii:56, 65, 68; Vaughan i:118.
14. TSP iii:71, 73, 87, 89, 95, 99, 105, 107, 453.
15. TSP iii:35, 112, 147, 185; Bod: Rawl MSS A22, f. 109.
16. TSP iii:137.
17. TSP iii:230, 336, 338, 350; CPSD 1655:78.
18. TSP ii:259, 298, 371, 372, 376, 382, 394, 398; Vaughan i:152.
19. Clarendon: *Rebellion* iii, part 2, 561.
20. TSP ii:466, 574, 594, 601; iii:492; iv:303, 477; Bod: Rawl MSS A24, f. 66.
21. TSP i:644; ii:373, 434, 490, 502, 568, 585, 684, 710; further reports from Adams are in Bod: Rawl MSS A17, ff. 148, 285, 354, 396.
22. CPSD 1655:192, 212, 220; TSP iii:190, 301, 338, 343, 355, 358, 384, 458, 591; Underdown: *Royalist Conspiracy,* 163–4; Clarendon: *Rebellion* iii, part 2, 565–8; BL: Egerton MSS 2542, f. 177.
23. Clarendon: *Rebellion* iii, part 2, 568–9; CPSD 1655–6:73. For Manning's examination see *Nicholas Papers* (ed. Warner) iii:149–87.
24. Welwood 98–9; *Notes & Queries* 12th series, x, 281.
25. PRO: SP 18/102, ff. 195, 215; SP 18/154, f. 123; SP 18/200; TSP v:210; EHR (1897) 121.
26. PRO: SP 18/154.
27. TSP i:502; ii:134, 143, 186, 239, 244, 577.
28. BL: Add 19516, ff. 2, 11, 20; 34014, ff. 19, 30; TSP iv:333.
29. BL: Add 19516, ff. 24, 38, 52, 102, 126; 34014, ff. 62, 72; 34015; TSP iii:231, 530.
30. Bod: Rawl MSS A37, f. 257.
31. Firth: *Clarke* iii:61; TSP iv:143, 144, 245.
32. BL: Add 4157, f. 15; PRO: SP 77/31, f. 405; SP 18/154, f. 120; TSP vii:28.
33. TSP iv:250, 342, 700, 725, 741, 769; v:18; BL: Add 4157, ff. 37, 115.
34. TSP vi:378; CSPV 1655–6, 84fn; HMC Ormonde MSS new series, i, 327.
35. CSP ii:70, 73.
36. Carte ii:88, 102; TSP iv:698.
37. CSP iii:91, 109–10.
38. TSP iv:629; v:45.
39. TSP v:160, 169, 178.
40. BL: Add 4157, f. 90; TSP iv:132; v:272, 314, 316, 319, 334, 349, 521; Carte ii:111; Vaughan ii:32, 37.
41. TSP i:757.
42. Bod: Rawl MSS A41, f. 576; Underdown: *Royalist Conspiracy,* 182, 185–9, 195–7; *Notes & Queries* 12th series, x, 123.
43. TSP v:594, 602.
44. TSP v:653, 657, 667, 694; Bod: Rawl MSS A22, f. 279; CSPD 1656–7:196; CCSP iii:216.
45. Burnet i:78.

46. TSP v:774, 775.
47. CSPD 1656–7:239; Vaughan ii:87; Rutt i:331–3, 354, 368; TSP v:710; PRO: SP 18/154, f. 98.
48. Burnet i:78.
49. BL: Egerton MSS 2618, f. 51.
50. Rutt ii:2, 3, 6; TSP vi:184–5, 188, 194; CPSD 1656–7:335; CJ vii:521–2.
51. TSP vi:315, 560, 829, 832; Vaughan ii:184; Rutt ii:134fn; PRO: SP 18/113, f. 268.
52. CSPD 1657–8:361; Bod: Rawl MSS A58, f. 302; CSPV 1657–9:103; TSP i:748; vi:441, 447, 492.
53. CSPD 1656–7:346, 362, 375, 376, 378; 1657–8 3–5, 19, 71; TSP v:351, 475; vi:308, 439, 467–8, 836.
54. Bod: Rawl MSS 157, ff. 53, 139–41; A37, f. 228; TSP iv:581, 677.
55. TSP vi:538.
56. PRO: SP 78/113, f. 106, SP 84/161, f. 173; CSPD 1657–8:352.
57. TSP vi:706.
58. *Notes & Queries* 12th series, x, 123; Morrice 24.
59. TSP i:710, 715; vii:63.
60. TSP i:xvii, vii, 13, 46; Whitelock: *Diary*, 30 June 1658; Rutt ii:472, 473.
61. Corker's reports are in TSP i:707–19; vi:834, 835; and Bod: Rawl MSS A48, f. 135; A49, f. 275; A50, f. 274.
62. CSP iii:463.
63. TSP vii:591, 598, 659, 660, 685.
64. BL: Add 4158, f. 146.
65. CSP iii, 517; *Nicholas Papers* iv:169.
66. Firth: *Clarke* iv:304; Willcock 293fn.
67. Burnet i:66; Willcock 374.
68. TSP vii:367, 470, 601, 624, 785.
69. BL: Add 28094, f. 9.
70. EHR (1928) 33–65, (1954) 373–87; Underdown: *Royalist Conspiracy* 248; CCSP iii:533, 535, 542, 563, 724; iv:285; CSPD 1659–60:248.
71. CSP iii:333, 450, 585, 586; Rutt iv:367fn.
72. Willcock 294–5; BL: Add 28094, f. 10.
73. Willcock 374; TSP i:xv, xvi.
74. CCSP iv:223, 234, 238, 290, 361, 409, 426.
75. CSP iii:582, 665; Elizabeth Hamilton: *The Illustrious Lady* (1980) 21.
76. BL: Egerton MSS 2549, f. 24; CSP iii:743.
77. CSP iii:529; BL: Egerton MSS 2549, f. 24.
78. Beresford, 116, 119; CSP iii:612.
79. BL: Egerton MSS 2537, f. 279; 2549, f. 121; Add 28094, f. 10; John Evelyn: *Numismata* (1697) 141.
80. CSPD 1657–8:305; 1661–2:231–2; *Notes & Queries* 12th series, x, 123.
81. CPSD 1660–1:36, 37, 44, 46, 67, 82; 1661–2:64, 129; 1665–6:168; Bod: Rawl MSS A64, f. 237; A67, f. 235.
82. HMC Downshire MSS i:part ii, 610; Buccleuch and Queensberry MSS ii:part i, 49–51.

6   Political and Parliamentary Affairs, 1657–1660

1. Rutt ii:290; CSPD 1657–8:26, 27, 47.
2. CSPD 1657–8:33, 45, 50, 206; Vaughan ii:236, 249, 268.
3. PRO: SP 78/113, f. 288; CSPV 1657–9:104.

4. TSP v: 146; vi: 462, 477, 573, 599; CSPV 1657–9: 134; Burnet i: 83.

5. EHR (1903) 79; Lansdowne MSS 821, f. 107; CSPD 1657–8: 239; TSP vi: 568, 579, 599, 632, 658.

6. TSP vi: 590–3; RSLI ii: 419.

7. TSP vi: 609, 648.

8. CPSD 1657–8: 110; BL: Add 4158: 5, 66; CCRO Huntingdon: Prescott MSS, Henry Cromwell's letterbook; TSP vi: 745, 789.

9. Firth: *The Last Years* . . . ii: 27; Rutt ii: 316, 351.

10. BL: Add 22919, f. 11; Rutt ii: 351, 407, 462. I am grateful to Major Desmond Chute for access to a Chute family history.

11. TSP vi: 773, 779, 781, 793; Firth: *Clarke* iii: 140.

12. CSPV 1657–9: 169.

13. TSP vi: 813, 871; vii: 4, 17, 20, 425; Carte ii: 116.

14. CSPD 1658–9: 89.

15. TSP vii: 192; Vaughan ii: 468.

16. TSP vii: 227, 294.

17. CSPD 1658–9: 99; TSP vii: 320, 323.

18. TSP vii: 344, 364; Morrice 27.

19. Sherwood 67.

20. CPSD 1658–?: 136; BL: Add 22919, f. 44; 4158, f. 136; TSP vii: 370, 374; Ashley: *England in the Seventeenth Century,* 112.

21. TSP vii: 381; HMC *5th Report,* 300; PRO: SP 84/162, f. 167.

22. TSP vii: 405, 412; BL: Add 22919, ff. 51, 54; Guizot: *Richard Cromwell* i: 16.

23. TSP vii: 490, 497, 510; HMC *9th Report,* part 2, 444.

24. BL: Add 22919, f. 63.

25. Rutt ii: 517, 518.

26. Rutt ii: 518; Guizot: *Richard Cromwell* i: 268.

27. PRO: SP 18/204, f. 38.

28. BL: Add 22919, f. 66; Lansdowne 823, ff. 122, 138, 153; TSP vii: 541.

29. TSP vii: 559, 572, 584, 585, 587, 597; Rutt iii: 450.

30. TSP vii: 574, 594, 602.

31. Rutt iii: viii, 10; EHR (1899) 112.

32. Rutt iii: 3, 11, 25, 26, 30; BL: Add 22919, f. 75; TSP vii: 603.

33. Rutt iii: 87, 104, 130, 138, 161, 192, 269, 281, 284, 287.

34. Beresford 292.

35. BL: Add 22919, f. 86; Rutt iv: 68.

36. Rutt iv: 86, 90, 91, 148, 149, 160, 203, 243, 430fn, 433. The reference is to the notorious Dr Richard Busby, headmaster of Westminster School.

37. Rutt iv: 285, 286, 293.

38. Rutt iii: 59, 61–3, 256, 307–10; iv: 141.

39. Rutt iv: 365.

40. Rutt iv: 383, 388, 400, 401, 436, 438.

41. Rutt iii: 233, 238, 241, 252, 256; Hardacre 133; BL: Add 22919, f. 102.

42. Rutt iii: 48, 49; iv: 151–7.

43. TSP vii: 619, 620, 623, 626; Rutt iii: 449, 494–8.

44. Rutt iv: 253, 257, 260–3, 273; TSP vii: 639.

45. Rutt iv: 301.

46. Rutt iv: 306, 307; CSP iii: 446; *Nicholas Papers* iv: 85.

47. Rutt iv: 407, 410–12; Davies 73fn; TSP vii: 653.

48. TSP vii: 436, 447–49.

49. Rutt iii: 75fn, 223fn; BL: Add 22919, f. 59.

50. Guizot: *Richard Cromwell:* 38–9.
51. Rutt iv: 457, 461.
52. Rutt iv: 469, 482fn.
53. Rutt iv: 223fn, 472, 476, 481, 484, 484fn; Waylen 30.
54. BL: Add 22919, f. 96; PRO: SP 78/114, f. 248; Rutt iv: 485fn
55. BL: Add 22929, f. 100.
56. Ludlow 247–8; CSP ii: 506.
57. PRO: SP 78/114, f. 254; Ludlow 250; TSP vii: 679.
58. CSPV 1659–61: 17–18.
59. Guizot: *Richard Cromwell* i: 389–91, 404.
60. Firth: *Clarke* iii: 214, 217.
61. CSP iii: 477.
62. HMC Leyborne-Popham MSS 117; CSP iii: 491, 532.
63. CSPD 1659–60: 148, 565; Bod: Rawl MSS A259, f. 74.
64. Firth: *Clarke* iv: 304; CCSP iii: 493, 497, 565, 724; CCSP iv: 246; Rutt iv: 464.
65. TSP vii: 732, 734, 803; BL: Add 4158, ff. 164, 172; Clarendon: *Rebellion* iii: part 2, 730, 731; CSPD 1658–9: 156, 161, 339.
66. CSPD 1659–60: 27; Bod: Rawl MSS C179, f. 310; Firth and Davies 635.
67. Bod: Rawl MSS A259, warrants of 17 and 22 June 1659, C179, f. 127; Ludlow 258.
68. BL: Add 28094, f. 10.
69. TSP vii: 785.
70. PRO: SP 18/219.
71. BL: Add 5804, f. 45; CJ vii: 833; TSP vii: 807, 808; CPSD 1659–60: 325.
72. HMC *7th Report,* 83, 462; CJ vii: 855.
73. TSP vi: 863; Aylmer: *The State's Servants,* 238.
74. TSP vii: 830, 837, 859, 873.
75. HMC Bath MSS 144; CSP iii: 693; *Nicholas Papers* iv: 205.
76. TSP vii: 826.
77. TSP i: xviii, vii, 810, 861, 887, 895, 896, 897, 900.
78. TSP vii: 888, 895.
79. CSP iii: 707; Guizot: *Richard Cromwell* ii: 166, 382; HMC Leyborne-Popham MSS 224; BL: Add 32093, f. 120.
80. Guizot: *Richard Cromwell* ii: 396–7, 401, 437.
81. Whitelock: *Memorials* 701; CCSP iii: 735.
82. Clarendon: *Rebellion* iii: part 2, 742, 755, 756, 761; CSP iii: 543, 743.
83. CSP iii: 749; CJ viii: 26.
84. HMC *5th Report,* 153, 184, 208.
85. CSPV 1659–61: 148–9.
86. CSPV 1655–6: 296.
87. CJ viii: 28.
88. Hester W. Chapman: *The Tragedy of Charles II* (1964) 383.
89. HMC *5th Report,* 154, 184; CSP iii: 463, 701, 704.
90. CJ viii: 77; EHR (1918) 368–74.

7   Foreign Affairs, 1657–1668

1. Rutt ii: 142–45; TSP vi: 342.
2. Burnet i: 77; PRO: SP 78/113, f. 112.
3. CSPV 1657–9: 40.
4. Rutt ii: 115; PRO: SP 78/113, ff. 243, 253, 283.

5. TSP vi:55, 160, 290, 337; PRO; SP 78/113, ff. 118, 183, 191, 226, 304; Waylen 116.

6. PRO: SP 78/113, ff. 244, 263; CSP iii:353.

7. PRO: SP 78/113, ff. 183, 272, 274, 283, 324; TSP vi:647.

8. PRO: SP 788/113, f. 321; TSP vi:524, 538, 561, 579, 614, 618, 626, 637, 676.

9. PRO: SP 78/113, ff. 322, 333; TSP vi:630, 654.

10. TSP vi:195, 288, 302.

11. BL: Stowe MSS 185, ff. 187–200.

12. TSP vi:138, 216, 278, 279, 288, 309, 323, 331, 357, 393, 407, 419, 432, 433, 635; HMC 6th Report, 442.

13. TSP vi:655, 686, 716, 728, 744, 752, 773; vii:35.

14. TSP vi:478; EHR (1961) 429, 432, 435.

15. Carte ii:116; TSP vi:508.

16. PRO: SP 75/16, f. 241.

17. EHR (1892) 724; TSP vi:545, 614.

18. PRO: SP 84/162, ff. 7, 102, 103; TSP vi:872.

19. TSP vi:802, 838; BL: Add 4158, f. 89; EHR (1892) 79.

20. EHR (1892) 725, 727; BL: Add 4157, f. 201.

21. Firth: *The Last Years'* . . . ii:251–6; TSP vii:105.

22. HMC *6th Report,* 443.

23. EHR (1892) 731, 733.

24. Ibid., 735, 737, 738.

25. CSPD 1657–8:89.

26. Ibid., 733, 734, 737.

27. Ibid., 739–741; PRO: SP 75/16, f. 271; TSP vii:195, 247, 265.

28. CSP iii:248; PRO: SP 78/114, ff. 11, 17, 33, 44, 62; TSP vi:789.

29. Firth: *The Last Years'* . . . ii:66; TSP vi:842; vii:47.

30. Higgins and Colombos: *International Law of the Sea* (2nd edn, 1951) art 515, 576, 577; TSP vi:489.

31. TSP vii:2, 21, 24.

32. Firth: *Clarke* iii:149.

33. TSP vii:158, 173, 176; Guizot: *Richard Cromwell* i:402.

34. Welwood 99.

35. Ibid., 97; CSPD 1655:336.

36. BL: Stowe MSS 185, ff. 187–200; TSP vii:218.

37. TSP vii:207, 259, 281, 284, 308, 319.

38. CSPD 1658–9:3, 79, 101; TSP vi:613, 633, 846.

39. TSP vii:283, 286, 298.

40. Vaughan ii:334, 340, 341fn, 485; PRO: SP 84/162, f. 160.

41. BL: Add 22919, f. 57; TSP vii:467, 512; Meadowe 98, 101, 102.

42. TSP vii:496, 499, 504, 516, 519, 547.

43. PRO: SP 99/45, ff. 111, 113, 123, 133.

44. Firth: *Clarke* iii:172; CPSD 1658–9:186; TSP vii:581.

45. Rutt iii:376–85; CSPV 1657–9:285–96; Guizot: *Richard Cromwell* i:82; TSP vii:342.

46. Firth: *Clarke* iii:177; Rutt iii:441, 442, 444, 445; BL: Add 22919, f. 80; TSP vii:620.

47. Rutt iii:481–9.

48. Ibid., 489–93; TSP vii:620.

49. Rutt iv:42fn, 148fn; TSP vii:636; CCSP iii:442, 448.

50. Carte ii: 157, 167.
51. Ibid., 171, 172; BL: Add 22919, ff. 25, 91, 96.
52. Guizot: *Richard Cromwell* i: 231, 233, 237.
53. Ibid., 171, 172; BL: Add 22919, ff. 25, 91, 96.
54. Ibid., 277, 278, 291, 321.
55. Ibid., 352.
56. Ibid., 367, 375; Firth: *Clarke* iii: 195; BL: Add 22919, f. 102.
57. PRO: SP 84/162, f. 211; CSPD 1658–9: 110.
58. PRO: SP 84/162, ff. 226, 270, 291.
59. Guizot: *Richard Cromwell* i: 374–80.
60. BL: Add 22919, f. 110; Davies 204.
61. Firth: *Clarke* iii: 195; BL: Stowe MSS 185, ff. 187–200.
62. Firth: *Clarke* iv: 279; BL: Add 4158, ff. 164, 172; TSP vii: 732, 743, 803.
63. The original text in Latin, with six England and three Dutch signatures, is preserved at Auckland Public Library, New Zealand: RBR GMS 149. EHR (1892) 723.
64. TSP vii: 838, 905; Bod: Rawl MSS C179, f. 77; Whitelock: *Memorials,* 700; BL: Add 4159, f. 7.
65. CCSP iii: 529, 569; CJ vii: 795.
66. TSP i: xix; vii: 915.

8   Personal and Family Affairs from 1645

1. VCH Surrey iii: 454; Manning and Bray: *History of Surrey* (1974) 783; PRO: PCC Will 1641: 44, Evelyn.
2. Firth and Davies 348, 353, 354; PRO: PCC Will 1651: 20, Grey.
3. *Medallic Illustrations of British History* (reprinted 1969) 370, 371; George Vertue: *Works of Thomas Simon* (2nd edn, 1780) 33, 67.
4. TSP ii: 227, 247; v: 383; Bod: Rawl MSS A24, f. 262; BL: Add 4157, f. 100.
5. Wells i: 304, 308, 319; TSP iv: 485; v: 475.
6. S. C. Gardiner 8, 13, 14, 455; BL: Add 4158, f. 53; VCH Cambs iv: 181, 227, 243; CJ ii: 199.
7. PRO: C54/3678; Bod: Rawl MSS A22, f. 369; TSP iv: 409.
8. Bod: Rawl MSS A26, f. 36.
9. VCH Cambs iv: 247, 254.
10. HMC *9th Report,* 293–4; VCH Cambs iv: 268, 271; BL: Add 5804, f. 51.
11. Wisbech Library: Wisbech Corporation Records 3 April 1657; A. G.Matthews: *Calamy Revised* (1934) 437.
12. Wisbech Library: Wisbech Corporation Records 2 November 1657, 2 November 1658, 10 January 1659.
13. CSPD 1657–8: 11, 226; Bod: Rawl MSS A56, f. 364.
14. TSP iii: 18, 686.
15. TSP iv: 221, 222, 559; v: 46; BL: Add 18979, ff. 267, 268, 271.
16. BL: Add 4157, f. 191; 4158, ff. 132, 140; 6194, f. 59; TSP ii: 173, 242; iv: 250; vi: 126, 383, 438, 457, 461; vii: 53, 492, 563, 575; CPSD 1655–6: 46; Bod: Rawl MSS A35, ff. 5, 171.
17. PRO: A0 3/11. The word 'hanaper' denotes a hamper of willow twigs used for storing documents.
18. Prestwych 150.
19. Longleat: Whitelock papers xv, ff. 6, 88.

20. Taylor, *passim.*
21. Charterhouse MSS.
22. Bod: Rawl MSS AA65, f. 347.
23. TSP vi:777.
24. CSPD 1656–7:304.
25. Vaughan ii:95; CPSD 1657–8:434; TSP vi:552.
26. LPL: MS xxxiA/12, f. 226; Bod: Rawl MSS D715, ff. 118, 121, copy at LPL.
27. TSP vii:536.
28. CSPD 1659–60:215; TSP vii:785; RSLI ii:425, 432.
29. Ludlow 39; Admissions 24 February 1595, 26 May 1622, 23 January 1655; RSLI ii:299, 379, 403.
30. HMC *5th Report* 146, 201; BL: Stowe MSS 497, f. 103; Thomas Hardres: *Reports of cases adjudged in the Court of Exchequer* (1693) ii:130; Bod: Rawl MSS A67, f. 318.
31. VCH Oxon vii:117, 119; Bod: Gough MSS 48, f. 275.
32. VCH Oxon vii:119; BL: Lansdowne MSS 985, f. 74; Bod: Gough MSS 48, ff. 114–23, 126; Tatham 164.
33. Charterhouse MSS; Bod: Rawl MSS A67, f. 361; Spalding 232.
34. Charterhouse MSS.
35. RSLI ii:12; TSP i:v.
36. Tatham 248; CJ v:84; vii:37; Manning and Bray, op. cit., iii:475; Vaughan i:xv.
37. Whitelock: *Diary,* 2 June 1660; Bod: Rawl MSS C366, f. 270; TSP vii:914.
38. LJ xi:120.
39. CJ viii:61, 286; TSP vii:211.
40. CSPD 1660–1:207, 492; PRO: SP 29/11, f. 88.
41. PRO: SP 29/74, f. 4.
42. RSLI iii:15, 28, 29; CPSD 1663–4:204, 249.
43. CSPD 1663–4:287, 433, 461, 477, 547, 554.
44. Ramsey: 64, 166, 169; Bod: Rawl MSS C172, f. 161.
45. Upton 117; VCH Bucks iv:272.
46. PRO: PCC Will 1668.
47. Whitelock: *Diary,* 14 December 1667.
48. *Notes & Queries* 8th series, xi, 83.
49. Stroud, *passim.*
50. RSLI iii:68, 81, 82, 321.
51. VCH Bucks iv:270, 272; Bod: Rawl MSS D682, f. 68; RSLI iii:123, 134.
52. Upton 37, 42, 113.
53. Wisbech Library: Wisbech Corporation Records 21 June 1669, 26 October 1822; VCH Cambs ii:329.

9 Conclusion

1. TSP vii:269.
2. C. H. Firth: *Oliver Cromwell and the Rule of the Puritans in England* (1900) 484.
3. CJ ix:51; TSP vii:32, 49, 62.
4. Bod: Rawl MSS A477, f. 10.
5. EHR (1888) 747, 749; TSP vi:781.
6. Bod: Rawl MSS A477, f. 10.

7. Ibid.

8. Vaughan i:383, 392; *History Today* (1958) 551; Whitelock: *Diary,* 26 January, 17 February and 2 March 1654; CSPV 1655–6:142.

9. PRO: SP 99/5b, f. 81.

10. TSP v:535.

11. TSP vii:192.

12. EHR (1903) 78.

13. Willcock 259–61; TSP v:122.

14. Vaughan i:433; CSP iii:346.

15. TSP vi:695; Whitelock: *Diary,* 22 May 1667.

16. CSP iii:441.

17. TSP iv:58.

18. CSPV 1659–61:38.

19. *Macmillans Magazine* lxx (May–October 1894) 295; Ifor Ll. Williams: 'John Thurloe as Secretary of the Council of State under the Commonwealth and Protectorate' (unpublished MA thesis, University of Wales, 1970) 58 and app.

BIBLIOGRAPHY

Note: Place of publication given only for works published outside the United Kingdom.

I Primary

UNPRINTED

Auckland Public Library, New Zealand — RBR GMS 149–64.

Bodleian Library, Oxford
Carte 63, 73–4, 80, 103, 131, 223, 228, 239, 274.
Clarendon 45–59.
Gough 48.
Rawlinson A2, 9, 15, 17, 22–1, 26, 35, 37, 41, 48–50, 54, 56–8, 64–5, 67, 259, 328, 477.
Rawlinson C129, 172, 179, 366, 989.
Rawlinson D682, 715.
Tanner 51–2, 60.

British Library, Department of MSS
Additional 4156–9, 4200, 5804, 6194, 19516, 22546, 22919, 28094, 32093, 34014–15, 37347, 38100.
Egerton 2537, 2542, 2549, 2618, 2645.
Lansdowne 755, 821–3.
Sloane 4365.
Stowe 185, 497.

Cambridgeshire County RO, Huntingdon — Prescott 98: Henry Cromwell's letterbook – outletters.

Charterhouse, London — Minutebook of the Assemblies of Governors, 1657–62.

Essex County RO, Colchester
D/DU 472/14.
D/DC 23/356.

Lambeth Palace Library, London — xxiA/12.

Longleat
Devereux papers.
Whitelock papers.

Mount Stuart, Rothesay	Whitelock's Diary.
Public Record Office, London.	AO 3/11.
	C 54/3678.
	SP 18/102, 154, 200, 204, 219.
	SP 25/45, 47–60, 69, 73–8.
	SP 77/31.
	SP 78/113–14.
	SP 84/161–2.
	SP 99/5b, 45.
Wisbech Library	Wisbech Corporation Records.

PRINTED

Abbott, W. C. (ed.), *The Writings and Speeches of Oliver Cromwell* (4 vols. Cambridge, MA, 1937–47).

Baildon, W. P. (ed.), *The Records of the Honourable Society of Lincoln's Inn* (4 vols, 1897–1902).

Baildon, W. P. (ed.), *The Records of the Honourable Society of Lincoln's Inn: Admissions 1420–1893* (2 vols, 1896).

Birch, Thomas (ed.), *A Collection of the State Papers of John Thurloe, Esq.* (7 vols, 1742).

Bischoffshausen, Sigismund von, see appendix to his biography of Thurloe, cited as a secondary source.

Bruce, J. and Hamilton W. D. (eds), *Calendar of State Papers Domestic Series, Charles I 1625–1649* (22 vols, 1859–93).

Burn, A. S., 'Correspondence of Richard Cromwell', *English Historical Review* XIII (189).

Burnet, Gilbert, *Bishop Burnet's History of his own Time* (2 vols, 172–34).

Carte, Thomas (ed.), *A Collection of Original Letters and Papers Concerning the Affairs of England, 1641–1660* (2 vols, 1739).

Coke, Roger, *A Detection of the Court and State of England* (3rd edn, 1697).

de Beer, E. S. (ed.), *The Diary of John Evelyn* (6 vols, 1955).

Dick, O. L. (ed.), *John Aubrey's Brief Lives* (1949).

Firth, C. H. (ed.), *The Clarke Papers* (4 vols, 1891–1901).

Firth, C. H. (ed.), 'Secretary Thurloe', *Notes & Queries* 8th S, XI (1897).

Firth, C. H. (ed.), 'Thurloe and the Post Office', *English Historical Review* XIII (1898).

Firth, C. H., 'Secretary Thurloe on the relations of England and Holland', *English Historical Review* XXI (1906).

Firth, C. H., 'Cromwell's Instructions to Colonel Lockhart in 1656', *English Historical Review* XXI (1906).

Firth, C. H. and Rait, R. S. (eds.), *Acts and Ordinances of the Interregnum* (3 vols, 1911).

Gardiner, S. R. (ed.), *Constitutional Documents of the Puritan Revolution* (3rd edn, 1906).

Green, M. A. E. (ed.), *Calendar of the Proceedings of the Committee for Compounding &c 1643–1660* (5 vols, 1889–92).

Green, M. A. E. (ed.), *Calendar of State Papers Domestic Series, 1649–1660* (12 vols, 1875–6).

Hinds, A. B. (ed.), *Calendar of State Papers . . . Venetian.*

Historical Manuscript Commission: numerous reports have proved useful, particularly the Appendices to the *First* to *Eighth Reports* (1870–81) and the *House of Lords Manuscripts New Series IV* (1908).

Hyde, Edward, Earl of Clarendon, *The History of the Rebellion and Civil Wars in England* (3 vols, 1717).

Jenks, Edward, 'Some correspondence of Thurloe and Meadowe', *English Historical Review* VII (1892).

Kenyon, J. P. (ed.), *The Stuart Constitution* (2nd edn, 1986).

Latham, Robert and Matthews, William, *The Diary of Samuel Pepys* (11 vols, 1970–83).

Ludlow, Edmund, *Memoirs of Edmund Ludlow* (revised edn, 1751).

Meadowe, Philip, *A Narrative of the Principal Actions occurring in the wars betwixt Sweden and Denmark* (1677).

Morland, Samuel, *History of the Evangelical Churches in the Valleys of Piedmont* (1658).

Morrice, Thomas (ed.), *Collection of the State Letters of Roger Boyle* (1742).

Nickolls, John (ed.), *Original Letters and Papers of State addressed to Oliver Cromwell found among Milton's Political Correspondence* (1743).

Ogle, O., Bliss, W. H., Macray, W. D. and Routledge, F. J. (eds), *Calendar of Clarendon State Papers* (5 vols, 1869–1970).

Rushworth, J. (ed.), *Historical Collection of Private Passages of State* (7 vols., 1659–1701).

Rutt, J. T. (ed.), *The Diary of Thomas Burton, Esquire* (4 vols, 1828).

Scrope, R. and Monkhouse, T. (eds), *State Papers Collected by Edward, Earl of Clarendon, commencing 1621* (3 vols, 1767–86).

Steele, R. (ed.), *Tudor and Stuart Proclamations* (2 vols, 1910).

Underdown, David, 'Cromwell and the Officers, February 1658', *English Historical Review* LXXXIII (1968).

Vaughan, Robert, *The Protectorate of Oliver Cromwell and the State of Europe* (2 vols, 1839).

Warner, G. F. (ed.), *The Nicholas Papers* (3 vols, 1886–97).

Welwood, James, *Memoirs of the Most Material Transactions in England* (revised edn, 1820).

Whitelock, Bulstrode, *Memorials of the English Affairs* (1682).

Whitelock, Bulstrode, *Journal of the Swedish Embassy* (2 vols, 1772).

II   Secondary

BOOKS
Ashley, Maurice, *General Monck* (1977).

Ashley, Maurice, *John Wildman, Plotter and Postmaster* (1947).

Ashley, Maurice, *England in the Seventeenth Century* (1952).

Ashley, Maurice, *Financial and Commercial Policy under the Commonwealth and Protectorate* (2nd edn, 1962).

Aylmer, G. E., *The State's Servants* (1973).

Aylmer, G. E., *Rebellion or Revolution?* (1987).

Aylmer, G. E. (ed.), *The Interregnum* (1972).

Ball, William, *Lincoln's Inn, its History and Tradition* (1947).

Barnard, T. C. *Cromwellian Policy in Ireland* (1975).

Barnard, T. C., *The English Republic 1649–1660* (1982).

Beresford, John, *The Godfather of Downing Street, Sir George Downing* (1925).

Bischoffshausen, Sigismund von, *Die Politik des Protectors Oliver Cromwell in der Auffassung und Thätigkeit seinen ministers Staatsecretärs John Thurloe* (Innsbruck, 1899).

Bland, D. S., *Early Records of Furnival's Inn* (1957).

Brown, H. F., *Venetian Studies* (1887).

Brown, L. F., *Political Activities of the Baptists and Fifth Monarch Men* (Washington, 1912).

Brunton, D. and Pennington, D. H., *Members of the Long Parliament* (1954).

Capp, B. S., *The Fifth Monarchy Men* (1972).

Coward, Barry, *The Stuart Age* (1980).

Darby, H. C., *The Draining of the Fens* (1940).

Davies, Godfrey, *The Restoration of Charles II 1658–1660* (San Marino, 1955).

Davys, John, *An Essay on the Art of Decyphering* (1737).

Dawson, W. H., *Cromwell's Understudy* (1938).

Dow, F. D., *Cromwellian Scotland 1651–1660* (1979).

Evans, F. M. G., *The Principal Secretary of State, 1558–1680* (1923).

Firth, C. H., *The Last Years of the Protectorate 1656–58* (2 vols, 1909).

Firth, C. H., *Oliver Cromwell and the Rule of the Puritans* (1900).

Firth, C. H. and Davies, Godfrey, *The Regimental History of Cromwell's Army* (2 vols, 1940).

Frank, J., *The Beginnings of the English Newspaper 1620–60* (Cambridge, MA, 1961).

Fraser, Antonia, *Cromwell, Our Chief of Men* (1973).

Fraser, P. M., *The Intelligence of the Secretaries of State 1660–1688* (1955).

Gardiner, F. J., *History of Wisbech* (1898).

Gardiner, S. R., *History of the Commonwealth and Protectorate, 1649–1656* (4 vols, 1903).

Guizot, F. P. G., *The History of Oliver Cromwell and the English Commonwealth* (2 vols, 1854).

Guizot, F. P. G., *Richard Cromwell and the Restoration of Charles II*, trans. Scoble, A. R. (2 vols, 1856).

Hardacre, Paul H., *The Royalists during the Puritan Revolution* (The Hague, 1956).

Hause, E. M., *Tumbledown Dick: The Fall of the House of Cromwell* (New York, 1972).

Hearder, H. and Loyn, H. R. (eds), *British Government and Administration: Studies Presented to S. B. Chrimes* (1974).

Hill, Christopher, *God's Englishman* (1970).

Hirst, Derek, *Authority and Conflict* (1986).

Hobman, D. L., *Cromwell's Master Spy* (1961).

James, M., *Social Problems and Policy in the Puritan Revolution* (1930).

Jones, C., Newitt, M. and Roberts, S. K. (eds), *Politics and People in Revolutionary England* (1986).

Kenyon, J. P., *Stuart England* (1978).

Kynaston, D., *The Secretary of State* (1978).

Korr, C. P., *Cromwell and the New Model Foreign Policy* (Berkeley, CA., 1975).

Morrill, J. S. (ed.), *Reactions to the English Civil War* (1982).

Noble, Mark, *Lives of the English Regicides* (2 vols, 1798).

Noble, Mark, *Memoirs of the Protectoral-House of Cromwell* (2 vols, 1787).

Parry, R. H. (ed.), *The English Civil War and After* (1970).

Pennington, D. and Thomas, K. (eds), *Puritans and Revolutionaries: Essays in Seventeenth Century History Presented to Christopher Hill* (1978).

Prall, S. E., *The Puritan Revolution* (1969).

Prestwych, John, *Respublica* (1787).

Ramsey, R. W., *Henry Cromwell* (1933).

Ramsey, R. W., *Richard Cromwell* (1935).

Ramsey, R. W., *Studies in Cromwell's Family Circle* (1930).

Rogers, Malcolm, *William Dobson 1611–46* (1983).

Roots, I. A., *The Great Rebellion* (1966).

Roots, I. A. (ed.), *Cromwell: A Profile* (1973).

Roots, I. A. (ed.), *Into Another Mould: Aspects of the Interregnum* (1981).

Rowe, V. A., *Sir Henry Vane the Younger* (1970).

Shaw, W. A., *History of the English Church 1640–1660* (2 vols, 1900).

Sherwood, Roy, *The Court of Oliver Cromwell* (1977).

Spalding, Ruth, *The Improbable Puritan: A Life of Bulstrode Whitelock* (1975).

Stearns, R. P., *The Strenuous Puritan: Hugh Peter* (Urbana, IL., 1954).

Stephen, L. and Lee, S. (eds), *The Dictionary of National Biography* (22 vols, 1921–2).

Stroud, Dorothy, *The Thurloe Estate in South Kensington* (1959).

Tanner, J. R., *English Constitutional Conflicts of the Seventeenth Century* (1928).

Tatham, G. B. *The Puritans in Power* 1640–1660 (1913).

Taylor, William F., *The Charterhouse of London* (1912).

Turner, E. R., *The Privy Council of England in the Seventeenth and Eighteenth Centuries, 1603–1784* (2 vols, Baltimore, 1927).

Underdown, David, *Royalist Conspiracy in England 1649–1660* (New Haven, CT, 1960).

Underdown, David, *Pride's Purge* (1971).

Upton, William H., *Upton Family Records* (1893).

The Victoria History of the Counties of England: Buckinghamshire, Cambridgeshire, Essex and Oxfordshire.

Walker, Neil and Craddock, Thomas, *History of Wisbech and the Fens* (1849).

Waylen, James, *The House of Cromwell* (revised edn, 1897).

Wedgwood, C. V., *The King's War 1641–47* (1958).

Wells, Samuel, *Bedford Level* (1830).

Willcock, John, *Life of Sir Henry Vane the Younger* (1913).

Woolrych, A. H., *Commonwealth to Protectorate* (1982).

Woolrych, A. H., *England Without a King 1649–1660* (1983).

Worden, A. B., *The Rump Parliament 1648–1653* (1974).

Young, Peter, *Oliver Cromwell and his Times* (1962).

ARTICLES   (other than those appearing in collections listed above)

Anon., 'Mr Secretary Thurloe', *Macmillans Magazine* LXX (1894).

Baker, Edmund, 'John Thurloe', *History Today* VIII (1958).

Catterall, C. H., 'A Suspicious Document in Whitelock's Memorials', *English Historical Review* XVI (1901).

Catterall, C. H., 'The Failure of the Humble Petition and Advice', *American Historical Review* IX (1903–4).

Coate, Mary, 'William Morice and the Restoration of Charles II', *English Historical Review* XXXIII (1918).

Davies, G., 'The Army and the Downfall of Ricahrd Cromwell', *Huntington Library Bulletin* VII (1935).

Davies, G., 'The Election of Richard Cromwell's Parliament', *English Historical Review* LXIII (1948).

Firth, C. H., 'Cromwell and the Insurrection of 1655: Mr Palgrave's Theory Examined', *English Historical Review* IV (1889).

Firth, C. H., 'Scot's Confession', *English Historical Review* XII (1897).

Firth, C. H., 'Cromwell and the Crown', *English Historical Review* XVII (1902) and XVIII (1903).

Gaunt, P. G. I., 'Interregnum Governments and the Reform of the Post Office, 1649–59', *Historical Research* LX (1987).

Hall, Hubert, 'The Thurloe Papers', *Contemporary Review* CLIV (1938).

Hause, E. M., 'The Nomination of Richard Cromwell', *The Historian* XXVII (1965).

Hollings, Marjory, 'The Secret History of the Interregnum', *English Historical Review* XXXXIII (1928).

M., J. G., 'Sir Richard Willys, Traitor', *Notes & Queries* 12th S, X.

M., J. G., 'Sir Samuel Morland and Cromwell', *Notes & Queries* 12th S, X.

Palgrave, R. F. D., 'Cromwell and the Insurrection of 1655', *English Historical Review* III (1888).

Palgrave, R. F. D., 'A Reply to Mr Firth', *English Historical Review* IV (1889).

Ramsey, R. W., 'Elizabeth Claypole', *English Historical Review* VII (1892).

Rannie, David W., 'Cromwell's Major Generals', *English Historical Review* X (1895).

Roots, I. A., 'The Short and Troublesome Reign of Richard IV', *History Today* XXX (1980).

Taft, B., 'The Humble Petition of Several Colonels of the Army', *Huntington Library Quarterly* XXXXII (1978).

Underdown, David, 'Sir Richard Willys and Secretary Thurloe', *English Historical Review* LXIX (1954).

Wilson, T. A. and Merli, F. J., 'Naylor's Case and the Dilemma of the Protectorate', *University of Birmingham Historical Journal* X (1965–6).

Woolrych, A. H., 'The Good Old Cause and the Fall of the Protectorate', *Cambridge Historical Journal* XIII (1957).

Woolrych, A. H., 'The Collapse of the Great Rebellion', *History Today* VIII (1958).

Worden, A. B., 'Toleration and the Protectorate', *Studies in Church History* XXI (1984).

UNPUBLISHED DISSERTATION

Williams, Ifor Llewellyn, 'John Thurloe as Secretary of the Council of State under the Commonwealth and Protectorate' (MA thesis, University of Wales [Cardiff], 1970).

INDEX